Y0-BCR-801

THE President
AND Congress

THE President AND Congress

Collaboration and Combat
in National Policymaking

Second Edition

Lance T. LeLoup
Washington State University

Steven A. Shull
University of New Orleans

Longman

New York   San Francisco   Boston
London   Toronto   Sydney   Tokyo   Singapore   Madrid
Mexico City   Munich   Paris   Cape Town   Hong Kong   Montreal

Vice President/Publisher: Priscilla McGeehon
Executive Editor: Eric Stano
Marketing Manager: Megan Galvin-Fak
Production Manager: Charles Annis
Project Coordination, Text Design, and Electronic Page Makeup: Pre-Press Co., Inc.
Cover Designer/Manager: Nancy Danahy
Cover Photo: © AP/Wide World
Senior Manufacturing Manager: Dennis Para
Printer and Binder: Maple-Vail Book Manufacturing Group
Cover Printer: Lehigh Press, Inc.

For permission to use copyrighted material, grateful acknowledgment is made to
arttoday.com for the artwork that appears on the chapter openers.

Library of Congress Cataloging-in-Publication Data

LeLoup, Lance T.
    The president and Congress: collaboration and combat in national policymaking/
    Lance T. LeLoup, Steven A. Shull.—2nd ed.
        p. cm.
    Includes bibliographical references and index.
    ISBN 0-321-10041-7 (alk. paper)
        1. Presidents—United States. 2. United States. Congress. 3. Political planning—
    United States. 4. Public policy (Law)—United States. I. Shull, Steven A. II. Title.

JK585 .L45 2002
320'.6'0973—dc   2002072954

Copyright © 2003 by Pearson Education, Inc.

All rights reserved. No part of this publication may be reproduced, stored in a retrieval
system, or transmitted, in any form or by any means, electronic, mechanical, photocopy-
ing, recording, or otherwise, without the prior written permission of the publisher.
Printed in the United States.

Please visit our website at http://www.ablongman.com

ISBN 0-321-10041-7

1 2 3 4 5 6 7 8 9 10—MA—05 04 03 02

To Pammy and Janice

Contents

Preface

Much has happened since the publication of the first edition of *The President and Congress: Collaboration and Combat in National Policymaking*. The terrorist attacks of September 11, 2001 have had a profound impact on the American people and their government. George W. Bush, elected president in one of the closest, most controversial presidential elections in history, saw the nation rally around him to wage an international war against terrorism. It will take many years to fully realize the impact of 9/11 but we cover many of the immediate consequences on national politics in this edition and include the passage of the Anti-Terrorism (Patriot) Act of 2001 as one of the new cases in civil rights. While the terrorist attacks transformed the country in a way, we feel it is important to be circumspect about the prospects for long-term change in presidential-congressional relations. Despite this tragedy, the powerful, more capable Congress that has emerged in the last generation is not likely to relinquish its shared role in national policymaking.

This edition continues and strengthens the major themes of the first edition of *The President and Congress: Collaboration and Combat in National Policymaking*. The presidency-centered approach, focusing on the president as the main initiator in policymaking, simply does not reflect reality today. Rather, the **shared governance** perspective presented here, viewing Congress and the president as coequal partners, is much closer to reflecting the way policies are made. We identify and focus on four patterns of policymaking—presidential leadership, congressional leadership, consensus/cooperation, and deadlock/extraordinary resolution. It is more evident than ever that *no single pattern characterizes presidential-congressional policymaking*. The 1990s and early 2000s have witnessed presidential leadership on terrorism and tax-cutting, congressional leadership on education and campaign finance reform, consensus on banning gay marriages, cooperation on welfare reform, and continued deadlock over health care and Social Security reform.

While divided government neither precludes nor ensures effective policymaking, we continue to believe that divided or unified party control of government does matter in many important ways. Presidents Bill Clinton and George W. Bush both dealt with unified *and* divided government during their presidencies. Clinton forced a tough deficit reduction package through Congress without getting a single Republican vote under unified Democratic control in 1993. But the next year, despite Democratic majorities, health reform—the crown jewel of the first term—failed to even come to a vote. Conversely, under divided government 1995–2001, Clinton and the Republican Congress agreed on welfare reform and a balanced budget agreement but battled over Medicare and education. George W. Bush was able to convince Congress to pass the largest tax cut in 20 years under the brief period of unified Republican control in 2001. Under divided government, Congress passed his education bill but only after stripping out his desired voucher provisions. Despite the president's popularity, the Democratic Senate killed a major Bush judicial appointment and held up others, forcing the president to resort to a number of interim appointments in 2002. Although the *amount of legislation* enacted may not depend on unified or split party control, both the *content of policy* (such as the composition of budget agreements) and the *conduct of politics* (such as the level of conflict between branches) is strongly influenced by divided government.

Many important changes have been made in the second edition in addition to including the dramatic events of the past four years. We have updated the book to include research on Congress, the presidency, presidential-congressional relations, and divided government that has been published recently. We expand the discussion of current theories of Congress and pay more attention to the trends that have brought greater partisanship in national policymaking. Two new cases from the administration of George W. Bush, the Anti-Terrorism Act and the Bush tax cut, provide a chance to examine changes in the political environment before and after September 11. In all, we present sixteen separate cases across the areas of civil rights, foreign policy, economic and budget policy, and social welfare policy. The point of our conceptual scheme is not to make precise, definitive determinations of the boundaries between presidential leadership, congressional leadership, or some other pattern. Rather, our goal is to provide readers with the conceptual tools to examine these and other cases, to be able to identify key variables and relationships, and to develop their own conclusions about why certain patterns of policymaking develop and what difference they make.

The events of 9/11 seem to have reduced some of the cynicism towards government at all levels and clarified that in areas such as homeland security, there are legitimate needs for government. Public support for both Congress and the president increased after 9/11. Whether this remains so in the future is yet to be seen. Overall, we do know that collaboration and combat between branches will continue to occur, depending on issues and ideology, short-term political and economic forces, and leadership skills in the different branches. We hope that the framework, cases, and analysis in this book will increase understanding of the fascinating and crucial policy relationship between the president and Congress.

Acknowledgments

The President and Congress: Collaboration and Combat in National Policymaking, Second Edition is the result of a collaboration started in the early 1970s when we were graduate students at Ohio State University working under Professor Randall Ripley. As legislative staffers together in the Ohio Senate, we also experienced first-hand collaboration and combat with the governor's office. Our professional work together began with an article in *Social Science Quarterly,* progressed to a coedited book in the late 1970s, then to a book entitled *Congress and the President: The Policy Connection* in 1993, and continues now with the second edition of *The President and Congress: Collaboration and Combat in National Policymaking.* It has been a rewarding partnership with far more collaboration than combat.

Many people contributed to this project. We are grateful to the many reviewers who made helpful comments on this edition and the earlier edition including Roger Davidson, Steven Smith, Bruce Evans, Donald Freeman, Janet Martin, David Kozak, Harvey Lieber, Conrad McBride, Keith Nichols, Charles Tidloch, M. V. Hood III, David J. Hadley, Karen E. Dean, and Craig Allin. Brandon Prins from the University of New Orleans helped prepare several figures for the new edition. Lisa Janowski at Washington State was tremendously helpful in putting together the parts of this edition and assisting in the preparation of the manuscript. Cynthia Avery and Diane Berger at Washington State also helped make it possible to complete the project. We are pleased to work with Longman on this new edition and thank Eric Stano and Brian Van Buren in particular. Finally, we thank our families and our remarkable wives, to whom the book is again dedicated, for their continued love and support.

Lance T. LeLoup
Pullman, Washington

Steven A. Shull
New Orleans, Louisiana

About the Authors

Lance T. LeLoup is the C. O. and Mary W. Johnson Distinguished Professor of Political Science at Washington State University, where he has taught since 1996. He has chaired the department and directed the Thomas S. Foley Institute at W.S.U. and was recently named Professor of the Year by the Mortarboard Society. After receiving his B.A. from Georgetown University with honors, he earned an M.A. and Ph.D. from Ohio State University. His current research includes presidential-congressional relations, federal budgeting, political and economic transition in Central Europe, and anti-globalization movements in France and Europe. He is the author of numerous books including *Budgetary Politics* (four editions), *Politics in America* (three editions), and *The Fiscal Congress: Legislative Control of the Budget,* and most recently co-edited *East-West Cooperation in Public Sector Reform in Central and Eastern Europe* (2002). He has published in leading journals including *American Political Science Review, Public Administration Review, Polity, Journal of Politics,* and *Public Budgeting and Finance.* His work abroad has included serving as a Research Fellow at the University of Exeter in England, a Senior Fulbright Scholar at the Budapest University of Economics, a Visiting Professor at l'Universite Catholique de l'Ouest, France, and a Fulbright Senior Specialist at the University of Ljubljana in Slovenia.

Steven A. Shull is University Research Professor at the University of New Orleans. He earned an M.A. and Ph.D. from Ohio State University. He is the author of over 115 publications, including *Explaining Congressional-Presidential Relations; Presidential-Congressional Relations: Policy and Time Approaches; A Kinder, Gentler Racism?; American Civil Rights Policy from Truman to Clinton; Congress and the President; The President and Civil Rights Policy; Interrelated Concepts in Policy Research; President Policy-Making;* and *Domestic Policy Formation* and is editor or co-editor of six volumes including *Presidential Policymaking* and *The Two Presidencies.* His articles have appeared in the *Journal of Politics, Western Political Quarterly, Social Science Quarterly, Political Research Quarterly, American Politics Quarterly, Policy Studies Journal, Policy Studies Review, Social Science Journal, Legislative Studies Quarterly, Presidential Studies Quarterly, Politics and Policy,* and other journals and books. He has served on three journal editorial boards and was a Fulbright Professor at the Chinese University of Hong Kong (fall 1985) and the University of Innsbruck (Austria, fall 2001). He edits a series of books for Garland Publishing Inc. on *Politics and Policy in American Institutions.* He won the University-wide career achievement award for excellence in research in 1986.

CHAPTER 1

Patterns
of Policymaking

Partners or Partisans?

Let us agree to bridge old divides. . . . Bipartisanship is more than minding our manners, it is doing our duty.[1]

—George W. Bush, first address to joint session of Congress, 2001

Not over my dead body will they (the Democrats) raise your taxes![2]

—George W. Bush, speech in Ontario, California, January 2002

No relationship in American politics is more important. For almost 220 years, the connection between Congress and the president has helped steer the course of American public policy. The course has often been erratic, navigating obstacles created by the founders to ensure competition between executive and legislative branches. How effectively the president and Congress work together to make public policy—whether by the leadership of one branch over the other or through cooperation and compromise—has profound consequences. At stake are policies that affect economic prosperity, social justice, and the nation's role in the rapidly changing global arena.

The relationship between Congress and the president has many faces. It may reflect a consensus between branches, resulting in swift, concerted action. It may reveal cooperation, tough negotiation, and compromise. It may show presidential leadership of a reluctant Congress or, conversely, congressional leadership of the policy process with or without the support of the president. Finally, the president and Congress may bog down in stalemate, grinding the processes of governing to a halt, requiring some extraordinary means to resolve the deadlock. Patterns of presidential-congressional relations have evolved for more than 200 years, and today they seem more complex than ever. The last three presidents and the Congresses they faced produced a political roller-coaster ride.

In 2001, President George W. Bush took office after winning one of the closest and most controversial elections in history. Bush was the first president in over a century to win the vote in the Electoral College but lose the popular vote. His victory was not assured until the U.S. Supreme Court intervened to ensure his victory in Florida more than a month after election day. It was no wonder that he appealed for bipartisanship and a constructive relationship with Congress:

> Together we are changing the tone in the nation's capital. And this spirit of respect and cooperation is vital, because, in the end, we will be judged not only by what we say or how we say it, we will be judged by what we are able to accomplish.[3]

In his first year in office, Bush saw his fortunes with Congress ebb and flow dramatically. His main priority, a $1.3 trillion tax cut, was scaled back but passed in May of 2001. His education initiative also received support in Congress, but not before the critical provisions on school vouchers were gutted from the bill. He received strong bipartisan support on his handling of the downing of a U.S. spy plane in China, but was blasted by congressional Democrats for abrogating the Global Warming Treaty and the Missile Defense Initiative. Bush took office enjoying unified Republican control of Congress for the first time in nearly 50 years, even though by the narrowest of margins. But only five months into his presidency, Republican Senator James Jeffords of Vermont switched parties, giving the Democrats a 50–49 majority.[4] Bush found himself fending off congressional initiatives that he opposed, such as campaign finance legislation and a Patients' Bill of Rights.

When terrorists hijacked airplanes and crashed them into the World Trade Center and the Pentagon on September 11, 2001, the relationship between President Bush and Congress underwent a dramatic change. The agendas that both branches had been pushing before that date were swept away in a surge of patriotism that embraced a new war on terrorism. As in earlier major national crises such as the Civil War, the Great Depression, and the attack on Pearl Harbor, the country and Congress turned to the president for leadership. The same Congress that had accused the president of dipping into the Social Security surplus a few weeks earlier, without dissent gave the president twice as much as he asked for to fight terrorism and rebuild New York City. After three short weeks of negotiation over civil liberties, Congress approved the Patriot Act with the sweeping new powers that the administration had requested. Even with this new national unity, partisan politics crept back into Washington after only a few weeks as the House and Senate and White House sparred over new airline security measures, specifically whether or not to make airport security forces federal employees. As the U.S. economy fell into recession for the first time in a decade, the stimulus package to help the economy recover from the severe shock caused by the attack was deadlocked for months.

In 1996, Bush's predecessor, Bill Clinton, also faced majorities of the other party in both houses of Congress and made an appeal for cooperation:

> The American people returned to office a president of one party and a Congress of another. Surely they did not do this to advance the politics of petty bickering and extreme partisanship they plainly deplore.
>
> No, they call on us instead to be repairers of the breach and to move on with America's mission. America demands and deserves big things from us, and nothing big ever came from being small.[5]

Clinton's relations with Congress were even more volatile than his successor's. With unified party control of government during his first two years—for the first time since the 1970s—the president convinced Democratic majorities to adopt a tough deficit reduction package in 1993. Not a single Republican in the House and Senate voted for it. Later that year, Clinton won another big victory when he convinced Congress to pass the controversial North American Free Trade Agreement (NAFTA). After these two successes, his major domestic initiative, comprehensive healthcare reform, ended in disaster. It not only failed to pass the Congress or even be brought to a vote, but also provided impetus for stunning Republican victories in the 1994 midterm elections. For the first time in 40 years, Republicans captured both houses of Congress, and divided government was the rule once more. Led by Republican House Speaker Newt Gingrich (R-Ga.) and his "Contract with America," the 104th Congress, not the president, largely set the national agenda in 1995.

Congressional ascendancy was short-lived as well. The bruising battle over the budget resulted in government shutdowns largely blamed on the Republicans. As the economy soared, Clinton successfully won reelection to a second term in 1996, while Republicans held on to slim majorities in the House and Senate. The president faced the ultimate attack from Congress in 1998 when the House impeached him and the Senate tried him but failed to convict and remove him from office. Despite facing hostile majorities in both the House and Senate, Clinton continued to use the presidential veto and veto threat to win major concessions from Congress on a range of issues through the end of his term.

Before Clinton's eight-year term, President George Bush Sr. also experienced volatile relations with Congress. Despite his easy election in 1988, Bush Sr. faced strengthened Democratic majorities in the 101st Congress. Reacting to the divisiveness of the Reagan era and the knowledge that he faced a legislature with proportionately fewer party supporters than any incoming president in history, Bush called for a new engagement between president and Congress in his inaugural address:

> We need compromise; we've had dissention. We need harmony; we've had a chorus of discordant voices. . . . We've seen the hard looks and heard the statements in which not each other's ideas are challenged, but each other's motives.

The American people await action. They didn't send us here to bicker. They asked us to rise above the merely partisan. In crucial things unity—and this, my friends, is crucial.[6]

Despite this plea for cooperation, only weeks into his administration, Bush saw his nominee for Secretary of Defense, John Tower, defeated in a nasty Senate confirmation battle. Bush had the ignominious distinction of being the first president in 200 years to not gain approval of an initial cabinet nominee. Relations improved shortly afterward when Bush and Congress reached agreement over two of the most divisive issues of the 1980s: aid to the Nicaraguan Contras and the federal budget. Six months later, however, the budget deal collapsed. In 1990, after a year of haggling over the deficit, a deal backed by both Bush and Democratic leaders was rebuked on the floor of the House. Despite Bush's promise of a "kinder, gentler nation," the president locked horns with Congress over social policy and civil rights as well, vetoing a family leave bill and a controversial civil rights bill. The Gulf War changed the tone in Washington in 1991 as the United States led a coalition of international forces to expel Iraq from Kuwait. President Bush enjoyed unprecedented public approval ratings, as high as 90 percent. Yet once again, the pattern was short-lived. Only a year later, his popularity plummeted, the economy headed into recession, he faced sharp attacks from Congress, and was defeated in the 1992 election.

Why do presidents seem to talk about collaboration but end up in combat with Congress? How can we comprehend these rapidly changing patterns of policymaking and volatile institutional relationships? What do these sharply divergent trends mean for future policymaking and the governing of the country in the twenty-first century?

Today, no single, simple pattern characterizes presidential-congressional policymaking. The days when either the legislative or executive branch could consistently dominate policymaking across a wide range of issues are gone, if they ever truly existed. In addition, *different patterns of presidential-congressional policymaking can occur across different policy areas at the same point in time.* The goal of this book is to provide a framework for better understanding the various patterns that occur. We will use that framework to analyze the way Congress and the president interact to make national policy, and determine what difference it makes. Does "better" policy emerge from cooperation or conflict? Presidential leadership or congressional leadership? To get a real-world understanding of the dynamics of presidential-congressional policymaking, we will analyze case studies of different patterns across various policy areas. To establish the context of the cases and their implications, we will explore constitutional foundations and the historical development of the presidency and the Congress. In this chapter, we develop a typology of legislative-executive policymaking, and specify explanatory factors, including the political environment, election results and resulting policy preferences, institutions, leadership, and the nature of the policy agenda. We begin by considering various perspectives on legislative-executive relationships.

Perspectives on Legislative and Executive Power

CONSTITUTIONAL PRINCIPLES

The common starting point for studies of presidential-congressional policymaking is separation of powers—the division of executive, legislative, and judicial branches in the Constitution. It is perhaps the most prominent structural feature of American government. Yet the phrase *separation of powers* itself is misleading.[7] The Constitution intermingles powers among branches, overlapping responsibility for governing. It is more accurate to think of separation of powers as Richard Neustadt characterizes it: "separated institutions sharing powers."[8] This sharing of powers makes possible the related constitutional doctrine of checks and balances.

The founders pursued several conflicting goals in creating a government for the United States. They wanted to devise a national government powerful enough to govern, but not so powerful as to infringe on individual liberties and state prerogatives. Protecting liberty was foremost in the minds of the framers of the Constitution. Separate institutions sharing power would prevent tyranny by blocking the accumulation of political power by any one branch. The framers accomplished this by placing one institution in conflict and competition with the others. James Madison, the principal architect of the Constitution, described it in Federalist #51 as a system in which "ambition must be made to counteract ambition."[9]

This system of separation of powers is in contrast to parliamentary forms of government, which place greater emphasis on the ability to make policy. Parliamentary systems are characterized by the fusion of, rather than the separation of, powers. The executive head and cabinet members are drawn from the legislative majority; they share a common political base. Supported by principles of majority rule and party discipline, the prime minister and cabinet are virtually assured of the enactment of their programs by the legislature. For example, British Prime Minister John Major and the Conservatives were able to continue to govern and won all no-confidence votes, even when their majority was down to a single seat in 1996.

As the scope of government expanded and the institutional capacity of both Congress and the presidency increased, many concluded that, although the separation of powers protected liberty effectively, it often made governing more difficult. Critics of separation of powers, who admired parliamentary systems, became more vocal in the 1980s as institutional conflict and deadlock became more common.[10] However, parliamentary comparisons are of limited value in analyzing the U.S. Congress and president. More relevant are perspectives that emphasize one branch or the other in the governing process.

CONGRESSIONALIST PERSPECTIVES

Throughout much of American history, the prevailing view recognized congressional supremacy. Congress, the "First Branch," was the source of legislation and policy leadership. The president's job was only to make sure that the laws were "faithfully executed." This perspective emphasizes a literal reading of the Constitution.[11] It stresses Madisonian checks and balances and the representation of multiple interests and regions, a particular strength of the legislature. This "congressionalist" or literal view, distrusts presidential power and executive leadership and respects congressional prerogatives in taxing and spending, war making, and domestic policy areas. John C. Calhoun in 1817 expressed the essence of the congressional primacy view: "Congress is responsible to the people immediately, and the other branches of government are responsible to it."[12]

Does a congressionalist view have any relevance today? It does in several different ways. First, many members of Congress ardently defend their lawmaking prerogatives in the constitutional system. As Charles Jones observes, "A day hardly passes on Capitol Hill without a member expressing the theory of legislative primacy."[13] In recent decades, even members of Congress within the president's own party have not hesitated to challenge the president when they felt the institutional power of Congress was illegitimately threatened, or if they had major policy differences with the president. Even after the events of September 11 gave President George W. Bush added influence in shaping foreign and defense policy, columnist George Will argued that congressional supremacy was still the dominant pattern:

> Congressional supremacy is not a mere preference or cyclical phenomenon, it is a constitutional fact: there is little a president can do if a determined congressional majority opposes it. That. . . explains why presidents rarely feel powerful.[14]

Second, a somewhat different congressionalist or Congress-centered view comes from recent research on presidential legislative success with Congress. As we will examine in more detail below, some recent studies show that the most important variables in explaining what happens to presidential proposals or positions have to do with the partisan and ideological composition of Congress rather than characteristics of the presidency.[15] That is to say, the outcomes of the legislative process are more a function of the composition of Congress than the president's popularity or margin of electoral victory.

PRESIDENTIALIST PERSPECTIVES

As the policy agenda of government expanded in the twentieth century, perceptions of proper balance between the legislature and the executive branch shifted. Concern about the ability of government to solve problems quickly and effectively grew, with less emphasis on restricting majorities in order to protect liberty. Following the presidency of Franklin D. Roosevelt (1933–45), a "presidentialist" or presidency-centered view prevailed, including among scholars.[16] This perspective was reinforced by the institutionalization of the presidency, greatly expanding its capability in policymaking; by growing public expectations for presidential leadership; and by the weakening of political parties after World War II.[17] Presidents became less dependent upon political parties for their election with the advent of television and the increased use of primaries and campaign advisors in presidential elections.

Serious questions about the potential dangers of presidential government emerged in the 1960s and 1970s in response to an unpopular war, presidential abuses and scandals, and impeachment proceedings against President Richard Nixon in 1974.[18] Tension between legislative and executive branches escalated with growing congressional opposition to the Vietnam War and reassertion of its constitutional prerogatives in foreign affairs. Institutional combat grew fiercer as President Nixon and Congress clashed over control of the power of the purse. Congress responded by enacting the War Powers Resolution in 1973 and the Budget and Impoundment Control Act in 1974 to strengthen its capabilities in war making and budgeting. The Watergate scandal and perceived abuses of the executive branch led to impeachment proceedings and the subsequent resignation of Nixon.

Despite the reassessments of presidential power in the wake of the Johnson-Nixon era, the vast majority of studies of legislative-executive relations still focus on the president and his "success" with Congress. Most research starts with the president's legislative agenda and grades the effectiveness of the legislative process through a boxscore or other measure of presidential wins and losses. A significant body of literature exploring how to measure presidential legislative success has developed.[19]

THE SHARED GOVERNANCE PERSPECTIVE

In recent years, many scholars have taken a more balanced perspective on presidential-congressional power. Mark Peterson describes Congress and the president as "tandem institutions constituting the major components of the national legislative decisionmaking system."[20] This conveys the notion of a partnership in which both branches must engage if there is to be a response to policy issues. Charles Jones makes a related set of arguments for a "separationist" perspective rather than congressional or presidential:

> Focusing exclusively on the presidency can lead to a seriously distorted picture of how the national government does its work. The plain fact is that the United States does not have a presidential system, it has a *separated* system. . . . I propose a separationist, diffused-responsibility perspective that I find more suited to the constitutional, institutional, political, and policy conditions associated with the American system of governing. (italics his)[21]

Recent work by Shull expands this approach by analyzing four aspects of interbranch relations across policy areas and over time.[22] Even actions such as executive orders are conditioned on the broader environment, including the president. In looking at a wide range of presidential-congressional interactions, there is evidence that a complex array of factors are necessary to explain outcomes.[23]

We believe that what we call a "shared governance" approach is essential for understanding the complex and changing ways in which Congress and the president interact to make policy today. A two-year Congress or four-year presidential term cannot be characterized by a single pattern of policymaking. At the same time that Congress and the president may be cooperating on balancing the budget, they may be in a confrontational battle over healthcare or abortion. Even in an exceptional period of presidential leadership, such as after the September 11 terrorist attacks, different patterns of legislative-executive relations were shortly in evidence. The move away from the once-dominant presidency-centered approach toward a shared governance perspective is particularly important in terms of expectations concerning divided party control of the presidency and Congress and how it affects policymaking.

Partisan Control and Divided Government

An important factor in understanding presidential-congressional relations is party control of the presidency and Congress. More than at any other time in U.S. history, elections are producing divided government: the presidency under the control of one party, and one or both houses of Congress under the control of the other party. This has occurred about two-thirds of the time since 1945.[24] As divided government has become more prevalent, it has been given a more prominent role in analyses of national policymaking. Much of the blame for government "deadlock," "stalemate," or "gridlock," and the often combative, ill-tempered atmosphere between Congress and the president, is attributed to divided government. Even the nature of divided government is in flux. Before the 1990s, it appeared that Republicans had a lock on the presidency (winning five of six elections from 1968 to 1988) and that the Democrats had permanent control of the Congress (majorities in one or both houses from 1955 to 1995). But the events of the 1990s confounded those assumptions. From 1995 to 2001, a Democratic president faced a Republican Congress. Table 1.1 looks at the cases of divided government since 1900.

The primary cause of divided government is the weakening of voters' ties to political parties and their willingness to split their tickets, voting for a candidate of one party for Congress and another for president. Is divided government accidental or chosen intentionally by voters? Some researchers suggest that "policy balancing" may be taking place—that voters feel more secure with the Democrats managing one branch to guarantee delivery of popular benefits, but with the Republicans in control of the other branch to ensure fiscally conservative management.[25] Opinion polls have shown that as many as two-thirds of voters say they prefer divided government, lending some credence to this theory. By 1996, however, only 50 percent of respondents said they favored divided government, and more than 75 percent of voters chose a member of the House of Representatives and a presidential candidate

Table 1.1 Divided Government since 1900

President	Party	Congress		House Control	Senate Control
Taft	R	62nd	(1911–1913)	D	R
Wilson	D	66th	(1919–1921)	R	R
Hoover	R	72nd	(1931–1933)	D	R
Truman	D	80th	(1947–1949)	R	R
Eisenhower	R	84th	(1955–1957)	D	D
Eisenhower	R	85th	(1957–1959)	D	D
Eisenhower	R	86th	(1959–1961)	D	D
Nixon	R	91st	(1969–1971)	D	D
Nixon	R	92nd	(1971–1973)	D	D
Nixon	R	93rd	(1973–1974)	D	D
Ford	R	93rd	(1974–1975)	D	D
Ford	R	94th	(1975–1977)	D	D
Reagan	R	97th	(1981–1983)	D	R
Reagan	R	98th	(1983–1985)	D	R
Reagan	R	99th	(1985–1987)	D	R
Reagan	R	100th	(1987–1989)	D	D
Bush	R	101st	(1989–1991)	D	D
Bush	R	102nd	(1991–1993)	D	D
Clinton	D	104th	(1995–1997)	R	R
Clinton	D	105th	(1997–1999)	R	R
Clinton	D	106th	(1999–2001)	R	R
Bush	R	107th	(2001–2003)	R	D*

*Although the Senate was tied 50–50 after the 2000 election, when Senator James Jeffords of Vermont left the Republican party in June, 2001, the Senate came under Democratic control.

of the *same* political party, the highest rate since 1952.[26] In recent years, the percentage of voters casting split tickets has begun to decline.

Many observers view divided government with great alarm. A century ago, Woodrow Wilson wrote that, "If you want to release the force of the American people, you have got to get possession of the Senate and the presidency as well as the House."[27] More recently, James Sundquist observed that under divided government, "all of the normal difficulties of attaining harmonious and effective working relationships between branches are multiplied manifold."[28]

In the mid-1980s, frustration over big budget deficits and persistent conflicts between President Reagan and the Democratic Congress led to some serious efforts to propose constitutional reforms that would lessen the probability of divided government or break deadlocks if they existed. The Committee on the Constitutional System, a blue-ribbon panel of scholars and public officials, reported at the bicentennial of the Constitution that separation of powers and checks and balances had led to "government stalemate and deadlock, to indecision and inaction in the face of urgent problems."[29] But is divided government as detrimental to policymaking as critics claim?

The most significant challenge to critics of divided government comes from David Mayhew's study, *Divided We Govern*.[30] In a comprehensive study of major legislation and congressional investigations between 1947 and 1990, Mayhew concludes that divided control has *not* made a difference in whether important policies are enacted. Comparing periods of unified and divided government, the results do not show meaningful differences in legislative output. Mayhew concludes that divided government does not inevitably lead to deadlock or preclude policy enactment, and has spurred a great deal of new research on the subject.

A number of studies in the last decade clarify or contradict his findings. A study using a more stringent definition of important legislation finds that divided government *did* produce less key legislation as well as greater conflict on roll call votes.[31] Another finds that divided government is more prone to gridlock and dampens legislative performance.[32] Mayhew measures only the supply of legislation, not the demand for legislation, so one cannot be certain that divided government has not prevented certain major legislative initiatives from being enacted. Divided government also increases the level of institutional conflict between branches.[33] The content of legislation—whether it proved to be good or bad policy—is also not tested by Mayhew's study. One recent study comparing policy content and results concludes that divided government inhibits the executive's ability to conduct free trade policy.[34]

What can we conclude about divided government? While divided government does not always paralyze policymaking as constitutional critics claim, it does make a difference. First, divided government affects the nature of the policy bargaining and hence, the content of legislation. For example, the deficit reduction agreements in 1990 and 1997 under divided government are very different in terms of the balance of tax increases and spending cuts than the Democrat's deficit reduction plan adopted under unified government in 1993. In general, facing a president of a different party who possesses veto power truncates the range of bills that Congress can adopt.[35] Second, it appears that divided government leads to greater reliance on extraordinary means of resolving deadlocks, outside of the normal procedures of the legislative process. The increased use of bipartisan commissions and interbranch summits are examples. Benjamin Ginsberg and Martin Shefler argue that as national elections increasingly fail to provide coherent governing coalitions, both branches resort to "politics by other means" in order to influence policy. They argue that growing institutional combat disrupts the system of shared powers and leads politicians to attempt to batter the other branch through revelation, investigation, and prosecution.[36]

The shared governance perspective embraces a more balanced approach to unified or divided party control. It cannot be assumed a priori that divided party control precludes effective policymaking. We will present cases that show several kinds of party divisions. *Partisanship* occurs when both parties are generally unified and opposed to each other. *Bipartisanship* exists when the divisions over an issue do not follow party lines or a majority of both parties support a policy. In the case of *cross-partisanship,* divisions largely follow party lines, but enough members defect to the other party to give them a working majority.[37] Divided versus unified party control of government is important, but it does not in itself dictate any one particular kind of interaction between the parties or the branches.

Examining Policymaking

POLICY APPROACHES

Ultimately, politics is about what the government does, the policy decisions and collective choices it makes. Hence, in addition to the shared governance perspective, we use a public policy approach, analyze case studies, and develop a framework to help compare and assess different patterns. In a simplified way, policymaking in national government can be seen as a sequence or a cycle.[38] Most commonly, the stages of policymaking include the following:

1. **Agenda Setting:** Determining what issues or problems government will address. Congressional parties and the presidency each have agendas with some overlapping and some competing items.
2. **Formulation:** Putting together the specific details of a proposed policy, such as drafting a bill or a rule. Legislation may be formulated in the legislative or executive branch, and submitted to Congress by a sympathetic member.
3. **Adoption:** The process by which a policy is approved and enacted. In terms of legislation, it often involves negotiation between branches, after which it is passed by both houses of Congress and signed by the president (except when a veto is overridden).
4. **Implementation:** The process of carrying out or enforcing a policy. It often involves the federal bureaucracy, the courts, and the states, but in many cases, Congress and the presidency are involved in oversight and monitoring to ensure effective implementation.
5. **Results:** The outcome of the policy—did it produce the desired ends and/or were there unintended consequences? The results, good or bad, often influence the policy agenda, starting a new cycle.

Thinking about the policy process in distinct sequential stages can be helpful in analyzing the case studies we present, but has its limitations. Policymaking often has no clear beginning or end, policies often overlap, and the stages are often blurred. Policymaking is often characterized by continuous feedback, where the consequences of one policy shape the decisions on subsequent policies. Traditionally, the sequential approach to policymaking has associated the presidency with the formulation stage and Congress with the adoption stage. In fact, as we shall see, the legislative and executive branches are involved at *all* stages of the policy process. For example, Congress and the president may have quite different policy agendas depending on their partisan and ideological composition. Congress as well as the White House formulates proposals. The presidency is deeply involved with adoption, often negotiating details of legislation with congressional representatives.

Although bureaucracy dominates policy implementation, Congress is increasingly active in shaping and overseeing implementation.

Policymaking can also vary across substantive areas. There are many ways to categorize policies, from a simple foreign policy-domestic policy dichotomy, to a list of very specific issues such as monetary or water resources policies. We will examine four broad policy areas: foreign and defense, civil rights, economic and budgetary, and social welfare.[39]

We complement the policy focus with the use of case studies, which allows us to explore similar patterns across the different issue areas. It is important to note that we did not choose a random sample of cases but rather a sample that represents different and instructive patterns. Multiple case studies analyzed systematically not only provide significant pedagogical contributions, but can also contribute to increases in cumulative knowledge.[40] We utilize the case studies to examine a series of explanatory factors, patterns of policymaking, and policy outcomes. To foster comparability, the 16 cases focus on *legislation* as opposed to appointments, investigations, oversight or other forms of presidential-congressional interaction.

DIMENSIONS OF POLICYMAKING RELATIONSHIPS

More than 107 Congresses and 43 presidents have managed to engage in nearly every conceivable kind of political relationship over the past two centuries. Patterns have ranged from the aggressive post-Civil War Congress that nearly drove Andrew Johnson from office because he opposed its radical agenda, to the quiescent Democratic majorities anxious for Franklin D. Roosevelt to lead them out of the Great Depression. Between these extremes lie a wide range of political patterns. While many variables can be used to describe legislative-executive interaction, two dimensions seem particularly useful: One is the level of conflict over a policy issue between legislative and executive branches, and the second is to what extent the legislative or the executive branch shaped the policy.

How Much Interbranch Conflict? In sharing power and responsibility for making national policy, relations between Congress and the president range from consensus and close cooperation to open political warfare. Interbranch conflict can vary along a continuum from little or none to moderate to extreme. Divisions between the two branches can stem from a variety of factors. In some cases, the conflict is institutional, based on protecting constitutional prerogatives, disagreement about the proper role of each, and a perception that the relationship between branches is out of balance.[41] For example, in 2001, when President Bush issued an executive order to try terrorists in military tribunals rather than civilian courts, members of both parties in Congress criticized the president for not consulting them for this important step. Under divided government, interbranch conflict is often partisan, springing from ideological differences, disagreements over policy, and the desire to gain electoral advantage over the opposing party. Because Congress consists of different party caucuses and factions, we assess interbranch conflict based on the conflict between the president and prevailing congressional majorities on that issue. The level of conflict between the White House and Capitol Hill plays a major role in determining the pattern of policymaking that emerges.

Which Branch Shapes Policy? Consistent with the shared governance perspective, the second dimension concerns the relative impact of each branch on policy decisions. This, too, can be conceptualized as a continuum ranging from cases where the presidency and executive branch determine the content of policy, to cases where both branches are approximately of equal importance in shaping policy, to cases where Congress largely determines the result. Many factors affect which branch has more influence in framing issues and affecting outcomes. In some instances, the relative salience of an issue for Congress compared to the president may be a factor. The president may simply not care about some issues of great concern to legislators and is content to let Congress do as it pleases. Presidents often defer to Congress on pork-barrel bills, for example, recognizing that the political costs of interference may far outweigh the benefits. Conversely, Congress may care little about certain presidential initiatives or fear the consequences of opposition, and therefore acquiesce to the Chief Executive. One branch may defer to the other on legal or constitutional grounds, acknowledging greater legitimacy to act on the part of the other branch. Finally, which branch shapes policy is often determined on the basis of power politics: Can the president exercise the muscle to ram an initiative through Congress without compromise, or can Congress gather the two-thirds majorities needed to override a presidential veto? Between the extremes are the more common cases of shared policymaking, where each side wins some and loses some in the political process.

PATTERNS OF POLICYMAKING

Combining these two dimensions of policymaking relationships across a vertical and a horizontal axis makes it possible to create a typology of policymaking patterns. Of course, we do not suggest that it is possible to locate policy cases along each continuum with precision. We can, however, make some *rough comparative assessments* of where a case falls within the two dimensions. Dividing the typology into four quadrants, we suggest four general patterns, as illustrated by Figure 1.1. The four patterns are *presidential leadership, congressional leadership, consensus/cooperation,* and *deadlock/extraordinary resolution.* We mean "leadership" in a relative sense: one branch has a greater role in shaping the policy result than the other branch. Other scholars refer to essentially the same phenomenon as presidential or congressional "primacy" or "ascendancy."[42] Here, however, we categorize individual bills and laws, not entire sessions or time periods. Note that there can be considerable variation between two cases within the same quadrant and close proximity between two cases in different quadrants. We will therefore analyze and compare cases both between different patterns and within the same patterns.

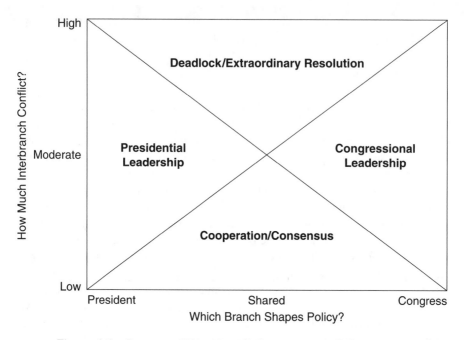

Figure 1.1   Patterns of Presidential-Congressional Policymaking.

Presidential Leadership. Policymaking shaped more by the president than Congress characterizes presidential leadership. It is marked by the executive providing direction and leadership with Congress sharing some part of shaping policy or largely following behind. Presidents can lead policymaking in a highly conflictual environment if they have sufficient power or resources. At the other extreme, presidential leadership can occur when there is relatively little interest or opposition from Congress. Presidential leadership can be partisan if the president controls working majorities in both houses of Congress, cross-partisan if he can attract enough defectors of the other party to win, or bipartisan if a significant number of members of both parties are willing to follow the president. As conflict increases, presidential leadership becomes less likely and deadlock becomes more probable. Conversely, at low levels of conflict, the legislation is more likely to fit the pattern of cooperation/consensus than presidential leadership.

Historically, presidential leadership tends to occur in times of national crisis, such as during the Civil War when President Lincoln, without the formal approval of Congress, established a draft, appropriated monies, blockaded southern ports, and suspended the writ of habeas corpus. In the 1930s, the economic crisis of the Great Depression with 25 percent unemployment, widespread bank failures, and pervasive hunger and homelessness, created a temporary environment that invited presidential leadership. In President Roosevelt's first few days in office, congressional leaders demanded action on legislation that had only been submitted hours earlier. "Vote!" one member exclaimed. "The house is burning down and the President of the United States says this is the way to put out the fire!"[43]

Today, when presidential leadership takes place, it is much more fleeting and contingent, displaying different kinds of party divisions. Presidential leadership can also occur in both less public and controversial cases. President Reagan succeeded in getting his controversial economic and budget package in 1981 because of Democratic defections in the House, a pattern of cross-partisanship. President Bush Sr. convinced a skeptical Democratic Congress to approve the use of force in the Gulf War, also a cross-partisan division. President Clinton passed a tough deficit reduction plan in 1993, despite unpopular large tax increases, in a partisan vote. And George W. Bush received strong bipartisan congressional support for his pursuit of the war against terrorism but needed cross-partisanship to pass his $1.3 trillion tax cut earlier in 2001.

Congressional Leadership. Policymaking shaped more by Congress, either with the cooperation of or over the objections of the president, characterizes the pattern of congressional leadership. As with presidential leadership, the boundaries in Figure 1.1 suggest that as interbranch conflict increases, the possibility of congressional leadership is reduced and the possibility of deadlock enhanced. Conversely, at low levels of conflict, the pattern is more likely to be one of consensus or cooperation. Perhaps the clearest examples of congressional leadership are when both houses override a presidential veto, as the Democratic Congress did to President Reagan with the Civil Rights Restoration Act in 1988, and the Republican Congress did to President Clinton with the Shareholder Lawsuits Act in 1995. Congressional leadership may be partisan, particularly under divided government. In the case of overriding presidential vetoes, however, whether under unified or divided government, congressional leadership is usually bipartisan or cross-partisan since one party rarely enjoys a two-thirds majority. Congressional leadership is usually bipartisan if interbranch conflict is institutional or constitutional, such as the enactment of the War Powers Resolution in 1973 and the Budget and Impoundment Control Act in 1974 over President Nixon's opposition. At moderate levels of conflict, and with some policy participation from the executive, Congress may still have an edge in determining the content of certain policies.

In the Republic's first century, congressional leadership was the norm for long periods of time, punctuated only briefly by assertions of presidential authority. The post-Civil War Congress that impeached and nearly removed President Andrew Johnson was clearly dominant in most instances. Congress continued to lead policymaking in most areas through the late nineteenth century although it was much more difficult when opposed by the president. President Grover Cleveland, in his attempt to block certain congressional actions, cast 583 vetoes during his two terms in the White House.

Even in the modern era, which puts more focus on the presidency, Congress frequently plays a leading role in making domestic policy. Congress played a major role in expanding civil rights and has been influential in shaping economic policy and social welfare policy. In the 1970s, Congress was the force behind the enactment of a number of laws to protect the environment, such as the Clean Air Act and the Water Pollution Control Act. During the Reagan era, a bipartisan coalition of congressional Republicans and Democrats both wrote and enacted comprehensive trade legislation in 1988. While the trade bill could not have become law without the participation and support of the Reagan administration, it was a congressional initiative largely shaped on Capitol Hill.

Cooperation/Consensus. The third pattern of executive-legislative policymaking is marked by moderate or low levels of conflict and constructive conflict management. Consensus occurs when opposition in either branch is unorganized, co-opted by informal agreements, or where no real disagreement exists—typically with "motherhood and apple pie" issues.[44] Either branch may play a leading role in formulating policy, or they may share the role equally, but lack of substantial organized opposition is the common characteristic. Important policy innovations can emerge from consensus, such as the National Aeronautics and Space Act of 1958, a reaction to the Soviet Union's successful launching of *Sputnik* the previous year. Both the Eisenhower administration and congressional leaders helped formulate and enact the space program. More frequently, consensus occurs with more symbolic or less important policy issues.

Cooperation differs from consensus in terms of higher political stakes, more substantial and organized opposition, and higher levels of conflict. Compromise, where neither side gets exactly what it wants, is the common denominator of cases falling into this pattern. Although bargaining and compromise take place in virtually all cases of presidential-congressional policymaking, it is often more dramatic here, with opposing sides moving significantly from their original positions. While many of the policy conflicts in this pattern reflect ideological or partisan cleavages, cross-partisanship and bipartisanship is the norm. Techniques to moderate conflict and create the basis for reaching compromise are frequently employed, including prior consultation and negotiation. Some measures—such as money bills where differences can be split—are more conducive to cooperation than either/or choices, such as school prayer or abortion. While one branch may play a greater role in shaping policy, in most cases, both branches work together to formulate and enact public policy.

The enactment of the sweeping Clean Air Act Amendments in 1990 is an example of the cooperation pattern of presidential-congressional policymaking. Although there were sharp differences in positions and competing environmental and economic interests, both branches made a commitment to see the process through.

While much of the detailed legislating and brokering of the act took place in Congress, it could not move forward without the president's support and leadership. The legislative process in Congress, from initial consideration through the adoption of a conference report, included consultation with administration officials and a number of closed sessions to resolve differences. Cooperation can characterize policymaking in foreign policy as well as domestic affairs. Constructive negotiation and compromise often settle issues such as free trade agreements, foreign aid, and choices of weapons systems.

Deadlock/Extraordinary Resolution. The final pattern is characterized by the inability to resolve a policy dispute, or the use of unusual means outside the normal legislative process to break an impasse. Deadlock often occurs because of constitutional checks and balances such as the presidential veto or by congressional rules such as the Senate filibuster, which require supermajorities (three-fifths or two-thirds of the legislators) to enact laws.[45] The term "political gridlock" became popular in the 1980s as recurrent interbranch conflicts captured the headlines. Yet significant variation can exist within this general pattern as with the other three. This pattern encompasses two distinct phenomena. The first is deadlock: a breakdown of the normal policy process, leading to inaction in a situation where there is sentiment that a problem needs to be addressed. This may occur by Congress not acting upon or defeating a presidential initiative. It may occur because of a presidential veto of congressional legislation where majorities are insufficient to override. Many proposals remain deadlocked for years because of consistent and concerted opposition in Congress or the White House. Welfare reform was deadlocked for decades until 1996 when Clinton and Republican leaders finally reached an agreement. Partisan disagreement over campaign finance reform, even despite the fund-raising scandals, led to a stalemate that was not broken until 2002.

Unlike campaign finance or welfare reform, some policies simply cannot remain deadlocked for long periods of time. The inability to resolve differences through normal governing processes can pose severe risks for the nation. For example, the government cannot function without a budget no matter how divergent the president and congressional majorities are on taxing and spending. Government cannot allow the Social Security system to go bankrupt. It is unthinkable that the federal government default on insurance programs guaranteeing deposits in banks and savings and loans, leaving millions of Americans without their life savings. Such situations characterize the second component of this pattern: extraordinary resolution.

Extraordinary resolution of policy deadlocks is often forced by the imperative nature of the decision. Under these circumstances, Congress and the president look to alternative means or "ad hoc arrangements" to break the stalemate.[46] Three main kinds of extraordinary resolution characterize presidential-congressional relations over the past 20 years. First, summits between leaders of both branches were increasingly employed to resolve divisive budget issues in the 1980s and the 1990s. With this type of resolution, small subgroups of leaders from both branches meet in private, usually away from the Capitol, to try to find common ground. Second, bipartisan commissions, with members appointed by the president and congressional leaders, have been created to break deadlocks over contentious issues such as the Social Security system and the closing of military bases. As much as anything, these kind of official commissions are formed to give members of Congress and the adminis-tration "political cover" to make unpopular decisions. Third, attempts to resolve policy deadlocks have been made by creating "automatic devices," that without pos-itive action by Congress, will automatically result in a certain policy. The best ex-ample is the 1985 Gramm-Rudman-Hollings law, which forced across-the-board budget cuts if Congress and the president were unable to reach designated deficit targets.[47] When the executive-legislative partnership proves incapable of resolving policy conflict through the normal processes, and deadlock poses unacceptable dan-gers to the nation, Congress and the president resort to extraordinary means to re-solve their differences.

The relationship between Congress and the president over two centuries reflects many variations of these four patterns. As we saw in the introduction to this chapter, the experiences of Presidents Bush, Clinton, and Bush indicate that patterns can change quickly and vary across policies. We believe that the typology provides a useful tool for analysis and comparison, but it is often difficult to categorize com-plex and multidimensional cases. Some cases may fall between categories, while over time, other cases may change patterns. Deadlock can become cooperation be-cause of an election, a world event, or other significant change in the environment. The objective is to identify and compare similarities and contrast differences to bet-ter understand the dynamics of policymaking.

That leads to two essential questions remaining to explore: What determines the pattern of policymaking and what difference does it make? What factors are impor-tant in shaping the way that Congress and the president make policy together? Research on legislative-executive relations suggests a number of factors that seem to be important. Some reflect characteristics of the presidency, some reflect character-istics of Congress, and some are external to both. First, the manner in which Congress and the president legislate together depends on the *political environment*, such as the state of the economy, public opinion, and world events. Second, *election results* determine the *party composition* of government and *policy preferences* of the presidency and Congress. Third, *institutions* in both branches are important, estab-lishing rules and the capacity to formulate and enact policy. Fourth, the *leadership* skills of the president and congressional leaders and the nature of the *policy agenda* affect patterns of presidential-congressional interaction. Certain policies may be more conducive to presidential leadership while others may be more conducive to congressional leadership.

Determinants of Policymaking Patterns

THE POLITICAL ENVIRONMENT

The state of the nation, the state of the world, and public expectations are among the many factors that help define parameters for policymaking and shape presidential-congressional relations. The terrorist attacks on September 11, 2001, caused a more profound change in the environment for American politics than any single event or trend since World War II. In a blink, public expectations changed. Citizens viewed government as more of a force for good than harm in protecting domestic security and pursuing the global war on terrorism. Although partisan disputes and presidential-congressional conflicts resumed relatively quickly, many of the changes in the environment had longer impacts.

Public Demand or Expectations for Change. At certain junctures in history, the political environment is conducive to change, such as during the Civil War or the Great Depression. Scholars such as Arthur Schlesinger Jr., James David Barber, and James Sundquist suggest that American politics unfolds in cycles.[48] Schlesinger and Barber argue that public expectations shift from demands for dramatic departures from the past, to a period of consolidation, and then to a period of reaction and retrenchment. Sundquist emphasizes the existence of particular cycles in presidential-congressional relations. The greater the expectations for change, the more dominant the president will be. Conversely, the greater the public desire for consolidation, the greater the influence of Congress and the more constraints the president will encounter. While the evidence supporting the existence of cycles is ambiguous, changes in public expectations do affect patterns of policymaking.

Presidential Popularity. Using public opinion data and congressional roll call voting patterns, a number of studies conclude that presidential popularity correlates with increased voting support from members of Congress.[49] During war, the public tends to "rally around the flag," boosting approval of the president and enhancing his influence. The president's popularity tends to increase when the United States is involved in some military action or national security crisis. Following the terrorists attacks, President Bush's public approval ratings were extremely high, hitting 90 percent in some surveys. Research shows, however, that the popularity boost is often short-lived and does not necessarily translate into increased domestic success. More enduring is the link between the state of the economy and public approval of the president.[50] Inflation, unemployment, and poor economic performance damage public approval ratings. Eisenhower, Reagan, and Bush Sr.—all popular presidents—saw their approval ratings bottom out around the time that unemployment peaked. How much presidential popularity affects success in Congress has been increasingly challenged by recent empirical research that suggests the impact is marginal at best.[51]

Public Approval of Congress. Public approval usually has less effect on Congress because of the divergence between public assessments of individual members and the institution as a whole.[52] Except for the period following Watergate and the impeachment proceedings against Richard Nixon in 1974, public approval of Congress has remained lower than other government institutions. But as measured by incumbent reelection rates (roughly 95 percent success by House incumbents and 80 percent for Senate incumbents over the past two decades), individual members enjoy strong public support. The popularity of incumbents minimizes some of the negative consequences of low approval ratings for the institution and can insulate legislators from a popular president. Even Congress may benefit from the rally-around-the-flag phenomenon. Congress enjoyed higher approval ratings in the wake of the Persian Gulf war in 1991 and the terrorist attacks in 2001. After the takeover of Congress in the 1994 elections, Speaker Gingrich and the Republicans were much more aggressive initially—when they enjoyed higher public support—than they were in 1996 following the budget deadlock and government shutdowns largely blamed on them.

Mass Media and Interest Groups. The mass media and interest groups are also important components of the political environment. Presidents attempt to use the media to their advantage. Employing the strategy of "going directly to the people over the heads of Congress," presidents use televised appeals, news conferences, and major addresses to mobilize public pressure on Congress to support the president's program.[53] On the other hand, presidents often see the media as the enemy lying in wait for any error or weakness. The media played a major role in the downfall of Richard Nixon, for example. Presidents often attack the credibility of the media to counter unfavorable press, but with mixed results. Congress is more difficult for the media to cover and the legislative process is hard to portray accurately in short broadcasts. Nonetheless, parties in Congress have become much more oriented toward "message politics," using the media to convey their issues to the public.[54] Members of Congress also attempt to use the media to their advantage through leaks, off-the-record interviews, and press conferences. For both institutions, the media play an important role in agenda setting and in creating a context of public expectations about critical issues.

Interest groups have influenced interbranch relations for more than two centuries and continue to be an important factor. Both branches respond to interest group pressure and attempt to use these groups to build political support.[55] Members of Congress are subject to lobbying and depend on political action committees (PACs) for much of their campaign funding. With the collapse of campaign funding rules by the 2000 election and the explosive growth of soft money, interest groups play an increasingly important role in financing the election of the president as well as members of Congress.[56] Many believe this influence is reflected as well in subsequent agendas and legislative negotiations on the part of both branches. A major campaign finance reform bill that curbs soft money was passed by Congress and signed by President Bush in 2002.

ELECTION RESULTS, PARTY COMPOSITION, AND POLICY PREFERENCES

Congressional Elections and Resulting Majorities. Election results shape the context for presidential-congressional policymaking by establishing partisan majorities in Congress. Based on their research, Jon Bond and Richard Fleisher conclude that the size of congressional majorities is the single most important factor in determining a president's success in getting programs adopted by Congress.[57] As discussed earlier, elections determine whether the presidency and Congress are under unified or divided party control. Elections also determine the distribution of policy preferences (ideology) of members. Some scholars believe that the distribution of policy preferences is more important than party. Rather than focusing on what party is in control, these scholars think of members as arrayed from right (conservative) to left (liberal).[58] The location of the "average" member (median member) is crucial, as well as whether most members are distributed close to the average, or toward the extremes.[59]

Research has shown that in recent years Republicans and Democrats in Congress have become more ideologically cohesive *and* polarized.[60] With the elimination of many conservative Democrats and moderate Republicans, the most liberal Republican today is to the right of the most conservative Democrat. With cohesive and sharply divided parties, unified party control of government should be more helpful to a president's legislative success. Clinton, for example, had a much higher level of success in Congress in his first two years with a Democratic Congress (88 percent) than in the years following the Republican takeover (28 percent).[61] On the other hand, given the distribution of policy preferences of members of Congress and institutions such as the Senate filibuster and presidential veto, gridlock is still common even under unified government.[62]

Policy outcomes are determined by the extent to which the president and members of Congress share policy preferences resulting from the previous election.[63] The degree to which the president's policy preferences are close to or far away from the midpoint of congressional ideology often determines what policy options are available and whether cooperation, deadlock, or dominance by one or the other branches occurs.

The President's Ability to Claim an Electoral Mandate. Election results create the basis for a president to claim a mandate. Leverage with Congress is assumed to be greater for a president elected by a landslide—Johnson and Reagan, for example—than for a president elected by a narrow margin—John Kennedy and George W. Bush, for example—or not elected at all, like Gerald Ford. The following observation reflects this conventional wisdom:

You ought to think of the presidency as an engine. Each president enters office facing the same model—the horsepower is generally stable and the gears are all there. What differs is the fuel. Different presidents enter with different fuel. Lyndon Johnson entered office with a full tank, while Ford entered on empty.[64]

The importance of electoral mandates seems to have declined in elections since 1988. In particular, George W. Bush entered office in 2001 with the weakest mandate imaginable—he did not win the popular vote, and he only won the electoral vote after a controversial ruling by the U.S. Supreme Court on the Florida vote. Nonetheless, Bush showed relatively effective leadership during his first six months in office, and strong presidential leadership after the terrorist attacks mobilized the country behind him.

INSTITUTIONS

The formulation, adoption, and implementation of policy depend on the institutions of national government and how effectively they work. Institutions can be both formal—such as legislative committees or an executive budget process—and informal—such as congressional norms and practices. Institutions help shape individual behavior and collective policy choices. From a public policy perspective, institutional capability refers to capacity to function effectively, to reach decisions and carry them out.[65] Two of the most important institutions affecting the legislative process are supermajority institutions—the Senate filibuster, often requiring 60 votes (three-fifths of the Senate) to pass legislation, and the presidential veto, requiring a two-thirds majority to override.[66] The constitutional institution of bicameralism—the existence of a Congress made up of two separate chambers—also contributes significantly to legislative gridlock.[67]

Congressional Institutions. How does the internal organization, written and unwritten rules, and processes of the House and Senate affect their ability to legislate and work with the president? As Congress became modernized at the beginning of the twentieth century, many key institutions developed: a stable committee system, party leadership organizations, the seniority system, and other behavioral norms. The degree of centralization or fragmentation of power among members has important consequences for Congress's ability to enact policy as well as the president's ability to lead Congress. It is difficult to build stable coalitions in a highly decentralized, fragmented legislature. A more centralized Congress, with powerful leaders, is no easier for a president to lead and is generally better able to compete with the president in the policy process. By the 1980s, as interbranch conflict intensified, Congress became more centralized through changes in the budget process, the emergence of more powerful leaders, and the rise of a new "committee oligarchy."[68] This increased the capability of Congress to challenge the president and affected patterns of national policymaking.

Presidential Institutions. The development of presidential institutions enhanced the power of the president and his relations with Congress. Much of the "institutionalized presidency" emerged in the 1940s, increasing the ability of the president to initiate policy, respond to crises, and manage government. The set of permanent institutions in the Executive Office of the President and the White House staff remain important elements in policymaking relationships with Congress. How well presidents utilize this "state apparatus" affects an administration's effectiveness in national policymaking.[69] When institutional performance suffers, reform and restructuring often take place. For example, Kennedy reacted to Eisenhower's formal, hierarchical decisionmaking style with a more wide-open, fluid style. Bush responded to Reagan's detached management style with a more hands-on approach. The president's Office of Legislative Affairs is important in determining how well the president's agenda is treated on Capitol Hill.[70]

LEADERSHIP AND THE POLICY AGENDA

Presidential Leadership. Many studies of presidential-congressional relations focus on the importance of individual leadership. Social scientists disagree about the importance of leadership in the overall policymaking equation. Many argue that environmental and institutional factors are more critical, but the style, personality, and skills of the president continue to attract attention.[71]

Attempts have been made to conceptualize presidential personality and leadership skills. Perhaps best known is James David Barber's fourfold scheme based on style and character to explain presidential performance.[72] Other studies focus on the personal skills needed to succeed, such as selling and management abilities rather than psychological attributes.[73] Empirical evidence about the effects of presidential leadership skills are mixed. Several studies of roll call voting conclude that leadership skills have only a slight effect on how members of Congress vote.[74] Presidential leadership may be reflected in ways other than final floor votes, however. A skillful president may be able to manage an ambitious agenda and make strategic decisions before bills reach the floor.[75]

Leadership also encompasses the ability to employ effective strategies, such as timing. The notion of a presidential "honeymoon" with Congress is widely accepted and premised on the belief that a president has a limited pool of "political capital" on which to draw. James Pfiffner has written of the need for presidents to "hit the ground running."[76] Paul Light argues that presidents must "move it or lose it" to push the legislative agenda with Congress quickly before their influence is reduced.[77] Lyndon Johnson alluded to this phenomenon after his landslide election over Barry Goldwater in 1964:

I was just elected president by the biggest popular margin in the history of the country—16 million votes. Just by the way people naturally think and because Barry Goldwater simply scared the hell out of them, I've already lost about 3 of those 16. After a fight with Congress or anything else, I'll lose another couple of million. I could be down to 8 million in a couple of months.[78]

Countering this cycle of decreasing influence is the view that delay can help the president—that further into his term, his skill and competence increase. Kennedy and Bush Sr. did not launch major legislative initiatives until they had been in office for some time and Jimmy Carter had more success in his second year than his first. However, one study concludes that presidents are no more successful with Congress early in their tenure, and that the stage of a president's term does not matter.[79]

At best there is limited evidence to support the relationship between presidential leadership skills and legislative success. One study finds that presidents are slightly more successful when journalists report favorably about their legislative skills.[80] Another study indicates evidence of presidential leadership skills influencing support between initial consideration and the final approval of a bill.[81] Another scholar finds that the more frequently a president mentions an issue, the more support he will receive with key supporters in Congress.[82]

Congressional Leadership. Congressional leadership is also important from a shared governance perspective. It is much simpler to focus on one person than on 535 members of Congress or even a handful of party and committee leaders. But the personalities, use of resources, and skills of House and Senate members are also instrumental in determining policymaking patterns and results. Norman Ornstein asserts that:

> . . . individual talent and adaptability matter. Certain eras may call out for strong (congressional) leaders, but for various reasons the individuals who find themselves elected or appointed to leadership posts do not measure up. At other times, clever, assertive, and adaptable leaders may be able to overcome considerable institutional impediments to provide surprisingly strong leadership.[83]

Congressional leadership styles have varied sharply in recent years. Republican Speaker of the House Newt Gingrich (1995–99) centralized power in the House to an extent not seen since the beginning of the twentieth century. He handpicked committee chairs, breaking the seniority system and weakening their power. He was followed by Dennis Hastert (R-Ill.) as Speaker. Hastert had a dramatically different, less confrontational style and gave more power to committees. Committee leadership—committee chairs and ranking minority members—can exert significant influence over legislation. Informal groups and caucuses increasingly provide policy leadership in Congress. Certain members, regardless of their seniority or position, act as "issue" leaders, playing a major role in defining the agenda and shaping outcomes.[84] Other members are particularly important as coalition builders because of their expertise, popularity, or personal skills.

The importance of congressional party leadership may not be based on the personality and skills of leaders. The work of Brady and Cooper suggests that there are certain times when rank and file members are willing to cede power to strengthen party leaders.[85] Rohde refines this argument with his theory of conditional party government. He argues that members are likely to grant more power to their leaders in circumstances where strong intraparty unity and interparty conflict exist.[86] These characteristics have existed in the United States since the 1980s, particularly after the 1994 elections gave Republicans majorities in the House and Senate.

Control of the Policy Agenda. Patterns of policymaking between Congress and the president also depend on the policy agenda and who sets it. Presidents may have had the advantage in setting the national agenda, but with the prevalence of divided government today, Congress increasingly frames, publicizes, and pursues its own agenda. Mark Peterson examined 300 policy initiatives and found presidential leadership in only 11 percent of the cases, opposition party dominance in Congress 20 percent of the time, compromise 24 percent of the time, and no action 25 percent of the time.[87] This is highly suggestive that the two branches share control more equally than is often assumed.

Agenda Size. Overly ambitious, unfocused agendas can result in lower overall success.[88] For example, Reagan focused almost exclusively on his budget and economic plan in his first year and saw its major provisions adopted. Carter, on the other hand, had a diverse and unfocused agenda in his first year. Reagan sent 107 issues to Congress compared to 232 for Carter.[89] Looking back, Carter concluded:

> With the advantages of hindsight, it now seems that it would have been advisable to have introduced our legislation in much more careful phases— not in such a rush. We would not have accomplished any more, and perhaps less, but my relations with Congress would have been smoother and the image of undue haste and confusion could have been avoided.[90]

Congressional agendas may follow the same rules. Newt Gingrich succeeded in focusing the congressional agenda in 1994–95 with the 10 major proposals contained in the Contract with America. Although fewer than 30 percent of the proposals became law in the first year, eventually 70 percent of the bills were adopted.[91]

Difference Among Policies. Issues themselves may help determine the relationship between Congress and the president and which branch is more likely to shape the final result. The most obvious example is the "two presidencies" thesis, which suggests that presidents are much more dominant in foreign affairs than domestic affairs.[92] Since 1965, differences between foreign and domestic success rates have narrowed considerably.[93] Some recent studies conclude that the phenomenon holds only for Republican presidents—who have greater success in foreign policy votes—rather than for Democratic presidents—who do equally well in both. Others suggest a reemergence of the "two presidencies" phenomena is due more to presidential weakness than congressional strength.[94]

In an earlier study, we compared congressional approval of presidential initiatives across the policy areas we are using in this study. Congressional approval ranged from 55 percent in *foreign and defense policy*, to 50 percent in *social welfare policy*, to 37 percent in *economic and budget policy*, to a low of 26 percent in *civil rights*.[95] While this suggests that policy area is related to policymaking patterns, the variation in overall success between individual presidents was just as great, ranging from a high of 57 percent for Johnson to a low of 31 percent for Ford. Rather than looking at legislative success only from the president's vantage point, we will utilize these four policy areas to examine different patterns of shared governance.

Consequences of Presidential-Congressional Policymaking

What difference do the patterns make? The answer requires identifying characteristics of policies and establishing criteria for judging "good policy." For example, are policies resulting from a dominant president more coherent and timely than policies dominated by Congress? Does a pattern of congressional leadership result in policies representative of more diverse interests and distributing benefits more widely? Are policies adopted through a pattern of consensus or compromise more or less effective than policies that emerge from extraordinary means of resolution? What are the consequences of inaction or deadlock? Does the policy work? Does it solve the problem? Are there unintended consequences?

Michael Mezey suggests that good public policy should be responsive and accountable by democratic standards, and informed, timely, coherent, effective, and responsible by managerial standards.[96] These criteria provide an important basis for evaluating policies.

> *Timeliness and Responsiveness.* Does the policy respond to a popularly perceived problem? Are policies adopted in a timely fashion and respond to immediate problems and needs, or does delay cause additional difficulties?
>
> *Representativeness.* Are a wide range of interests and concerns reflected in the process? Does the final result represent the public interest rather than a narrow special interest?

Symbolic or Substantive. Are policies more show than substance, avoiding fundamental issues for the sake of taking some action? Are policies sufficiently informed by expert information and analysis? Are policies adopted primarily for political purposes or to solve problems in a realistic, honest way?

Accountability. Do citizens know who is responsible for policies that are enacted or not enacted, or is responsibility for a policy obscured, limiting the capacity of citizens to hold policymakers accountable?

Nature of Benefits. Do policies primarily provide private goods that benefit groups or individuals or public goods that benefit the larger society? Are the costs and benefits of policies targeted to achieve a desired result, or diluted and dispersed so that everyone gets a piece of the pie but overall impact is reduced?

Consistency and Coherency. Are policies clear, relatively unambiguous, moving in a single general direction, or are they contradictory and internally inconsistent? Do policies correspond reasonably to government actions in other areas or do they conflict with other related policies?

Effectiveness. Do policies have the desired impact and results, making progress toward their objectives? Or do they require constant reconsideration and reformulation, often creating undesired, inadequate, or unintended results? Do policies meet long-term needs as well as short-term demands?

Conclusion

To better understand the dynamics of presidential-congressional policymaking, much of the book looks at case studies in foreign and defense policy, civil rights policy, economic and budget policy, and social welfare policy. Each chapter explores the evolution of policy, the current agenda and major issues, and particular features of the political environment, leadership, and institutional structure. Each of the four general patterns we identify occurs in various forms across each policy area. In nonrandomly selecting cases, therefore, we have chosen one each of presidential leadership, congressional leadership, consensus/cooperation, and deadlock/extraordinary resolution across the four policy areas. *It is clearly not meant to imply, however, that each pattern is equally prevalent across policy areas.* We know, for example, that presidential leadership is more common in foreign and defense policy than in social welfare policy. Drawing on the literature and many other cases not detailed here, we discuss which patterns are more typical or unusual in a given policy area.

Table 1.2 presents the cases that will be examined in Chapters 5 through 8. At the conclusion of each of these chapters we will take an overview of presidential-congressional interactions in that policy area and the prevalence of certain patterns. In the concluding chapter we will assess each of the four patterns across policy areas, summarizing policy characteristics and consequences.

Table 1.2   Cases of Presidential-Congressional Policymaking

Pattern of Interaction

POLICY AREA	PRESIDENTIAL LEADERSHIP	CONGRESSIONAL LEADERSHIP	CONSENSUS/ COOPERATION	DEADLOCK/ EXTRAORDINARY RESOLUTION
Foreign Policy	Gulf War (1991)	Cuba Sanctions Act (1996)	Panama Canal treaties (1978)	Aid to Contras (1983–1989)
Civil Rights Policy	Antiterrorism (Patriot) Act (2001)	Civil Rights Restoration Act (1988)	Same-Sex Marriage Act (1996)	Civil Rights Act (1991)
Economic and Budget Policy	Tax cut (2001)	Shareholder Lawsuits Act (1995)	Tax Reform Act (1986)	Balanced Budget Plan (1995–1996)
Social Welfare Policy	Economic Opportunity Act (1964)	Catastrophic Healthcare Insurance (1988–1989)	Welfare Reform Act (1996)	Social Security Bailout (1983)

Before the cases are presented, Chapter 2 explores more fully the constitutional foundations of Congress and the presidency and traces the evolution of their relationship over two centuries. Chapters 3 and 4 examine the presidency and Congress as policymaking institutions in more detail. Chapters 5 through 8 examine the policy areas before presenting the cases and their results. In Chapter 9, we review general policy consequences across the four patterns and assess the shared governance. In doing so we hope to expand understanding of the way in which Congress and the president make public policy and how the process and results might be improved.

Notes

1. *CQ Weekly* (March 3, 2001): 495.
2. Quoted in *Newsweek* (January 14, 2002): 34.
3. *CQ Weekly* (March 3, 2001): 498.
4. Jeffords actually became an Independent but caucused with the Democrats, giving them a working majority in the Senate.
5. Inaugural address of William Clinton, January 20, 1997, in *Congressional Quarterly Weekly Report* (January 25, 1997): 252–253.
6. From the Inaugural Address of President George Bush, January 20, 1989, reprinted in Gerald M. Pomper, *The Election of 1988* (Chatham, NJ: Chatham House, 1989): 209–210.
7. Louis Fisher, *The Constitution Between Friends* (New York: St. Martin's, 1978): 7–13.
8. Richard Neustadt, *Presidential Power* (New York: Wiley, 1960): 26.
9. James Madison, Federalist Paper #51 (New York: Modern Library, 1965).
10. Lloyd Cutler, "To Form a Government: On the Defects of Separation of Powers," in Thomas Cronin (ed.), *Rethinking the Presidency* (Boston: Little, Brown, 1982): 62.
11. Roger H. Davidson, David Kovenock, and Michael O'Leary, *Congress in Crisis: Politics and Congressional Reform* (Belmont, CA.: Wadsworth, 1969): 17–25.

12. Quoted in Charles S. Hyneman and George W. Carey (eds.), *A Second Federalist* (New York: Appleton-Century-Crofts, 1967): 151.

13. Charles Jones, *Separate But Equal Branches* (Chatham, NJ: Chatham House, 1995): 8.

14. George W. Will, "Devil's Island! Guillotines!" *Newsweek* (December 10, 2001): 84.

15. Jon Bond, Richard Fleisher, and Glen Krutz, "An Overview of the Empirical Findings on Presidential-Congressional Relations," in James Thurber (ed.) *Rivals for Power: Presidential-Congressional Relations* (Washington D.C.: CQ Press, 1996): 103–139.

16. Thomas E. Cronin, *The State of the Presidency* (Boston: Little, Brown, 1975): 25–30.

17. James P. Pfiffner, "Divided Government and the Problem of Governance," in James Thurber (ed.), *Divided Government* (Washington, D.C.: CQ Press, 1991): 39.

18. Arthur M. Schlesinger, Jr., *The Imperial Presidency* (Boston: Houghton Mifflin, 1973).

19. George C. Edwards III, *At the Margins* (New Haven, CT: Yale University Press, 1989); Jon R. Bond and Richard Fleisher, *The President in the Legislative Arena* (Chicago: University of Chicago Press, 1990); Douglas Rivers and Nancy Rose, "Passing the President's Program: Public Opinion and Presidential Influence in Congress," *American Journal of Political Science,* 29:2 (May 1985): 183–186.

20. Mark A. Peterson, *Legislating Together* (Cambridge, MA: Harvard University Press, 1990): 4–7.

21. Charles Jones, *The Presidency in a Separated System* (Washington, D.C.: Brookings Institution, 1994): 2–3.

22. Steven A. Shull, *Presidential-Congressional Relations* (Ann Arbor: University of Michigan Press, 1997).

23. Steven A. Shull and Thomas C. Shaw, *Explaining Congressional-Presidential Relations* (Albany, N.Y.: SUNY Press, 1999).

24. Lloyd Cutler, "The Cost of Divided Government," *New York Times* (November 20, 1987).

25. Morris Fiorina, *Divided Government,* second edition (Boston: Allyn and Bacon, 1996).

26. Rhodes Cook, "A New Dynamic Splits the Vote," *Congressional Quarterly Weekly Reports,* April 19, 1997: 934.

27. Woodrow Wilson, quoted in Pfiffner (1991): 44.

28. James L. Sundquist, "Needed: A Political Theory for the New Era of Coalition Government in the United States," *Political Science Quarterly* 103 (Winter, 1988–1989): 629.

29. Donald Robinson (ed.), *Reforming American Government: The Bicentennial Papers of the Committee on the Constitutional System* (Boulder, CO: Westview Press, 1985).

30. David R. Mayhew, *Divided We Govern* (New Haven, CT: Yale University Press, 1991).

31. Sean Kelley, "Divided We Govern: A Reassessment," *Polity* 25 (1993): 475–484.

32. Sarah Binder, "The Dynamics of Legislative Gridlock, 1947–96," *American Political Science Review, Vol. 93, No. 3* (September 1999): 519–533.

33. George C. Edwards III, Andrew Barrett, and Jeffrey Peake, "The Legislative Impact of Divided Government," *American Journal of Political Science* 41 (May 1997): 545–563: and Shull (1997).

34. David Epstein and Sharyn O'Halloran, "Divided Government and the Design of Administrative Procedures," cited in Fiorina (1996): 167.

35. Cary R. Covington and Andrew Bargen, "The Effect of Divided Government on the Ideological Content of Bills Enacted by the House of Representatives," paper presented at the annual meeting of the American Political Science Association, San Francisco, August 30–September 2, 2001. Also see Keith Krehbiel, *Pivotal Politics* (Chicago: University of Chicago Press, 1998).

36. Benjamin Ginsberg and Martin Schfler, *Politics by Other Means* (New York: Norton, 1999).

37. Jones (1994): 30.

38. See Charles O. Jones, *An Introduction to the Study of Public Policy* (Pacific Grove, CA: Brooks Cole, 1984) for a description of the process. For an empirical test, see Steven A. Shull and Dennis W. Glieber, "Testing a Dynamic Process of Policymaking in Civil Rights," *Social Science Journal,* 31 (1994): 53–67.

39. These four policy areas have been important parts of the government agenda for decades and are suggested in part by Aage R. Clausen, *How Congressmen Decide: A Policy Focus* (New York: St. Martin's,

1973); and John H. Kessel, "Parameters of Presidential Politics," *Social Science Quarterly* 55 (June 1974): 8–24.

40. Bruce M. Russett, "International Relations Research: Case Studies and Cumulation," in Michael Haas and Henry Kariel (eds.), *Approaches to the Study of Political Science* (San Francisco: Chandler, 1970): 425–440. Examples of such integrative case studies include Irving Janis, *Groupthink,* second edition. (Boston: Houghton Mifflin, 1982) and Charles Bullock III and Charles Lamb, *Implementing Civil Rights Policy* (Pacific Grove, CA: Brooks/Cole, 1984).

41. Peterson (1990): 9.

42. Jones (1994): 11.

43. Quoted in James M. Burns, *Roosevelt: The Lion and the Fox* (New York: Harcourt Brace, 1956): 165.

44. Barbara J. Nelson, *Making an Issue of Child Abuse: Political Agenda Setting for Social Problems* (Chicago: University of Chicago Press, 1984): 27–29.

45. David W. Brady and Craig Volden, *Revolving Gridlock,* (Boulder, CO: Westview, 1998).

46. John B. Gilmour, "Summits and Stalemates: Bipartisan Negotiations in the Postreform Era," in Roger H. Davidson (ed.), *The Postreform Congress* (New York: St. Martin's, 1992): 233–256; Pfiffner (1991): 82

47. Michael L. Mezey, *Congress, the President, and Public Policy* (Boulder, CO: Westview Press, 1989): 147–188: Walter Oleszek, "The Context of Congressional Policymaking," in Thurber (1991): 82.

48. James D. Barber, *Pursuit of the Presidency* (Englewood Cliffs, NJ: Prentice-Hall, 1980); Arthur Schlesinger Jr., *The Cycles of American History* (Boston: Houghton Mifflin, 1986); and James L. Sundquist, *Decline and Resurgence of Congress* (Washington, D.C.: Brookings Institution, 1981).

49. George C. Edwards III, *Presidential Influence in Congress* (San Francisco: Freeman, 1980); Douglas Rivers and Nancy Rose, "Passing the President's Program: Public Opinion and Presidential Influence in Congress," *American Journal of Political Science* 29 (May 1985): 183–196.

50. Michael B. MacKuen, "Political Drama, Economic Conditions, and the Dynamics of Presidential Popularity," *American Journal of Political Science* 27 (1983): 165–192.

51. Bond, Fleisher, and Krutz (1996): 127; Shull and Shaw (1999): 90.

52. See John Hibbing and and James T. Smith, "What the American Public Wants Congress to Be," in Lawrence C. Dodd and Bruce I. Oppenheimer, *Congress Reconsidered,* seventh edition, (Washington, D.C.: CQ Press, 2001): 45–66.

53. Samuel Kernell, "Explaining Presidential Popularity," *American Political Science Review* 72 (June 1978): 506–522; MacKuen (1983).

54. C. Lawrence Evans, "Committees, Leaders, and Message Politics," in Dodd and Oppenheimer (2001): 217–244.

55. Norman Ornstein and Shirley Elder, *Interest Groups, Lobbying, and Policymaking* (Washington, D.C.: CQ Press, 1978).

56. Anthony Carrado, "Financing the 2000 Elections," in Gerald M. Pomper (ed) *The Election of 2000* (New York: Chatham House, 2001): 92–124

57. Bond, Fleisher, and Krutz (1996).

58. Krehbiel (1998).

59. Keith Poole and Howard Rosenthal, *Congress: A Political-Economic History of Roll Call Voting* (New York: Oxford University Press, 1997).

60. Robert S. Erikson and Gerald C. Wright, "Voters, Candidates, and Issues in Congressional Elections," in Dodd and Oppenheimer (2001): 67–96.

61. Bond, Fleisher, and Krutz (1996): 125.

62. Brady and Volden (1998): 1–10.

63. Bond, Fleisher, and Krutz (1996): 105.

64. Quoted in Charles O. Jones, "Presidential Negotiations with Congress," in Anthony King (ed.), *Both Ends of the Avenue* (Washington, D.C.: American Enterprise Institute, 1983): 102.

65. Lester M. Salamon and Michael S. Lund, *The Reagan Presidency and the Governing of America* (Washington, D.C.: Urban Institute Press, 1983): 3.

66. Brady and Volden (1998): 2–5.

67. Binder (1999): 519–533.
68. Laurence C. Dodd and Bruce I. Oppenheimer, *Congress Reconsidered,* fourth edition. (Washington, D.C.: CQ Press, 1989): 49–50.
69. Colin Campbell, *Managing the Presidency: Carter, Reagan, and the Search for Executive Harmony* (Pittsburgh: University of Pittsburgh Press, 1986): 11.
70. Paul C. Light, *The President's Agenda: Domestic Policy Choice from Kennedy to Carter* (Baltimore: Johns Hopkins University Press, 1982).
71. Neustadt (1960) emphasizes individual or personal leadership, for example, whereas Campbell (1986) emphasizes institutional factors.
72. James D. Barber, *The Presidential Character*, fourth edition. (Englewood Cliffs, NJ: Prentice-Hall, 1992).
73. Marcia Whicker and Raymond Moore, *When Presidents Are Great* (Englewood Cliffs, NJ: Prentice-Hall, 1988).
74. Clausen (1973); Edwards (1980).
75. Terry Sullivan, "Headcounts, Expectations, and Presidential Coalitions in Congress," *American Journal of Political Science* 32:3 (August 1988): 567–589; Peterson (1990): Chapter 2.
76. James P. Pfiffner, *The Strategic Presidency: Hitting the Ground Running* (Chicago: Dorsey, 1988).
77. Light (1982).
78. Quoted in Doris B. Kearns, *Lyndon Johnson and the American Dream* (New York: Harper & Row, 1976): 226.
79. Richard Forshee and Russell D. Renka, "What Helps and Hurts Presidents? A Logit Model of Roll Call Voting," paper delivered at the annual meeting of the Midwest Political Science Association, Chicago, April 13–15, 1989.
80. Brad Lockerbie and Stephen A. Borrelli, "Getting Inside the Beltway: Perceptions of Presidential Skill and Success in Congress," *British Journal of Political Science 19* (January 1989): 97–106.
81. Terry Sullivan, "Explaining Why Presidents Count: Signaling and Information, "*Journal of Politics 52* (August 1990): 939–962.
82. Patrick J. Fett, "Presidential Legislative Priorities and Legislative Voting Decisions: An Exploratory Analysis," *Journal of Politics 56* (May 1994): 502–512.
83. Norman Ornstein, "Can Congress Be Led?" in John J. Kornacki (ed.), *Leading Congress* (Washington, D.C.: CQ Press, 1990): 16–17.
84. Susan Webb Hammond, "Committee and Informal Leaders in the U.S. House of Representatives," in Kornacki (1990): 62:63.
85. Joseph Cooper and David W. Brady, "Institutional Context and Leadership Style: The House from Cannon to Rayburn," *American Political Science Review 75 (*1981): 411–425.
86. David Rohde, *Parties and Leaders in the Post-Reform House* (Chicago: University of Chicago Press, 1990).
87. Peterson (1990).
88. Charles W. Ostrom Jr. and Dennis M. Simon, "Promise and Performance: A Dynamic Model of Presidential Popularity," *American Political Science Review* 79:2 (June 1985): 334–358.
89. Fett (1994).
90. Jimmy Carter, *Keeping Faith: Memoirs of a President* (New York: Bantam, 1982): 87.
91. Darrell M. West and Burdett A. Loomis, *The Sound of Money* (New York: Norton, 1999): 139.
92. Steven A. Shull (ed.), *The Two Presidencies: A Quarter Century Assessment* (Chicago: Nelson Hall, 1991), which reprints Aaron Wildavsky, "The Two Presidencies," *Transaction* 4 (December 1966).
93. Lance T. LeLoup and Steven A. Shull, "Congress Versus the President: The 'Two Presidencies' Reconsidered," *Social Science Quarterly* 59 (March 1979), reprinted in Shull (1991).
94. Jon Bond and Richard Fleisher, "Are There Two Presidencies?: Yes, but Only for Republicans," *Journal of Politics* 50 (August 1988): 747–767; Richard Fleisher, Jon Bond, Glen Krutz, and Stephen Hanna, "The Demise of the Two Presidencies," *American Politics Quarterly,* 28 (January 2000): 3–25.
95. LeLoup and Shull (1979).
96. Ibid., 8–9

CHAPTER 2

The Constitution and Shared Governance

. . . by so contriving the interior structure of the government, as that its several constituent parts may, by their mutual relations, be the means of keeping each other in their proper places.

—James Madison, *Federalist* #51

To a remarkable degree the connection between the Congress and the president of the United States still runs along a path that the founders laid out by more than two centuries ago. Throughout history, scores of court decisions, precedents, traditions, and innovations have helped shape legislative-executive politics. Chapter 1 introduced the shared governance perspective, the policy approaches, the patterns of presidential-congressional policymaking, and their causes and potential consequences. This chapter explores the foundations and development of legislative-executive policymaking: Why did the founders write the language of Articles I and II as they did? What were the key decisions and the philosophy underlying them? Once the Constitution was ratified, how did relationships between branches evolve and to what ends? How did the political environment, institutional capacity, leadership, and the policy agenda affect presidential-congressional relations over two centuries? What role has the Supreme Court played as an arbiter of disputes between branches, interpreting the constitutional boundaries between Congress and the president?

Prelude to Constitution Making

In the summer of 1787, 55 delegates from 11 of the 13 colonies met to amend the Articles of Confederation. Of course, they did more; they drafted an entirely new blueprint for government—one that was unprecedented in the history of the world.

As one eminent historian noted, "The Framers . . . virtually invented both the concept of a written frame of government and the ideal of constitution making by convention".[1] Since 1787, nearly all constitutions around the world have followed the American model of written constitutions produced by a representative assembly. Even more important than the constitution making process is the unique structure created by the founders, which shapes policymaking today.

THE COLONIAL EXPERIENCE

Colonists did not even think of themselves as "Americans" until the 1770s when the prelude to the Revolution began to create a sense of national identity separate from the British. When war became inevitable, the Declaration of Independence expressed radical sentiments about the natural rights of citizens relative to government. Influenced by philosopher John Locke, the Declaration proclaimed that government must be based on the consent of the governed.[2] The colonists' experience in the 1770s during the war, and during the 1780s as a confederation of states, had a profound effect on the thinking and actions of the framers.

American colonists had developed a strong distaste for executive powers. For them, King George III was a powerful symbol of an arbitrary, capricious executive. These feelings were enhanced after 1765, when the British Crown became displeased with the role of the 13 colonies during the French and Indian Wars. The Stamp Act and Navigation Acts were enacted to force the colonies to pay some of the war costs. Prior to 1765, American colonies had been governed relatively loosely, so these measures to exert more control ran counter to the rising tide of American nationalism. Colonial governors were increasingly viewed as extensions of the impervious authority of the Crown; their actions exacerbated resentment against the monarchy. As tensions mounted in the early 1770s, colonial governors often suspended rights previously enjoyed by the colonists: habeas corpus, trial by jury, and the sanctity of private homes. England reacted harshly to the Boston Tea Party in 1773, virtually rescinding the charter of Massachusetts. American political activity increased along with the growing hostility.[3] War with England broke out soon after independence was declared on July 4, 1776.

GOVERNMENT UNDER THE ARTICLES OF CONFEDERATION

Articles of union for the 13 independent states were drafted in 1777 and submitted by the Continental Congress to the state legislatures for ratification. The Articles of Confederation were not actually ratified until 1781, when seven states relinquished claims on land to their west. It was a weak central government: Each state was guaranteed "its sovereignty, freedom and independence, and every power, jurisdiction and right" not granted to the national government. This nominal national government consisted of a unicameral legislature—the Confederation Congress—made up of one representative from each state. Congress was granted the power to make treaties, coin money, regulate trade with the Indians, build a navy, and create a post office. Major decisions required unanimous agreement by all the states.

It was at best a feeble union, with severe structural deficiencies. The national government lacked the power to raise revenues since the Crown had abused this power. Without that power a national government could hardly function. There was virtually no head of government or executive branch. John Hanson was elected the first "President of the Confederation Congress of the Confederacy" in 1781. John Hancock was later elected to the post but never bothered to show up! There were no national courts. What little power the states ceded to the national government under the Articles belonged to the legislature.

The United States could barely make policy under the Articles of Confederation in the 1780s. The nations of the world did not know with whom to negotiate and lacked respect for the new country. Efforts to revise the Articles gained momentum. Only five states had sent delegates to a convention in Annapolis, Maryland, in 1786 to discuss trade between the states, but those in attendance ended their meeting by calling for a convention in Philadelphia the next year. Congress approved the convention for the "sole and express purpose of revising the Articles of Confederation." However, the delegates would go far beyond their legal mandate—they created an entirely new government structure.

Shaping Legislative and Executive Branches

Fifty-five delegates gathered in Philadelphia in the sweltering summer of 1787. It was a distinguished group, including Benjamin Franklin, James Madison, Alexander Hamilton, and James Wilson. The country's most prominent statesman and war hero, George Washington, presided. As a group they were wealthy, politically experienced, and powerful men. They were not only practical politicians but well educated, conversant with the books and dominant ideas of the day. Many had read Locke and Montesquieu, whose ideas helped Madison conceptualize the new government.

The founders' difficult challenge was to create a national government powerful enough to run the country effectively, but not so powerful as to infringe on the liberties that the country had won. At the first week of the convention, they agreed to create a national government with three separate branches. The presumption changed from reforming the Articles of Confederation to creating a new national government in which powers were separated. Convention politics and decisions reached in Philadelphia reflected various interests: large states versus small states, slave states versus nonslave states, and advocates of a strong executive versus those who wanted a weak executive. Their choices still influence the course of policymaking today.

The Congress

The new legislature was the most democratic creation of the founders. Its preeminence was reflected in its very position as Article I. Determining how seats would be apportioned in the new Congress was one of the thorniest conflicts of the convention. James Madison and the Virginia delegation proposed the Virginia Plan, which largely set the agenda for the convention. Madison advocated a strong central government dominated by Congress. The plan called for a bicameral Congress with both houses apportioned on the basis of population. The Senate, the upper chamber, would be elected by the House, and the House would be elected by the people.

Delegates from the smaller states were concerned about several aspects of Madison's proposals. They felt the national government would be too strong and that their states would lose too much autonomy. With both houses of Congress apportioned on the basis of population, their voices would be lost in a government dominated by large states. They wanted each state to have equal voice in the new union, as they had under the Articles of Confederation. The small states offered counterproposals, referred to as the New Jersey Plan. It called for a unicameral legislature where each state—regardless of population—had equal representation.

These fundamental differences over the power of the national government and representation in Congress threatened to cause the collapse and failure of the convention. On the brink of disaster, a committee of one delegate from each of the 11 states in attendance met over the Fourth of July weekend. This committee arrived at the most critical compromise of the convention. The Connecticut or Great Compromise proposed two houses of Congress: the House of Representatives, apportioned on the basis of population elected by the people, and the Senate, with each state having two senators who would be appointed by the state's legislature. Representatives would be elected every two years, while senators would be appointed on a staggered basis for six-year terms. The compromise on the shape of the bicameral legislature went a long way toward assuring the success of the convention. Extraordinary resolution prevented near deadlock.

The Presidency

Disagreements over the shape of the executive branch were less threatening to the convention itself, but views were strongly held and passionately debated. Madison's original plan had called for a single executive to be elected by Congress. The New Jersey Plan called for a plural executive who would be relatively weak. The debate over the nature of the presidency reflected the founders' uncertainty about government power—more specifically, executive power.[4] Those who wanted a weak executive, subservient to the legislature, were suspicious of anything that smacked of monarchy. As Madison noted in his diary, Roger Sherman of Connecticut argued in debate that the president should be "nothing more than an institution for carrying the will of the legislature into effect, that the person or persons ought to be appointed by and acceptable to the legislature only."[5] One delegate proposed a plural executive representing different sections of the country, to lessen the threat of a drift toward monarchy. Other delegates, troubled by the inability to govern under the Articles, favored a strong executive with independent veto power over the legislature.

Over the course of the summer, the shape of the presidency took form. Delegates finally agreed on a single executive, as advocate James Wilson argued, to ensure "energy, responsibility, and dispatch" in the presidency. The means of selection was extensively debated. Those who wanted a powerful, independent executive argued for direct election. Those who wanted a subservient president lobbied for selection by Congress. In the end, they compromised on the Electoral College, with election by the House of Representatives in case no individual won a majority of electoral votes. The Electoral College was made up of electors chosen by the various states, one for each senator and representative. Not anticipating the rapid development of the party system, the founders generally assumed that after George Washington, many presidential elections would be decided in the House.

Delegates also disagreed on the term of office for the presidency and provisions for removal. Some favored a single six- or seven-year term, without the possibility of reelection, to put the president "above politics." The convention originally agreed to a single seven-year term but later reversed itself and accepted a four-year term, with no limitation on reelection. The ultimate sanction of the legislature was impeachment and removal of the president from office in cases of "treason, bribery, and other high crimes and misdemeanors." The presidency became more of a national symbol than the founders wanted and they would undoubtedly be surprised at its modern-day scope.

DIVIDING AND INTERMINGLING POWERS

As we saw in Chapter 1, the founders created separate institutions sharing powers. Using the ideas of Montesquieu, James Madison believed that separate branches would prevent the accumulation of political power and tyranny. The result is a complex mix of powers specifically delegated to one branch or the other, with many powers divided between the two branches.

Congress was granted the power to approve all legislation and to override a presidential veto by a two-thirds vote of both houses. The Constitution grants to Congress a number of economic and budget powers. Congress was also explicitly delegated powers dealing with foreign and military affairs, as well as the power to make laws "necessary and proper" for the execution of their other powers. Over the years, broad interpretation of this provision by the courts not only established national supremacy over the states, but made it possible for Congress to legislate in the areas of social welfare policy and to amplify later constitutional amendments—particularly the First and Fourteenth Amendments—by enacting civil rights legislation.

The powers delegated to the president in the Constitution were more restrictive. The president was granted the power to recommend measures to Congress, call special sessions, provide information on the state of the union, veto legislation, and ensure that the laws are faithfully executed. In the realm of foreign affairs, the president was named commander-in-chief of the armed forces and delegated the power to nominate ambassadors, recognize nations, and negotiate treaties. All executive power was delegated to the president. Thus, subsequent executive branch institutions have legal authority but possess no direct constitutional power.

"Separate" institutions actually share intermingled constitutional powers. In a sense, the Madisonian system of checks and balances institutionalized interbranch conflict, by dividing responsibility to ensure that ambition would counteract ambition. Congress checks the president through the power to impeach and remove from office, to override vetoes, to confirm nominations, and to ratify treaties (Senate only). The president's veto power checks the legislature. The courts were included in the division of powers as well: The president nominates judges and justices, and the Senate has the power to confirm them. The ability of the Supreme Court to declare an act of Congress or the executive branch unconstitutional, established in the case of *Marbury v. Madison* (1803), became the Court's most potent check on the other two branches.

Over the years, the powers of the national government and both legislative and executive branches expanded far beyond those specifically delegated in the Constitution. In the case of *McCulloch v. Maryland* (1819), the Supreme Court recognized implied powers of national government, which could be exercised even if not expressly enumerated in the Constitution. Today, both branches are engaged in activities beyond the imagination of the founders. The powers of the two branches are not only those formally enumerated in the Constitution and implied by the Constitution (often as interpreted by the courts), but also those powers that *evolved* informally through custom and precedent. Table 2.1 compares some powers of Congress and the president.

Table 2.1   Executive and Legislative Powers

CONGRESS	PRESIDENT
Enumerated powers	
Accept or reject legislation	Recommend legislation
Override veto by two-thirds vote	Veto legislation
Accept or reject nominations by majority vote	Nominate executive and judicial officials
Determine qualifications of members	Advise Congress on state of the union
Raise taxes and appropriate funds	Call special sessions
Create and define executive departments	Enforce the laws
Support army and navy	Grant pardons/reprieves
Ratify treaties	Negotiate treaties
Declare war	Recognize countries
Remove president by impeachment and conviction	Commander in chief
Implied powers	
Instruct agencies	Executive privilege
Legislative veto	Formulate and submit budget
Enact congressional budget	Manage economy and submit economic reports
Produce economic and budget reports	Impoundment, reprogramming
Review executive agreements	Make executive agreements
Oversight and investigations	Central clearance and submission of legislative program
Audit federal agencies	Issue executive proclamation and orders
Send delegations abroad	Regulatory review
Expand legislative staff and agencies	Organize White House staff
Coordinate communications and media	Media and news management

Despite over two centuries of change, the fundamental, inherent competition between branches remains: Madison's system of separation of powers and checks and balances has effectively protected individual liberty by preventing tyranny. However, it has also created a political system that does not make policy through a single dominant pattern of executive-legislative interaction. As a result, leaders sometimes have difficulty in making policy quickly and effectively, and interbranch conflict and opposition may obscure accountability. The patterns of interbranch relations today and their consequences depend not only on the constitutional foundation, but on over 200 years of customs, precedents, and conflicts among Congress, the president, and the courts.

Policymaking Patterns in the Early Republic

A LIMITED PUBLIC POLICY AGENDA

Government and public policy were so fundamentally different in the 1790s that it is difficult to conceptualize today. The new United States was an agrarian nation with a dispersed population. People had to be self-reliant, independent, and individualistic; they simply had no other choice. The policy agenda was limited and simple: conducting foreign affairs, facilitating commerce, and providing those few needed services that people could not provide for themselves. Delivering the mail and paying soldiers were among the most costly expenses of government. Roads and canals were often built with public money. Some of the most important early issues were economic: trade and tariffs, whether to maintain a national bank, and questions of debt.

Yet despite the limited policy agenda, divisions in government may have been deeper in the first 20 years of the Republic than at any other time, with the exception of the Civil War. As George Washington and the early Congresses began the task of governing, the political environment was a nation dividing into two camps. The creators of the first political parties disagreed in fundamental terms over the power and scope of the national government. The two emerging political parties, as one expert has noted, "regarded themselves not as parties but as embodiments of the nation's will."[6] Alexander Hamilton's Federalists supported a strong national government as exemplified by the national bank. George Washington and Alexander Hamilton's economic program fostered commerce and attempted to protect domestic manufacturing. The National Bank, authorized in 1791, was a key component.

In growing opposition to the Federalists were Thomas Jefferson's Democratic Republicans, who would soon drop the latter part of their name and become the Democratic party. Jefferson feared that the Federalists would erode federalism (particularly the autonomy of the states) and the entire concept of limited government. Even their choice of name was meant to imply that the Federalists were not "republicans" but rather tilted toward monarchy. The Federalists favored manufacturing over agriculture while the Democratic Republicans were strongly agrarian in their roots and sentiments. Jefferson's followers supported the French Revolution as an extension of the American Revolution, pitting the common people against their masters—in contrast to John Adams and the Federalists who saw it as a dangerous threat to order and society.

DEVELOPING POLITICAL INSTITUTIONS

In terms of institutional development, both Congress and the presidency were in their infancy. The House of Representatives was the more active of the two legislative chambers, engaging in lively public debate over the issues of the day. The Senate, in contrast, met in secret, kept no records, and senators spoke quietly and decorously.[7] John C. Calhoun found life in the Senate stifling, choosing to resign and run for the more lively House of Representatives. Neither branch remained in session for long periods of time. Travel to and from Washington made the job of serving in Congress rather a hardship on family and career. It often took weeks to obtain a quorum. The first Senate, meeting in the Capitol in New York City, was delayed for over a month waiting for enough senators to arrive. Turnover was high. Most members served for only one of two terms before retiring from public life. It remained a citizen legislature, in which influence was based on individual character rather than longevity. Henry Clay was elected Speaker of the House in his very first term in 1810. However, a few members served for many terms and were among the important early American leaders.

The presidency, too, was in its infancy in terms of institutional development. George Washington created the first Cabinet by assembling the secretaries of the four original Cabinet departments: State, Treasury, Justice, and War. These remain today the most important Cabinet positions, sometimes called the "Inner Cabinet."[8] Hamilton, Washington's first secretary of the treasury, presented the administration's program on the floor of Congress, even though he was a member of the executive branch. By 1793, growing animosity led Congress to ban Hamilton from the floor.[9] President Washington knew many of the members of the first Congresses. Later, he made a personal trip to the Capitol to consult with senators concerning an Indian treaty and was not well received. He was furious with his treatment by the Senate and vowed never to go to Congress in person again. This precedent diminished the Senate's role from advising the president to giving or withholding consent after a presidential appointment or treaty had been made.[10] Washington also asserted the power of executive privilege—that the president could withhold certain sensitive information from Congress.

LEGISLATIVE-EXECUTIVE RELATIONS

Washington made efforts to establish informal ties with Congress and began the long presidential tradition of "wining and dining" members of Congress, initiating the custom of dinners for legislators at the president's residence. One attendee noted, "The president is a cold, formal man; but I must declare that he treated me with great attention."[11] Washington was perhaps more of a statesman than a politician, and his overall record with Congress was relatively successful. Washington cast two vetoes, in both cases on the grounds that the legislation was unconstitutional.

Presidential leadership changed with the election of John Adams in 1796. Divisions had become increasingly bitter and Adams lacked Washington's status and political skills. He would become the only president of the first five to be defeated for reelection and not serve two terms. With the election of Thomas Jefferson as president in 1800, the Democratic Republicans eclipsed the Federalist party. Despite being a bitter opponent of the Federalists, Jefferson adopted a position favorable to a strong national government and consummated the Louisiana Purchase in 1803. Jefferson was the first president to use the party caucus as a way to lead Congress. He frequently met with members of his party and submitted legislation through friendly members.

By today's standards, Jefferson was extremely deferential to Congress, which was still seen as the most important branch of the national government. Congressional dominance was the normal pattern of national policymaking. Jefferson cast no vetoes because, by maintaining good relations with congressional majorities, he did not need to. He placed great emphasis on courting legislative support, holding small dinner parties almost nightly while Congress was in session. It was once observed that, "food and wine were standard accessories of political persuasion [and] the secret of Jefferson's influence."[12] Madison and his immediate successors were not as successful or skillful as Jefferson, but by the end of the War of 1812, the United States had entered a period of one-party politics. The Federalists ceased to be a significant political force, and presidents were content to let Congress handle the main responsibilities for governing. In foreign affairs, however, presidential leadership had already begun to assert itself, such as with the declaration of the Monroe Doctrine.

Policymaking Patterns from the Jackson Era to the Civil War

New Issues in a Growing Nation

Economic issues continued to be a critical part of the policy agenda as the nation expanded and grew. The economies of the North and South diverged, with the South relying on a slave-based plantation economy, and the North on a growing industrial and manufacturing base. The National Bank was still a major national controversy 30 years after its original charter. In the area of foreign policy, the Monroe Doctrine helped define the role of the United States in the world and allowed presidents to concentrate on westward expansion rather than European affairs. The question of slavery was never far below the surface of national politics, even after the Missouri Compromise of 1820. Closely related to the question of slavery was that of the power of the national government versus the power of the states. Neither question would be answered until the Civil War.

Until the election of Andrew Jackson in 1828, the national government had little enough to do, and Congress could do most of it. Then changes in the political environment and presidential leadership demonstrated the potential power of the presidency. The American electorate expanded dramatically throughout the 1820s, during a period of national growth and democratization. The right to vote had previously been limited to landowners, but as the nation grew and moved west, most states dropped property qualifications for voting. Between 1824 and 1828 alone, the number of eligible voters tripled.[13] The sharpening of divisions between political parties also changed the political environment. The era of one-party politics was over; Andrew Jackson and his supporters emerged as the Democratic party, vociferously opposed by a new conservative party, the Whigs, and other political factions.

AN ENHANCED VIEW OF PRESIDENTIAL POWER

Based on his appeal to the expanded American electorate, President Andrew Jackson demonstrated what more aggressive leadership could attain. He claimed coequality with Congress in governing the nation and a more legitimate voice of the electorate. He considered himself the "Tribune of the People" compared to Congress, which he maintained represented local, parochial interests. His opponents branded him a tyrant and labeled him "King Andrew the First." This did little to dim his popularity with the people, demonstrating the importance of public support as a political resource for any president. Jackson was the first president to use the veto for political reasons rather than purely constitutional ones: He asserted that he had the power to veto any bill Congress passed, even if he deemed it constitutional. His 12 vetoes were more than double the total of all the previous presidents combined. Jackson was opinionated, stubborn, energetic, and combative, and his relations with Congress were rocky. Forty years after the Constitution was drafted, the potential political separation between branches became clearer.

However, Jackson's successors did not build on his precedent of a stronger presidency. His political opponents went so far as to promise to reverse Jackson's stance. President William Henry Harrison, for example, in his few weeks in office before succumbing to pneumonia, "foreswore any executive interference in the legislative process."[14] Both he and President Millard Fillmore took legislative positions on the divisive issue of admission of new states, ultimately leading to the Compromise of 1850. A succession of presidents—Tyler, Polk, Pierce, and Buchanan—served only one term and demonstrated little interest in challenging Congress. Only James Polk laid out much of a presidential agenda.

INSTITUTIONAL DEVELOPMENTS

Institutional development of both branches was modest but steady. The executive branch grew very slowly; presidents relied on the cabinet and a few personal confidants and private citizens as advisors. President James Polk once complained about spending too much time correcting grammatical errors in State Department memos, a presidential task nearly incomprehensible today. In Congress, the committee system began to take shape, although the strong standing committees of later years did not yet take form. Presidents found themselves facing more numerous power centers when dealing with the legislative branch.[15] The decentralizing impact of the emerging committee system was in part countervailed by developing party organizations within Congress. The Senate gained in stature during this period, reducing the pre-eminence the House of Representatives had enjoyed in the early years of the Republic. But both branches would take a back seat to the presidency during the Civil War.

Presidential dominance of national government may have saved a nation torn apart by the Civil War. The Republican party, formed in 1856, won the presidency with candidate Abraham Lincoln in 1860. Lincoln, although elected by only 40 percent of the vote in a four-way race, was one of the most powerful presidents in American history. As other presidents would discover during crisis situations, the political environment was conducive to expanded presidential power. The public supported the presidency and other branches acquiesced in its exercise. Lincoln took a number of unprecedented actions as president, moving decisively to preserve the Union. Without the approval of Congress, he appropriated money, instituted a draft, ordered the blockade of southern ports, closed the post office, and suspended habeas corpus, allowing southern sympathizers to be jailed for the duration of the war without being charged with any crime. As a courtesy to Congress, Lincoln submitted some of these actions for approval after the fact. He based his actions on "popular demand and public necessity" and the "inherent" powers of the presidency.[16]

Policymaking Patterns from Reconstruction to the Depression

THE INDUSTRIAL REVOLUTION AND GROWING POLICY AGENDA

After the Civil War, the domestic political environment took a very different form. Foremost was the question of reconstruction: how to treat the defeated South. This issue, more than any other, split legislative and executive branches in the 1860s; the hostility between Congress and the president reached historic proportions. Congress, under the control of the Radical Republicans, was determined to punish the South, and no presidential interference would be tolerated. Also, in reaction to the dominance of President Lincoln, leaders of the House and Senate were anxious to reassert their control of policymaking in the postwar era. When the ineffective Andrew Johnson, Lincoln's successor, proved meddlesome, he was impeached by the House and nearly convicted by the Senate in 1868.[17] The presidency was in a weakened state, and Congress dominated national politics for decades after.

As the United States became more industrialized and urbanized, the policy agenda of Congress in this period focused heavily on civil rights and economic policies designed to promote the growth of private industry. The Thirteenth, Fourteenth, and Fifteenth Amendments to the Constitution, adopted in the 1860s, abolished slavery, guaranteed due process and equal protection to all citizens, and protected the right to vote regardless of race or previous condition of servitude. For the first time, blacks were elected to Congress. However, the Supreme Court in 1873 placed the most narrow possible interpretation on "privileges and immunities" of blacks. Congress responded by passing a series of civil rights laws in the 1870s, forbidding discrimination in public accommodations such as hotels and restaurants. The Court subsequently unraveled these protections as well, and allowed states to pass so-called "Jim Crow" laws, which reinstituted a system of legal segregation of the races in the South.[18]

Economic policy continued to hold the attention of president and Congress in the late nineteenth century. The Civil War had destroyed the slave-based economy of the South, and the harsh reconstruction policies of Congress prevented a timely recovery. For the rest of the nation, however, it was an era of prosperity. The Civil War provided a direct stimulus to the development of industry; the economy was reshaped in ways favoring industrialization.[19] The Republican party, which dominated national government in this era, passed legislation that promoted the interests of industrial capitalists. The National Bank Act gave favored status to large commercial banks. The Homestead Act helped the railroads by giving settlers free land in the West, thus creating a market and dependency on the railroads. The Morrill Act created the great land-grant universities of the Midwest and West, helping agriculture and encouraging industrialization by increasing the supply of technically skilled labor. At the same time, economic interest groups became a more prominent part of the national political environment.

PRESIDENTIAL LEADERSHIP

Party competition was often fierce in this era. Republicans dominated the presidency, with Grover Cleveland and Woodrow Wilson the only Democrats to win the presidency between 1868 and 1932. However, Democrats often did better in congressional elections, building on the one-party "solid" South and their strength in big cities. Divided government sometimes resulted. Political leadership also continued to influence legislative-executive relations. Grover Cleveland attempted to reassert presidential authority in the 1880s and ran into congressional opposition. In two terms, Cleveland cast a record 583 vetoes, only 7 of which were overridden. Teddy Roosevelt was an assertive leader, using the presidency as his "bully pulpit." Roosevelt believed that the president could engage in any action not expressly forbidden by the Constitution. Roosevelt was also willing to use innovative tactics with Congress. When Congress refused to appropriate enough money to send the U.S. Navy on a muscle-flexing world tour, Roosevelt sent the Navy halfway around the world on available funds, then demanded that the legislature spend the money to bring the ships back. His successor, William Howard Taft, had a less-expansive view of the presidency, believing presidential power should be limited only to what the Constitution expressly granted.

Woodrow Wilson's notions of presidential leadership were heavily influenced by parliamentary forms of government. From early in his career as a professor of government to the end of his political career, Wilson recognized the importance of overcoming the fragmentation caused by the constitutional system. In the 1880s, when Congress still dominated national government, he expressed concern with the impervious authority of the standing committees.[20] By the time he was elected president in 1912, Wilson believed in a strong presidency with a Congress that behaved like the British House of Commons. Key to this approach was a strong party system, and Wilson accordingly based his presidency on partisan appeals. He boldly proposed a parliamentary-like transition of power if he were to lose the 1916 election. He suggested that rather than wait months for the inauguration, he would appoint his opponent as secretary of state (then second in line for the presidency) and then he and his vice president would immediately resign. Wilson was a powerful and effective president whose influence was enhanced by World War I. However, his parliamentary and partisan approach ultimately came back to haunt him. Alienated Republican senators blocked ratification of the Treaty of Versailles, which contained his dreams for the League of Nations and his blueprint for the international order after the war.

The executive branch grew as the functions of government expanded. The Interstate Commerce Commission—the first regulatory agency—was created in 1889. During the late nineteenth century, a number of reforms were proposed to improve legislative-executive relations. George Pendleton of Ohio introduced legislation to permit Cabinet officials to "occupy seats on the floor of the House of Representatives" and respond to direct questions during sessions.[21] Others proposed allowing members of Congress to serve in the president's Cabinet. Overall, however, the presidential office remained limited compared to today. Perhaps the most important institutional development occurred in 1921, with the enactment of the Budget and Accounting Act. This law created the Bureau of the Budget (BOB) and led to a national budget assembled by the president and his budget director.

Maturing Congressional Institutions

Significant institutional developments affecting congressional policymaking took place in this era. Between 1865 and 1932 Congress had modernized. It evolved from a part-time citizen legislature to a professional one. Service in the House and Senate became a career: The average length of service went from two to eight years. As turnover declined, Congress became a more stable institution, with established rules, norms, and legislative procedures. Workloads and the length of sessions increased.[22] Whereas Congress had met less than six months a year in the nineteenth century, by the twentieth century it remained in session throughout the year. With less turnover, the committee system became the bulwark of congressional decisionmaking. The seniority system (giving committee chairs to the member of the majority party who had been on the committee the longest) became the key to power within the legislature. Party leadership organizations—floor leaders and whips—were established by 1900. The powers of the Speaker of the House expanded in the 1880s and 1890s, until a revolt by rank-and-file members in 1910 stripped the Speaker of important powers. This further strengthened the committee system and committee chairs—who, along with party leaders, became the key focal point for presidential negotiations with Congress.

The United States had became one of the world's leading economic powers by the end of World War I. With its economic strength came greater military strength and an enhanced role in world affairs. Congress had evolved significantly as an institution, while the strength of the presidency continued to depend largely on the leadership skills and policy agenda of the incumbent. Presidents Harding, Coolidge, and Hoover in the 1920s were relatively weak and unassertive. However, the presidency would be permanently changed when the nation faced its greatest economic crisis and elected Franklin Delano Roosevelt to the presidency.

Policymaking Patterns in the Modern Era

GROWTH IN THE SIZE AND SCOPE OF GOVERNMENT

The Great Depression dominated the political environment when Roosevelt was inaugurated in 1933. The dire consequences of the global economic collapse gripped the nation: 25 percent unemployment, industrial output cut in half, millions of homeless and hungry, and failures of banks and businesses at the rate of hundreds per day. As president, FDR responded to this situation with an ambitious new agenda and proved to be a dominant leader. When he left office, he not only left a legacy of strong leadership, but he also left the presidency permanently changed as an institution.

Roosevelt came into office promising decisive action to make the government a more active partner in reversing the economic decline. Confident that Congress would go along, he warned that if Congress failed to act:

> I shall not evade the clear course of duty that will then confront me. I shall ask the Congress for the one remaining instrument to meet the crisis—broad executive power to wage a war against the emergency, as great as the power that would be given to me if we were in fact invaded by a foreign foe.[23]

The environment was more than conducive to such leadership; the public and Congress demanded it. The president was extremely popular and had swept into office with huge Democratic majorities in both houses of Congress. Roosevelt declared a "bank holiday," closing the nation's banks while asking Congress for additional powers to help solve the banking crisis. The new Congress convened a special session to receive the emergency request. After only 40 minutes of debate, the bill, which was only partially written, was passed and sent to the president. In his first 100 days, Roosevelt led and the Congress followed in a flurry of policymaking activity. Within a few months, the president proposed and Congress enacted the Agricultural Adjustment Act, the Civilian Conservation Corps, unemployment relief, securities and stock market regulations, the Tennessee Valley Authority, emergency railroad legislation, the National Recovery Act, and dozens of other measures.

The policy agenda of government for the first time expanded to encompass social welfare legislation. The centerpiece was the Social Security Act of 1935, which laid the foundation of the nation's social welfare system for the next half-century. It created Old Age Survivors and Disability Insurance (OASDI), unemployment compensation, Aid to Families with Dependent Children (AFDC), and aid to the blind and disabled. In dealing with the Depression, Roosevelt took a new approach to budgetary and economic policy. Using the theories of British economist John Maynard Keynes, the government played a much more active role in managing the economy by using deficit spending in the budget to stimulate economic growth. Civil rights did not yet play a prominent role on the policy agenda, but the efforts of such organizations as the National Association for the Advancement of Colored People (NAACP) sowed the seeds of the civil rights movement in the 1950s and 1960s.

When the United States entered World War II, all other issues took a backseat to the task of winning the war. Presidential government emerged; the commander in chief used emergency powers to direct the war effort through the growing bureaucracy in Washington. Congress kept a watchful eye on the executive branch, overseeing spending and management. Roosevelt died in 1945 shortly before the war ended, leaving a profound mark on the presidency and national government.

PRESIDENTIAL GOVERNMENT

Roosevelt's tenure transformed the presidency into the office we recognize today. The White House staff grew from a handful of aides to hundreds of domestic and foreign policy advisors. The Executive Office of the President (EOP) was created in 1939, giving future presidents a permanent organization to assist them. The Budget Office was moved to the EOP and became a powerful instrument for presidential influence over economic policy and budget priorities. The 1946 Employment Act made the national government responsible for economic management and created the Council of Economic Advisors to assist the president. In 1947, Congress passed legislation creating the National Security Council (NSC) as part of the institutionalized presidency.

Franklin D. Roosevelt not only helped change the institutions, his personal leadership helped redefine popular conceptions of the presidency as a source of policy innovation. He was a skilled politician, adept at working with Congress. Although he had his occasional problems—such as the ill-fated "court-packing plan" by which he attempted to add justices to the Supreme Court—his legislative record was unparalleled. He was also the first "media president," enhancing his power by effectively communicating with the American people through his fireside chats, broadcast on radio.

Roosevelt created expectations for "presidential government" and left behind institutions with which to achieve it. His immediate successors inherited what has been called the "heroic" presidency, based on the view that presidential leadership is the most effective pattern of interbranch policymaking.[24] The postwar policy agenda was darkened by confrontation and the nuclear threat underlying the cold war between the Soviet Union and the United States. In the atomic age, members of Congress increasingly deferred to Presidents Truman, Eisenhower, and Kennedy in foreign affairs. While the pattern of presidential dominance became more prominent, Congress did not abdicate responsibility in the domestic realm, despite the more powerful presidency. Economic issues also were a key element of the policy agenda as Congress and the president attempted to promote prosperity through economic policies. Federal spending and the budget grew. Congress and the president often battled over economic policies and budget priorities, particularly under divided party control of government.

Civil rights became a critical policy issue during this period, but not initially an issue where the presidency led. President Truman integrated the nation's armed forces through an executive order, but it was the Supreme Court rather than the legislative or executive branch that took the lead on civil rights. The landmark decision in *Brown v. Board of Education* (1954) declared segregation in public schools to be unconstitutional, marking the culmination of years of struggle through the courts and the commencement of legislative battles to protect the civil rights of blacks. Congress played a leadership role in enacting the 1957 and 1960 civil rights bills, whereas the Civil Rights Act of 1964 and the Voting Rights Act of 1965 reflected legislative support for strong presidential leadership.

Social welfare issues, so dramatic in the 1930s, were dormant in the 1940s and 1950s. In the 1960s, however, concerns about poverty, healthcare, and the elderly resurfaced, making social welfare policy once again a high priority on the policy agenda of both the Congress and the president. The Economic Opportunity Act of 1964 created a host of antipoverty programs. The Medicare Act of 1965 provided entitlements to pay for healthcare for the elderly and those who fell below the poverty line.

The Vietnam War and the Watergate scandal not only shattered myths of the "heroic" presidency but instigated a period of heightened conflict between branches that prevails today. Vietnam was an undeclared presidential war that ended the bipartisan consensus in Congress and abruptly halted congressional acquiescence to the president. Although President Johnson claimed that the 1964 Gulf of Tonkin Resolution passed by Congress gave him the legal authority to commit ground troops in Vietnam, by the late 1960s a growing number of members believed that the war was not only immoral, but illegal. Senate Foreign Relations

Committee Chair J. William Fulbright (D-Ark.) held televised hearings that challenged both the wisdom and the constitutionality of the war. Resolutions to stop the war, although never adopted, commanded increasing support and publicity.

Hostility between branches continued after the inauguration of Richard Nixon in 1969. His administration's secret bombing in Cambodia set off a string of protests and riots on college campuses across the nation in 1970. The presidency, in the words of historian Arthur Schlesinger Jr., had become "imperial": isolated, aloof, above the law, unchecked by Congress.[25] The Watergate scandal and the fall of the Nixon administration seemed to confirm this view. Richard Nixon became the first president to resign from office in the face of certain impeachment by the House and conviction by the Senate for his role in the cover-up and his attack on democratic processes and institutions.

CONGRESSIONAL RESURGENCE

In response to growing concerns over the imperial presidency, Congress took a number of steps to increase legislative power in both the foreign and domestic realms. The Case Act of 1972 limited the president's ability to use executive agreements rather than treaties to circumvent the need for Senate approval. The War Powers Resolution limited the president's ability to commit troops in hostile situations without congressional approval. It required prior consultation with Congress, notification of the commitment of troops, and limited their stay without congressional approval. Congress also beefed up oversight of intelligence agencies and limited the president's emergency powers.

In the domestic realm, Congress attempted to increase its influence over budgetary and economic policy by adopting the Budget and Impoundment Control Act of 1974. This legislation limited the ability of the president to impound monies, as well as created budget committees, the Congressional Budget Office, and a new legislative budget process. Congress increased administrative oversight and scrutiny of presidential nominations for positions in both the executive and judicial branches. The legislative veto—an arrangement giving Congress the opportunity to block certain agency actions—became increasingly popular. Table 2.2 summarizes some of the actions taken by Congress in the 1970s to check the power of the presidency.

Congress succeeded in changing the balance of political power between the White House and Capitol Hill. However, the difficulties of Presidents Nixon, Ford, and Carter made some observers wonder whether the "imperial" presidency had become the "imperiled" or the "impossible" presidency.[26] The political environment seemed to change in 1980 with the election of Ronald Reagan and a Republican Senate. Reagan succeeded in pushing a dramatic economic and budget plan through Congress. However, the process bogged down into recurring stalemate after 1982. Continued budget crises forced President Bush Sr. to abandon his pledge not to raise taxes; he compromised with Congress in a budget agreement in 1990.

Table 2.2 Congressional Resurgence in the 1970s

PRESIDENTIAL ACTION	CONGRESSIONAL RESPONSE	IMPLICATIONS FOR PRESIDENT
Committing troops	National Commitments Resolution, 1969	Sense of the Senate resolution requires the president to seek the consent of Congress.
War making	War Powers Resolution, 1973	President must immediately report any use of the armed forces to Congress and must terminate the use of the military within 60 days unless Congress has declared war; the president can get a 30-day extension. After 90 days, Congress can, through a concurrent resolution, terminate the action.
Emergency powers	National Emergencies Act, 1976	President must notify Congress in advance and identify laws intended to be used in a national emergency. Emergencies are limited to six months. Either house of Congress can vote to end the emergency at any time.
Executive agreements as treaties	Case Act, 1972	The secretary of state must submit within 60 days the texts of any executive agreements.
Impoundment	Budget and Impoundment Control Act, 1974	The president must report any delays in implementation of the budget. Congress established the Congressional Budget Office.
Secrecy	Creation of Senate and House Intelligence Oversight Committees, 1975	House and Senate exercise budgetary control over the CIA and other intelligence agencies.
Reprogramming	Increased use of legislative veto	Congress exercises tighter control over executive branch actions.

Presidential-congressional relations returned to unified government with the election of Bill Clinton to the presidency in 1993, following 12 years of divided government under Reagan and Bush. After two years of reasonably cooperative relations, the Republicans took over both chambers of Congress as a result of the midterm elections in November 1994. Republicans in the House, who had not controlled that body in 40 years, chose fiery Newt Gingrich (R-Ga.) as Speaker. They drew up the "Contract with America" as a conservative agenda to counter what many considered to be Clinton's liberal policies. This set the stage for two potential constitutional crises concerning impeachment and the Electoral College.

In 1998, the House voted to impeach President Bill Clinton on two of the four charges submitted by the Judiciary Committee. Although the Senate did not convict him, partisan rancor ran high. Democrats charged that this effort ran strictly along partisan lines, more akin to the decision against Andrew Johnson more than 100 years ago rather than the bipartisan impeachment proceedings against Richard Nixon in 1974 that eventually resulted in his resignation. The case against Clinton itself raised serious constitutional issues concerning the presidency. On his last day in office, Clinton admitted lying under oath in a deal with federal prosecutors that let him avoid being charged once he was out of office.

Less than two years later, Republican George W. Bush won the electoral vote but lost the popular vote for president to Democrat Al Gore in 2000. Bush was well aware that, like John Quincy Adams, he was the only other president's son to attain the nation's highest office, and both had done so under the cloud of losing the popular vote. Bush also hoped to avoid the unhappiness of Adams' single term in office. The intervention of the Supreme Court, which determined that voting regularities in Florida did not preclude the state from certifying that Bush electors had won the election and, thus, the presidency, prolonged the bitterness after this election. The month-long battle that preceded the Supreme Court's actions had shown fallabilities in state voting systems, and a no-holds-barred partisanship on the part of both political parties to capture the White House. George W. Bush had a most inauspicious start to his presidency in terms of political capital and an electoral mandate. As we saw in Chapter 1, the political environment was made more difficult for Bush in 2001 when a party switch turned over the Senate to the Democrats. Nonetheless, Bush was able to get both his education and tax cut bills through Congress by the end of his first year, and after September 11, few people remembered the election controversy.

Scholars and journalists continue to debate the role of the two branches in policymaking. As we saw in Chapter 1, many observers consider the president better suited for effective leadership, particularly in foreign affairs. They echo Hamilton's view that the president's advantages over Congress include unity, dispatch, representativeness, and secrecy.[27] In modern literature, advocates of presidential leadership emphasize that the diverse and fragmented nature of Congress is unlikely to produce the needed clarity of policy and speed of action.[28] In recent years, even in the area of foreign policy, a growing number of scholars support an enhanced or even an equal role of Congress and the president, disputing assumptions about the inherent advantages of the presidency.[29] In particular, the end of the cold war and the breakup of the Soviet Union have weakened arguments about the necessity of presidential leadership.

In the nation's third century under the Constitution, many questions remain unanswered about the balance between legislative and executive institutions and which branch shapes (or should shape) public policy. The review of interbranch relations suggests that patterns of policymaking have shifted over time, depending on the political environment, the state of institutional development, the policy agenda, and the effectiveness of leadership. Policymaking today is not dominated by Congress as it was in the nineteenth century, nor by the president as it was in the mid-twentieth century. We find instead a shifting array of patterns, including cooperation or deadlock as well as dominance by Congress or the president. Yet many questions about the constitutional basis for interbranch competition remain unanswered.

On occasion, legislative and executive officials have turned to the courts—the third branch of government—for remedies. Throughout the Republic's more than

200 years, the Supreme Court has periodically served as the final arbiter in disputes between legislature and executive, defining the limits of power of each branch. Next, we consider the role of the courts in helping to define the balance of power between Congress and the president.

The Impact of the Courts on Legislative-Executive Power

Two important points help describe the role of the courts in shaping the boundaries of legislative-executive power. First, the courts have attempted to avoid getting involved with disputes between the other two branches. They have refrained from ruling on so-called "political" disputes between branches or in any cases that have become moot (already resolved). Second, when the courts have intervened, they have rarely dealt with fundamental issues of presidential and congressional power. Most frequently, court decisions have nibbled at the edges of the separation of powers. In cases of national emergency or wartime, the courts have usually deferred to the expansion of presidential power, even when that expansion is in obvious violation of the Constitution. Despite these limitations, several court decisions have had an important effect on the constitutional balance between branches and specific policy questions. In addition, with institutional conflict on the increase, the courts have been called on to intervene more than ever in the past three decades. Table 2.3 shows the number of statutes and presidential decisions that the Court ruled unconstitutional during various time periods. The challenges to Congress and the presidency have increased since the 1950s and were particularly extensive against Richard Nixon, who averaged nearly five challenges per year in office. Except for Nixon, however, recent presidents generally have fared better than Congress with the Supreme Court.

Table 2.3 Supreme Court Decisions Against Congress and Presidents

	LEGISLATIVE STATUTES VOIDED			RULINGS AGAINST PRESIDENTS		
Dates	(Years)	No.	(No./Year)	Presidents	No.	(No./Year)
1789–1864	(76)	2	(.03)	Washington–Lincoln	13	(.19)
1865–1910	(46)	33	(.72)	A. Johnson–Taft	6	(.13)
1911–1930	(20)	24	(.83)	Wilson–Hoover	8	(.40)
1931–1936	(6)	14	(.43)	F. Roosevelt	8	(.75)
1937–1953	(17)	3	(.30)	Truman	3	(.30)
1954–1968	(15)	25	(.60)	Eisenhower–L. Johnson	5	(.08)
1969–1988	(20)	38	(.53)	Nixon (25)–Reagan	30	(.67)
1989–1998	(10)	20	(.50)	Bush–Clinton	3	(.25)
Totals	(210)	159	(.76)		76	(.38)

Compiled by the authors from the following sources: for *presidents*, Lyn Ragsdale, *Vital Statistics on the Presidency* (Washington, D.C.: CQ Press, 1998): 444; for *Congress*, Harold Stanley and Richard Neimi, *Vital Statistics on American Politics* (Washington, D.C.: CQ Press, 2000): 286.

Appointment and Removal Power

One set of questions that has occupied the courts is the interplay between presidential-congressional appointment, confirmation, and removal powers. Presidents nominate only the very top officials in the executive branch and all federal judges; those nominations are subject to Senate confirmation. All evidence suggests that the Senate generally defers to presidential appointees in the executive branch. Only two Cabinet nominees have been rejected in the modern era, Louis Straus as secretary of commerce under Eisenhower and John Tower as secretary of defense under Bush. Despite the publicity and controversy surrounding the rejection of Robert Bork, Reagan's nominee to the Supreme Court, the Senate was much more likely to reject presidential Supreme Court nominees in the nineteenth century than in the twentieth. Lyn Ragsdale recounts just over 30 instances in our nation's history where presidents encountered difficulties with their Supreme Court nominees.[30]

The question over who had the power to remove officials appointed by the president and confirmed by the Senate embroiled the first Congress and many congresses in subsequent years. After a lengthy debate in 1789, it was agreed that the president would have the power to remove Cabinet secretaries.[31] However, this did not mean that the president had the power to remove all executive branch officials, and questions about executive-legislative removal power remained. The controversy broke out again over Andrew Jackson's removal of the secretary of the treasury, against the wishes of Congress, in 1833. As we have seen, the removal power also lay behind the main impeachment charge against President Andrew Johnson in 1867. The Supreme Court finally confronted the issue directly in the case of *Myers v. United States* (1926).[32] The case arose over the removal of a postmaster in Portland, Oregon, by the Postmaster General, with the concurrence of President Woodrow Wilson. This action violated a law passed by Congress in 1876, which required the Senate to advise and consent on the removal of all postmasters. In the decision, the Supreme Court ruled that the president has broad powers to remove executive branch officials and that the removal power is vested in the president alone.

The Court's unqualified ruling on the removal power was amended a decade later in the case of *Humphrey's Executor v. United States* (1935).[33] Franklin D. Roosevelt removed one of President Hoover's appointees to the Federal Trade Commission (FTC) on policy grounds, rather than for neglect of duty or malfeasance, as specified in the FTC Act. The Court scaled back the broad decision in *Myers*, unanimously ruling against Roosevelt. The opinion noted that the FTC was not purely an executive agency, so Congress had the right to specify conditions for removal.[34]

The removal power has periodically reemerged as an issue between branches in recent years. With interbranch conflict running high during the Nixon administration, the courts stepped in on several cases. In 1973, President Nixon fired Watergate Special Prosecutor Archibald Cox because he was pressing the case against the president too forcefully. The event became known as the "Saturday Night Massacre," because the attorney general and the deputy attorney general resigned rather than carry out Nixon's order. Although Cox never got his job back, the federal court ruled that the president had illegally removed the special prosecutor from his post.[35]

Early in 1997, the Republican-controlled Senate debated a number of measures designed to limit President Clinton from appointing federal judges not to their liking. One of the devices would have expanded senatorial courtesy, usually reserved for district court nominees, to presidential nominees to the appellate courts. Any Republican senator from states within each of the 11 federal circuits could have objected to a presidential nominee. Another measure would have required advance approval of a nominee's ideological background. Some conservative Republican senators even made efforts to impeach Clinton-appointed judges they deemed too liberal. Part of the motivation for the proposals was to reduce the power over nominations from the Senate Judiciary Committee, where confirmation recommendations have traditionally resided, and place the decisions more in the Republican caucus as a whole. Confirmation of Clinton nominees was delayed. However, when Democrats recaptured the Senate in mid-2001, they too, slowed the approval process for Bush nominees.

RECENT COURT DECISIONS

In addition to the removal power, courts have intervened in battles between Congress and the president over questions ranging from legislative vetoes to executive privilege. Conversely, they have exercised judicial restraint in other areas, particularly decisions over war powers and control of foreign policy. A Supreme Court decision in 1974 helped force a president from office as the conflict between Congress and Richard Nixon reached its climax. The case arose when the special prosecutor, whose office Congress had created, subpoenaed the tapes that Nixon had secretly made of conversations in the White House Oval Office. The administration refused to turn them over on the grounds that executive privilege gave the president the right to withhold certain sensitive information. In the landmark case of *United States v. Nixon* (1974), the Supreme Court unanimously ruled that executive privilege was valid in some cases but not to the degree claimed by the president.[36] Nixon finally turned over the recordings and was forced to resign six weeks later because the evidence contained in the tapes proved he had knowledge of and participated in the cover-up of the Watergate break-in. Executive privilege became an issue again in Clinton's second term when top aides, such as Bruce Lindsay, called by the special prosecutor to testify about alleged sexual misconduct by the president, refused to testify on the grounds of executive privilege.

Other recent court decisions have affected presidential-congressional relations. The Supreme Court refused a lawsuit by U.S. Senator Barry Goldwater (R-Ariz.) against President Jimmy Carter who nullified a defense treaty with Taiwan. Carter took this action in an effort to improve relations with mainland China. The Court determined that the president has the right to abrogate as well as negotiate treaties. The U.S. Supreme Court also overturned a form of the line-item veto as a violation of separation of powers in 1998.

One of the key separation-of-powers decisions of recent decades arose in response to congressional attempts to exert control over rules and regulations developed by the executive branch. The "legislative veto" is a process where an action by the bureaucracy can be negated if Congress disapproves it. As the number of legislative veto provisions included in bills increased, provisions were included where rules could be disapproved by a vote of both houses, that of a single house, or in some instances the vote of a single committee. In the case of *Immigration and Naturalization Service v. Chadha* (1983), the Supreme Court declared the legislative veto unconstitutional because it blurred the distinction between branches created by the founders.[37] If Congress wants to "veto" a rule or regulation promulgated by a federal agency, a bill must pass both houses of Congress and be signed by the president. The *Chadha* decision invalidated portions of more federal laws in a single stroke than all previous courts had struck down in history.

Although the legislative veto was overturned, lawmakers continue to use variations of it. For example, members can adopt "report-and-wait" provisions that require agencies to submit proposed decisions to Congress. Legislators may pass joint resolutions as opposed to regular bills. Vetoes may be imposed through the appropriations process, denying resources to assure compliance with congressional wishes. Finally, informal understandings between the branches can preserve the legislative veto. Such accommodation might not be strictly legal, but may be necessitated by political realities. Therefore, despite the *Chadha* decision, the legislative veto continues in various reconstituted forms.

Several years later, the Supreme Court applied this narrow interpretation of separation of powers to congressional attempts to reduce massive federal budget deficits. The Gramm-Rudman-Hollings mandatory deficit-reduction law had provided that the Comptroller General of the United States—an official removable only by Congress—could order budget cuts in the executive branch. In the case of *Bowsher v. Synar* (1986), the Supreme Court ruled that this provision violated the separation of powers.[38] By focusing on the more narrow question of who could remove the comptroller general, the Court sidestepped the more fundamental question of the relative power of legislative and executive institutions in national government.

In 1988, the Supreme Court sided with Congress in a separation-of-powers dispute with the president. Under challenge was the law enacted after Watergate, creating special prosecutors (later called independent counsels) to investigate wrongdoing in the executive branch. Several Reagan-era officials who had been investigated and prosecuted under the statute challenged its constitutionality. In the case of *Morrison v. Olsen* (1988), the Court upheld the constitutionality of the independent counsel law. The justices did not accept the administration's claim that the law interfered with the president's authority over criminal prosecution.[39] On January 17, 1998, Clinton became the first sitting president ever to testify as a defendant in a court case, a sexual harassment suit filed against him by Paula Jones. The court ruled in *Clinton v. Jones* (1997) that the president has no immunity from sexual harassment protection while in office.

The separation-of-powers cases rejected by the courts in recent years are as instructive as the cases that they have heard. Particularly in the area of foreign affairs, the courts have steered clear of decisions. During the Vietnam War, the courts consistently refused to hear challenges brought by members of Congress concerning the constitutionality of an undeclared war. Despite the courts' unresponsiveness, legal challenges by members of Congress against the president have proliferated in recent years. A suit seeking to test the legality of U.S. presence in El Salvador was dismissed by a federal appeals court in 1983.[40] A suit challenging the invasion of Grenada was dismissed in 1985 because the invasion was over. Similarly, federal courts dismissed cases seeking to test the constitutionality of U.S. policy in Nicaragua and the sending of the U.S. Navy to the Persian Gulf in 1988.

Did President Clinton's confrontation with the court over his personal conduct result in decisions that will weaken the office for future presidents? The federal courts rejected executive privilege and presidential immunity from civil suits. Presidential scholar Peri Arnold worries about the office, stating that "Clinton's failed claims of presumed presidential immunities weaken the presidency."[41]

How important have the courts been in shaping the boundaries of legislative-executive power? Even though Congress and the president have increasingly turned to the courts in their battles with each other, the courts continue to avoid cases. When they cannot, they tend to decide cases on the narrowest grounds possible. While court decisions have had important impacts, they have not decisively changed the balance of power between branches. Political factors, rather than court rulings, continue to determine the balance of power. Without courts or any other mechanism to resolve decisively many of the constitutional disputes, a number of reformers suggest that the only solution is fundamental constitutional change.

Conclusion

Many critics argue that, whatever the genius of the constitutional system two centuries ago, it is inadequate for the governing needs of today. The system of separate institutions sharing powers is blamed for inaction or inadequate policies in the face of urgent problems. Most of the founders saw the Constitution as a good start, but an imperfect document. Thomas Jefferson believed that it would essentially be rewritten every generation or so. A century after its drafting, however, the Constitution tended to be seen as nearly perfect, not to be tinkered with. In the late nineteenth Century, British Prime Minister William Gladstone called it "the most wonderful work ever struck off at a given time by the brain and purpose of man."[42] Most modern-day observers are less sanguine in their assessment, but there has been little sentiment to change history's most durable written blueprint for government.[43]

After more than two centuries, separation of powers and checks and balances remain the constitutional foundation on which shared policymaking is based. Whatever the presumed merits of the arguments to amend the Constitution to reduce the separation between branches, the constitutional structure is here to stay. The relationship between Congress and the president is one of shared governance and responsibility for both foreign and domestic policy. As the cases in the chapters that follow will show, policy is made through a variety of patterns of legislative-executive interaction. To make the system work effectively, however, Congress and the president must find ways to work together constructively on the most difficult issues. How each branch makes policy through its own institutional arrangements and decisionmaking processes is the subject of the next two chapters.

Notes

1. Elmer E. Cornwell Jr., "The American Constitutional Tradition: Its Impact and Development," in Kermit L. Hall et al. (eds.), *The Constitution as an Amending Device* (Washington, D.C.: American Political Science Association, 1981): 4.
2. John Locke, *Second Treatise on Civil Government* (1690). See also Clinton Rossiter, *1787: The Grand Convention* (New York: Macmillan, 1966).
3. R. R. Palmer and Joel Colton, *A History of the Modern World* (New York: Knopf, 1965): 327.
4. Joseph Kallenbach, *The American Chief Executive* (New York: Harper Row, 1966): 26.
5. U.S. Congress, "Debates of the Federal Convention of 1787 as Reported by James Madison," in *Documents Illustrative of the Formation of the Union of the American States*, 69th Cong., 1st Sess., 1927: 664.
6. Paul Goodman, "The First American Party System," in William N. Chambers and Walter Dean Burnham (eds.), *The American Party Systems* (New York: Oxford University Press, 1975): 56–89.
7. Robert C. Byrd, *The Senate 1789–1989*, (Washington, D.C.: U.S. Government Printing Office, 1989): 28.
8. Thomas C. Cronin, *State of the Presidency* second edition (Boston: Little Brown, 1980).
9. Louis Fisher, *The Politics of Shared Power: Congress and the Executive* (Washington D.C.: CQ Press, 1981): 33.
10. James D. Richardson (ed), *A Compilation of Messages and Papers of the Presidents*, Vol. 1, (Washington D.C.: U.S. Congress, 1899): 64–115.
11. William Maclay, *Sketches of Debate in the First Senate of the United States* (New York: Ungar, 1965): 135, 172.
12. James S. Young, *The Washington Community, 1800–1828* (New York: Columbia University Press, 1966): 168.
13. Charles Williamson, *American Suffrage from Property to Democracy 1760–1860* (Princeton NJ: Princeton University Press, 1960).
14. James L. Sundquist. *Decline and Resurgence of Congress* (Washington, D.C.: Brookings Institution, 1981): 23–24.
15. Louis Fisher. *Politics of Shared Powers*, second edition (Washington, D.C.: CQ Press, 1987): 43.
16. J. G. Randall, *Constitutional Problems Under Lincoln* (Magnolia, MA: Smith, 1964): 58.
17. John F. Kennedy, *Profiles in Courage* (New York: Harper Row, 1956): Chapter 6.

18. Slaughterhouse cases (1873), civil rights cases (1883), and *Plessy v. Ferguson* (1896) essentially disenfranchised southern blacks.

19. Charles Beard and Mary Beard, *The Rise of American Civilization* (New York: Macmillan, 1927) and Louis Hacker, *The Triumph of American Capitalism* (New York: Columbia University Press, 1940).

20. Woodrow Wilson, *Congressional Government* (Columbus, OH: Bobbs Merrill, 1885).

21. Fisher (1981): 37.

22. Nelson Polsby, "Institutionalization in the U.S. House of Representatives," *American Political Science Review* 63 (1969): 787–807.

23. James M. Burns, *Roosevelt: The Lion and the Fox* (New York: Harcourt Brace, 1956): 165.

24. Cronin, (1980): 25–30.

25. Arthur Schlesinger Jr., *The Imperial Presidency* (Boston: Houghton Mifflin, 1973).

26. Geoffrey Hodgson, *All Things to All Men: The False Promise of the Modern American Presidency* (New York: Simon and Schuster, 1980) and Harold Barger, *The Impossible Presidency* (Glenview, IL: Scott Foresman, 1984).

27. John C. Donovan, *The Cold Warriors: A Policymaking Elite* (Lexington, MA: D.C. Heath, 1974): 57, 70; Dorothy B. James, *The Contemporary Presidency*, second edition (New York: Pegasus, 1973): 179; Robert A. Dahl, *Congress and Foreign Policy* (New York: Harcourt Brace, 1950); James A. Robinson, *Congress and Foreign Policy* (Homewood, IL: Dorsey, 1967).

28. I. M. Destler, *Presidents, Bureaucrats and Foreign Policy* (Princeton: Princeton University Press, 1974): 85; Robinson (1967): 65; Donovan (1974).

29. Sundquist (1981); Charles O. Jones, *The Presidency in a Separated System* (Washington, D.C.: Brookings Institution, 1994) and *Separate but Equal Branches* (Chatham, NJ: Chatham House, 1995).

30. Lyn Ragsdale, *Vital Statistics on the Presidency* (Washington, D.C.: Congressional Quarterly, Inc., 1998): 429–430.

31. Fisher (1981): 56.

32. *Myers v. U.S.* 272 U.S. 52, 61, 98 (1926).

33. *Humphrey's Executor v. U.S.* 295 U.S. 602, 618–619 (1935).

34. Fisher (1981): 68.

35. *Nader v. Bork* 366 F. Supp. 104 (D.D.C. 1973).

36. *U.S. v. Nixon* 418 U.S. 683 (1974).

37. *Immigration and Naturalization Service v. Chadha* 462 U.S. 919 (1983).

38. *Bowsher v. Synar* 478 U.S. 714 (1986).

39. *Morrison v. Olson* 108 SCT 2597, 101 L Ed 2d 569; on remand in re sealed case; 857 F2d 801 (1988).

40. *Congressional Quarterly Weekly Report* (January 7, 1989): 14.

41. Peri E. Arnold, "Bill Clinton and the Institutionalized Presidency," in Steven E. Schier (ed.), *The Postmodern Presidency: Bill Clinton's Legacy in U.S. Politics* (Pittsburgh: Univeristy of Pittsburgh Press, 2000): p. 39.

42. William Gladstone, "Kin Beyond the Sea", *North American Review* (September/October, 1878).

43. Donald Robinson (ed), *Reforming American Government: The Bicentennial Papers of the Committee on the Constitutional System* (Boulder, CO: Westview Press, 1985); Lloyd Cutler, "To Form a Government: On the Defects of Separation of Powers," *Foreign Affairs* (Fall 1980), excerpted in Thomas Cronin (ed), *Rethinking the Presidency* (Boston: Little Brown, 1982): 62; David Stockman, *The Triumph of Politics* (New York: Harper Row, 1987): 9; James Sundquist, *Constitutional Reform and Effective Government* (Washington, D.C.: Brookings Institution, 1986): 4; James Q. Wilson, "In Defense of Separation of Powers, in Cronin (1982): 179–182; Arthur Schlesinger, "Leave the Constitution Alone," in Robinson (1985): 53

CHAPTER 3

The Presidency and Policymaking

The powers of the presidency are often described. Its limitations should sometimes be remembered.

—JOHN F. KENNEDY, 1963

Under what conditions can the President of the United States set the agenda and lead government? Under what circumstances does Congress follow the lead of the president? As we saw in Chapter 2, both institutions have undergone profound changes in character and relative power over 200 years. The twentieth century witnessed a dramatic expansion in the American presidency; the president became the focal point of national politics. The dominant military and economic strength of the United States put the president in an even more powerful position.[1] Yet even in their most dominant periods, presidents faced a myriad of constraints. An enhanced presidency did not mean a diminished Congress. The roles of Congress, the bureaucracy, interest groups, and other actors remained important. As the aftermath of the September 11, 2001, terrorist attacks revealed, the country still turns to the president in time of national crisis and threat. But even in the period following September 11, Congress played a major role in determining national policy in both the domestic and foreign arenas.

This chapter explores several important questions about the president as a partner in national policymaking. First, what is the potential for presidential leadership, and what are the available political resources and the most difficult obstacles and limitations? Second, how do the factors identified in Chapter 1 (the political environment, election results and policy preferences, institutions, leadership, and the policy agenda) shape the president's role in policymaking? Finally, what is the legislative record of modern presidents? How can we measure and compare the relative performance of recent occupants of the White House in working effectively with Congress? What do those findings suggest about a shared governance perspective compared to a presidency-centered approach?

Considerable disagreement exists among presidential scholars over whether to study the office from individual or institutional perspectives.[2] Although it is useful to consider the presidency from different levels of analysis, the lines between them are not always distinct. Presidents want to succeed, to improve their standing in the polls, to push their philosophy of government, to enact good public policy, and to establish a historical legacy, but it may not be possible to achieve all of these at the same time. Individual actions by the president always involve various system and institutional factors. Understanding the president's role in policymaking depends on both individual leadership and institutional characteristics. It also depends on understanding the political resources and constraints of the American presidency.

The Potential for Presidential Leadership

POLITICAL RESOURCES AND SOURCES OF PRESIDENTIAL POWER

Although the powers granted to the president in the Constitution were not extensive, they form the foundation for presidential power today. Many of the disputes between branches, as we saw in Chapter 2, still involve fundamental constitutional interpretations. Did George Bush Sr. need congressional authorization for the use of force against Iraq in 1991, or did he have the authority as commander in chief to order the invasion on his own? Although he claimed to have the authority, the fact that he requested congressional approval suggests that the constitutional question remains unresolved. The presidential powers to appoint officials, to wield executive authority, and to see that the laws are faithfully executed are significant, but they do not assure the president success in the legislative arena. Informal and implied powers have proven more important as resources in shared policymaking with Congress.

Clinton Rossiter, expressing the view that a strong presidency is essential to effective policymaking, describes the expanded roles of the president: chief diplomat, chief legislator, party chief, chief of state, voice of the people, and manager of prosperity.[3] How would presidents be able to fulfill these expanded responsibilities? Developments not envisioned by the writers of the Constitution contributed to increases in the president's power. Because of greater governmental scope and complexity and the trend toward federal solutions to problems, the public came to expect more of the president, and more of the Congress as well. Presidents were expected to take a greater legislative role and provide more unified policy alternatives.[4] By the end of World War II, Congress and the country looked to the president to formulate a legislative agenda.[5] As crisis manager, the president was granted a number of emergency powers over the years to deal with foreign and domestic disasters.[6] The president may call up the national guard in the case of a civil crisis, as Eisenhower did in

Little Rock, Arkansas, in 1957. In addition, the dominant global role of the United States in the postwar era, the dangers of the cold war, and the threat of nuclear destruction further strengthened the role of the president.

Most of the president's political resources are not formal ones. Richard Neustadt notes that presidential power is primarily exercised not through the ability to command but through the ability to bargain and persuade.[7] Presidents succeed by consolidating and maximizing personal political power and by managing political resources skillfully. One of the most important resources is the ability to use the mass media to reach the people. Teddy Roosevelt talked about using the presidency as a "bully pulpit," but the advent of television significantly increased the president's ability to command the center stage of politics. Management of the news and public relations became important presidential resources.[8] Whether through an address to Congress, a visit to a foreign capital, a press conference, or a hike at Camp David, the president can make news instantly by going public.[9]

In addition to a vast public relations apparatus, the presidency has other perquisites that can enhance presidential power. The president controls several thousand appointments to the most important jobs in the executive branch. This can help shape rulemaking, enforcement, and policy implementation. The president has resources as the head of his political party, including the national party organization and elected members of the party. In addition, the president has tremendous fundraising potential, either for reelection as president or for the election of fellow party members. President Bush Sr., for example, raised nearly $1 million in a single fundraiser in 1991. President Bill Clinton elevated fund-raising to a new level by rewarding major campaign contributors with intimate meetings and sometimes even overnight lodging in the Lincoln bedroom in the White House. Both he and Vice President Al Gore were criticized for making solicitation phone calls from their White House offices, a practice that some considered a violation of federal law. George W. Bush signed campaign finance reform into law in the morning, then headed off to fund-raisers in the afternoon.

Sitting in the Oval Office in the mansion on Pennsylvania Avenue, the president enjoys the trappings of a chief of state. The White House sports a professional staff of some 400 individuals, with several thousand more close by in the Executive Office of the President. Air Force One, the president's private jet, and scores of helicopters are available. Lacking a king in the United States, the president must also serve as head of state. Presidents may try to emphasize the "regal" aspects of office. Nixon came up with fancy uniforms for the White House guards. Lyndon Johnson, for example, raised his desk and chair while lowering the other chairs in the office, reputedly noting "it's hard to bargain from your knees."

THE LIMITS OF PRESIDENTIAL POWER

Presidents cannot govern like kings. Despite the ability to command national and international media attention, the power of the presidency to direct the policymaking process in the United States is limited. Constraints became particularly evident after the Vietnam War and Watergate, when Congress was resurgent. Political scientist Harold Barger described what he called the "impossible presidency": an office whose expectations far exceeded its ability to produce.

> The presidency has grown impossible because of important changes in American life and because of dramatic alterations in the political and economic balance of power and influence globally. . . . During the post-World War II era, presidential authority over domestic and foreign policymaking increased, but forces leading to fragmentation in American politics already were beginning to chip away. . . .[10]

Changes in the international system also radically changed the ability of the American president to shape world affairs even though the United States is now the world's only superpower. The collapse of communism and the dismantling of the Soviet Union eliminated the crisis mentality of the cold war, which had favored presidential leadership. In addition, other economic and geopolitical changes altered the ability of the United States to act independently in the world in recent years. Increasingly, the United States depends on the global marketplace for its prosperity and no longer has a self-contained economy. In foreign affairs, multilateral cooperation and greater reliance on the United Nations, as in the Persian Gulf War in 1991, are increasingly important. Richard Rose suggests that the modern presidency, which began with the inauguration of Franklin D. Roosevelt in 1933, has ended and a new postmodern presidency has arrived:

> The difference between the modern and the postmodern presidency is that a postmodern president can no longer dominate the international system. . . . While the White House is accustomed to influencing foreign nations, the postmodern president must accept something less appealing: Other nations can now influence what the White House achieves.[11]

Many efforts at congressional reassertion (described in Chapter 2) had profound cumulative effects on the presidency by increasing policymaking constraints. Changes in elections and the decline of political parties in the United States magnified this trend. The growing independence of voters, the tendency toward ticket-splitting, and the decline in electoral competition for Congress sharply reduced presidential coattails. Republican landslides in the 1972, 1984, and 1988 elections failed to produce any significant Republican gains in Congress. Such gains came only after Democrat Bill Clinton had occupied the White House for two years. Republicans captured both chambers of Congress in the 1994 midterm elections and maintained control even after Clinton's decisive reelection victory over former Senate Majority Leader Bob Dole (R-Kan.) in the 1996 election.

George W. Bush won the electoral vote in a squeaker in the election of 2000. Republicans continued to hold a very slim lead in the House but, after the dust settled, the Senate ended up in a tie with 50 Republicans, 50 Democrats. An historic agreement gave both parties equal membership on committees, but due to the tie-breaking vote by Senate President (and Vice President) Richard Cheney, Republicans held on to control of all chairmanships. This bare GOP majority lasted only a few months when the Democrats recaptured the upper house after of a Republican senator defected. The terrorist attacks on the United States certainly enhanced the ability of President George W. Bush to dominate the government agenda. Given Bush's approval ratings of 80 percent, congressional Democrats decided not to challenge Bush on his conduct of foreign policy. But even in the aftermath of this national crisis, on domestic issues such as an economic stimulus package, congressional Democrats wanted equal voice with the president in determining national policy.

In addition to Congress, other institutions and actions constrain the president. The Supreme Court today is more likely to overrule past precedents. Interest groups remain a potent force in all stages of policymaking. The bureaucracy can be an obstacle to presidential leadership, particularly when the president's goals differ from the dominant norms and direction of an agency. An aide to John F. Kennedy once remarked, "Everyone believes in democracy until he gets to the White House and then you begin to believe in dictatorship, because it's so hard to get things done."[12] In short, although the presidency has expanded far beyond its constitutionally prescribed powers, other competitors for power are also stronger, and the nation is increasingly dependent on the global system.

PRESIDENTS IN THE POLICYMAKING PROCESS

Most studies of the presidency assume that the president plays a dominant role early in the policymaking process, especially in agenda setting and formulation.[13] This follows the conventional wisdom that "the president proposes and Congress disposes." Some scholars argue that this is particularly true in certain policy areas, such as foreign and defense.[14] In reality, both Congress and the president have important roles in virtually all stages of the policy process. They interact not only with each other, but with a host of other participants. Presidents not only formulate policy, but today they are often directly involved in bargaining with Congress over policy specifics in the adoption stage.[15] A veto threat is often a potent weapon in these negotiations. Presidents and certainly the executive branch are deeply involved in the process of implementation. We begin by examining the president's role in agenda setting before discussing important presidential actions in later stages of policymaking.

THE PRESIDENT'S AGENDA

In addition to the policymaking environment, presidential institutions, and leadership skills, the president's participation in the legislative process, (and ultimate success) depends on shaping the policy agenda. Clearly, presidents anxious to change the world face a greater challenge than those satisfied with consolidating and maintaining the status quo. Historically, the "two presidencies" phenomenon has been observed—that presidents have more influence and success in foreign affairs than in domestic politics. We will examine that proposition in detail in Chapter 5.

Three things are important to know in analyzing the impact of the president's agenda on policy outcomes. First is the nature of the president's agenda. Is it clearly defined? Is it sweeping or narrow? Does it generally advocate the expansion, maintenance, or retrenchment of government as a whole? Second, how much congruence or conflict exists between the president's agenda and the policy preferences of majorities in Congress? Third, how active is the president willing to be to pursue the agenda, to use the resources of the presidency as aggressively as possible, and to confront Congress? Presidents' assertiveness in pushing their agenda can be measured through content analysis of their State of the Union addresses and other sources of presidential statements. Much of what appears on the later government agenda can probably be traced to public presidential communications.[16]

The president's agenda, his orientation toward expansion, maintenance, or retrenchment of government, and his willingness to pursue that agenda in Congress are important determinants of the policymaking pattern that emerges. When the presidential agenda conflicts with congressional agendas, cooperation is likely to be required, to either make policy or avoid stalemate. Dominance by either branch is less likely. A president willing to be assertive with Congress is more likely to dominate than a more passive president; he is also more likely to risk deadlock when in conflict with Congress. The president shapes the agenda by proposing legislation to Congress. Presidents cannot formally introduce legislation themselves, but they can have a sympathetic member of Congress introduce bills for the administration. In the cases that begin in Chapter 5, we will see that the nature of the president's agenda and his willingness to pursue it helps determine which pattern of policymaking occurs.

THE PRESIDENT'S ROLES IN SUBSEQUENT STAGES OF POLICYMAKING

One important way that presidents can participate in the adoption of policy, the third stage of the policymaking process, is by taking positions on legislation pending in Congress whether the administration introduced it or not. (We will discuss this idea of presidential position taking later in this chapter.) Such matters are on the legislative agenda, which the president may seek to influence or block. Presidents can lobby Congress for legislation they favor and negotiate modifications of legislation to meet their objectives. An example is President George W. Bush's negotiations with Republican House member Charles Norwood (R-Ga.) over the proposed Patients' Bill of Rights. Even though the administration did not introduce or push such legislation, the president took an active role in formulation so that any policy that did eventually pass would be more acceptable to his policy preferences. In the last decade, presidents have been increasingly represented by their top White House staff advisors in high-level, closed-door negotiations with Congress. This can take the form of summits over the budget, or simply meetings to resolve pending legislative issues that are in dispute.

When the president cannot get his way by modifying legislation to his preferences, he may be forced to veto bills of which he does not approve. However, a president must use this technique sparingly because it is more a sign of weakness (e.g., the president was not able to get policy modified through negotiations) than strength.[17] Thus, the veto, which is also discussed at the end of this chapter, is a measure of last resort, to stop adoption in the hopes of getting legislation closer to the president's preferences. Occasionally, presidents turn to executive orders to adopt alternative policy if Congress does not accede to their wishes. For example, in the realm of foreign policy, international agreements have largely superceded treaties as foreign policy adoption. Because policy proposals normally must pass through many decision stages, there are multiple points of access and opportunities for influence by those both inside and outside government.

Presidents also play roles in even later stages of policymaking. Implementation refers to the execution or carrying out of public policy. Frequently it leads to substantive or procedural modification of laws because goals, intentions, and directives are not always clear. Responsibility for implementation is firmly entrenched in the Cabinet and the permanent bureaucracy. Partly because of its complexity, policy implementation is an activity that is less subject to presidential influence than either policy formulation or adoption. Indeed, presidents frequently complain of bureaucratic intransigence.[18] This perception seems true because the president must delegate the enforcement and coordination of programs to executive staff who do not always share his views, timetable, or outlook.[19] Policy implementation is an important function, but so staggering in scope, the president cannot always (or even usually) get his way. Few programs are self-executing. The rest of the executive branch can show support or nonsupport of the president in a variety of ways.

Evaluation refers to assessments of the effectiveness and consequences of actions and policies. Results are the "ultimate" end of public policy. However, empirical evidence on the impact of governmental programs is difficult to obtain, since it is usually attempted after the fact. Nevertheless, evaluation (including feedback from interested and affected groups) often leads to adjustments and refinements in public policy, which the president is sensitive to and affects the policy agenda. The public evaluation of the catastrophic healthcare insurance, a case detailed in Chapter 8, was highly unfavorable. President Bush Sr. decided it was probably better to leave it off the policy agenda altogether rather than try to change the policy for the better.

Elections and the Political Environment

PRESIDENTIAL ELECTIONS

At one time in American politics, a landslide presidential victory at the polls was usually accompanied by significant gains in Congress by the president's party. In 1936, Franklin Roosevelt was overwhelmingly reelected, carrying scores of new Democrats into Congress. In 1952, Dwight Eisenhower's massive electoral victory led to Republican party control of both the House and the Senate. In 1964, Lyndon

Johnson parlayed his landslide victory into expanded Democratic majorities in both houses. Since 1968, however, presidential coattails have diminished significantly.[20] Although Ronald Reagan exhibited coattail effects in 1980, helping the Republicans capture the Senate and reduce Democratic majorities in the House, the trend is for presidential and congressional elections to be increasingly decoupled. George Bush Sr. had no measurable coattails in 1988, and Republicans lost seats in both the House and Senate. He ended up taking office with a lower percentage of members of his own political party in Congress than any other president in history! President Bill Clinton failed to capture 50 percent of the vote either in 1992 or 1996, although he was close in '96.

Democratic presidential candidates in recent years have usually trailed the vote margin of Democratic congressional candidates. Since 1932, Democratic candidates for Congress, on average, have won 4 percent more of the popular vote than Democratic candidates for president. Table 3.1 ranks the last 12 Democratic presidential nominees by the percentage they ran ahead or behind congressional candidates of their parties. Only Roosevelt and Johnson ran ahead, and by relatively small amounts. Ironically, Al Gore was next in 2000 and his difference figure would have been higher had not Reform candidate Ralph Nader obtained 2.7 percent of the popular vote. Similarly, Independent Ross Perot cut into Clinton's popular vote margin even more in 1992 and 1996. However, these generally negative findings lead some to suggest the existence of "reverse coattails"; the popularity of Democratic congressional candidates may actually help increase voter support for the party's presidential candidate.

Table 3.1 Vote Differential Between Democratic Presidential Candidates and Congressional Running Mates (1932–2000, Figures beginning in 1975 are for House Democrats only)

PRESIDENTIAL CANDIDATE	DIFFERENTIAL
Johnson	+3.8%
Roosevelt	+2.8 (4 elections)
Gore	−1.4
Clinton	−2.5 (2 elections)
Truman	−2.8
Kennedy	−5.0
Stevenson	−7.2 (2 elections)
Humphrey	−7.3
Dukakis	−7.7
Carter	−7.8 (2 elections)
Mondale	−11.5
McGovern	−14.5
Average	−4.0

Source: Adapted from Norman J. Ornstein et al, *Vital Statistics on Congress* (Washington, D.C.: CQ Press, 1996; Lyn Ragsdale, *Vital Statistics on the Presidency* (Washington, D.C.: Congressional Quarterly, Inc., 1996: 155); data for 1996 and 2000 updated by Shull.

Although presidential and congressional elections are increasingly independent, there may be some residue of influence, even if it does not produce a policy-specific mandate. George Edwards suggests that elections still "provide a vehicle through which the public can express its general views to a congressman and can have an effect on congressional behavior without having detailed views on specific policies."[21] In terms of elections, as we have seen, the victory of George W. Bush was one of the narrowest and most controversial in history. Yet the fact that this did not notably harm him in his crisis-filled first year suggests the limits of electoral margins in explaining presidential power or success.

PUBLIC OPINION

Public opinion is an important presidential resource and it often is shaped by the political and economic environment of the country. One of the key elements of public opinion is public support for the president—the approval rating. Pollsters have measured the approval rating since the 1930s, allowing comparisons of presidents over time. Approval ratings are extremely volatile. In 1991, for example, George Bush's public approval ratings dropped some 40 percent in the nine months between the end of the Gulf War in March and the bottoming of public confidence in the economy in December of that year. Bill Clinton's popularity was low during his first term but actually improved at the beginning of his second term before dropping to 61 percent in late 2000. George W. Bush's popularity was in the mid to upper 50 percent until September 11. After that, it went as high as 85 to 90 percent and held at 80 percent six months after the attacks. Figure 3.1 shows the volatility of these popular approval ratings.

Studies show that certain factors consistently impact presidential approval ratings in a positive or negative way.[22] Presidents gain in popularity during an international crisis or other occasions when the American people "rally around the flag." This phenomenon occurs even in *unsuccessful* foreign operations: Kennedy gained in the polls after the abortive invasion at the Bay of Pigs in Cuba in 1961. Perhaps the most important factor that shapes presidential approval is the performance of the U.S. economy. Poor economic performance translates into declining presidential popularity as George Bush Sr., Ronald Reagan, and Jimmy Carter all discovered during their presidencies. Scandal or malfeasance in office can damage a president's standing: Truman's popularity dropped because of scandals involving his staff; Nixon's approval hit a record low for all presidents during Watergate; and Reagan's standing dropped noticeably after the Iran-Contra revelations. Finally, most presidents simply become less popular the longer they are in office. Although Eisenhower, Reagan, and Clinton seem to be exceptions, the trend holds for most presidents. This has important implications for a president's legislative strategies.

Presidents are not passive in the battle over public opinion; today, they actively attempt to bolster their support and sway public sentiment. The public relations apparatus of the federal government now costs well over $1 billion. Articulate spokespersons often present the president's views to the public. Release of good and

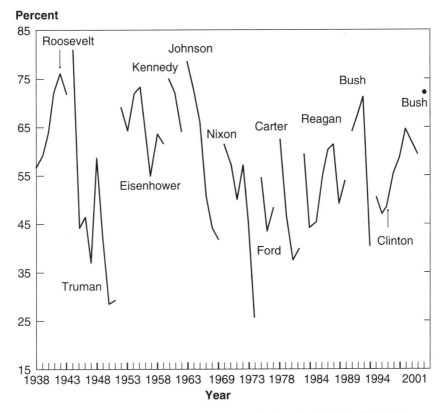

Percent

Figure 3.1 Presidential Popular Approval, Gallup Poll, 1938–2001. Percent who approve of the way [president's name] is handling his job as president.

Source: Gallup Organization. Values are annual averages of all polls conducted on presidential approval. Earlier data from Lyn Ragsdale, *Vital Statistics on the Presidency,* revised edition Washington, D.C., Congressional Quarterly, Inc., 1998. Updated by authors. Figure prepared by Brandon Prins.

bad news from the White House is timed accordingly to hit or miss the nightly television news. Presidents may manipulate economic or budget data to put the best possible face on results. Presidents and their public relations teams are often evasive and secretive about information that might have negative political effects. As President Carter's assistant Hodding Carter commented, "Government is not in the truth business. It is the presumed duty of an administration to govern, not to do reporters' work for them."[23]

Public support for the president is critical, because it may affect legislative success with Congress. Research finds that the greater the president's popularity in a congressional district, the greater the likelihood of support from that member on presidential proposals or on measures where the president takes a position.[24]

Edwards finds, for example, that increases in a president's popularity of 10 percent boosts legislative support by about 1.5 percent.[25] However, other scholars argue that popularity does not translate directly into enacted legislation; popular support is only one of many important environmental factors.[26] In addition, popularity seems to help presidents more during the earlier years in a president's term compared to later when party majorities in Congress become more important.

PARTY CONTROL AND STRATEGIES WITH CONGRESS

As we will discuss in the next chapter, political parties in the United States have reversed their decline in some important ways and party voting in Congress rose over the past generation. Republicans and Democrats also became more cohesive and more ideological, with sharper differences in policy preferences. As a result, party composition of Congress is one of the most important aspects of the political environment. Partisanship is a key element of presidential support and success in Congress. Presidents often begin building legislative coalitions with members of their own party, whether in the majority or the minority. Members of the president's party have greater incentives, both in terms of politics and policy, to go along with him. Studies show that the party occupying the White House tends to have more cohesive voting patterns in Congress than the other party, particularly on foreign policy issues.[27]

The alignment in Congress helps determine whether a president pursues a partisan (get a majority with members of your own party only), cross-partisan (try to attract a few defections from the other party to make a majority), or bipartisan (try to get a majority of members of both parties) approach with Congress. Although party government has worked on occasion in American political history, the legacy of Woodrow Wilson's inability to win ratification for the Treaty of Versailles in 1919 stands as a reminder of the consequences of excessive reliance on a partisan strategy in the U.S. system. More often than not, presidents need the votes of members of the other party to succeed legislatively.

Because of the divisions within the northern and southern wings of the Democratic party, Lyndon Johnson relied on and cultivated Republican help in his civil rights battles. With huge Democratic majorities in Congress, particularly after the 1964 landslide, he could afford to ignore Republican legislators on most other matters. Ronald Reagan, with the help of a small band of conservative Democrats (the so-called "boll weevils"), pursued a cross-partisan strategy in 1981–82. While his program was adopted in 1981, Democratic gains in the House in the 1982 congressional elections contributed to declining presidential legislative success, and increasing partisanship in congressional voting during the rest of his administration.[28]

Bill Clinton pursued a rare partisan strategy with Congress in 1993 with his deficit reduction plan while the Democrats controlled the Congress. He was successful in passing the huge deficit reduction plan—including a major tax increase—without a single Republican vote, but by the narrowest of margins. This is an extremely difficult pattern to follow and was not available after the Republicans captured Congress in 1994. Facing a Republican Congress for the rest of his term, Clinton changed his legislative strategy. He often threatened Congress with the veto and actually used it, as in the case of the budget confrontation of 1995–96 (see case in Chapter 7), and succeeded in winning major policy concessions from the Republicans in many cases. In other instances, he looked to build bipartisanship, but with the Republicans determined to pursue their own agenda, that tack was difficult. Moderate Senator John Breaux (D-La.) stated, "I'm hoping for some cooperation with a president who knows he has to govern from the center and a Congress that knows that compromise is not a dirty word."[29] One of the best examples of cooperation was welfare reform (see case in Chapter 8).

President George W. Bush followed a strategy of cross-partisanship in getting his top priority, a tax cut, enacted in May 2001. He attracted just enough moderate Democrats to provide a narrow victory (see case in Chapter 7). He succeeded with a bipartisan strategy with his second priority, education reform. By compromising on the most controversial aspect of his proposals (school vouchers) and giving in to Democrats' demands for more spending, he was able to get a majority of both parties to support the bill, which he signed in January 2002.

Despite the increase in party voting, Congress has not turned into a parliament. Party loyalty is still far from automatic. However, because members of a president's party support him more often than the opposition does, legislative success is related to party control of the House and Senate. Until the mid-1970s, presidents were successful 85 percent of the time when they had majorities in Congress, compared to only 65 percent when their party was in the minority.[30] Since then, presidential success has declined overall, but even Jimmy Carter (who was less popular than either Reagan or Bush), received greater support from Congress because of the partisan Democratic majorities. Of all the factors in the political environment, majorities in Congress remain the single best predictor of presidential support and legislative success.[31] Yet, other environmental, institutional, leadership, and agenda factors, which we shall consider next, mediate the influence of party.

Presidential Institutions

The informal advisory system that served Presidents Washington through Hoover proved inadequate in the 1930s when government expanded into the areas of social welfare, economic management, regulation, and other new activities. The Brownlow Report of 1937, commissioned by President Roosevelt, issued a number of recommendations for reorganizing the American presidency. Changes that were adopted permanently altered the nature of the office. The institutionalized presidency consists of the president and those who work directly for him: the inner circle of White House staff and presidential agencies that play a regular and important role in decisionmaking. The presidency is much more than a single individual, but much less than the entire executive branch. Three of the key elements of the presidency are the White House staff, the Executive Office of the President (EOP), and the Cabinet.

WHITE HOUSE STAFF, EXECUTIVE OFFICE, AND CABINET

Two years after the Brownlow Report, the White House staff and EOP were created. The White House staff includes domestic staff to care for the president and his family as well as the president's top advisors: press secretary, chief of staff, domestic affairs advisor, national security advisor, political affairs advisor, communications director, appointments secretary, congressional liaison, and others. These staff members serve two important functions. First, they are the president's ambassadors to groups and constituencies in the political system, ranging from Congress to civil rights groups to the business community. Second, the White House staff is an important decisionmaking group within the administration, working with the president in formulating foreign policy decisions, a legislative package, a budget, or an economic plan. The White House staff grew from 50 during the Roosevelt administration to around 500 in the early 1970s and is around 400 today.

The EOP forms a second circle around the president. It represents a mini-bureaucracy that works directly for the president. Most employees are physically located outside of the White House, usually in the Executive Office buildings nearby. One of the first agencies within the EOP was the Bureau of the Budget (BOB), which played a key role in the institutionalized presidency by compiling the budget for the executive branch. In 1970 BOB was reorganized into the Office of Management and Budget (OMB). Besides formulating the executive budget, OMB helped to manage the vast bureaucracy and, later, to review federal regulations.

The EOP also includes the National Security Council (NSC), created by the National Security Act of 1947. This postwar legislation, based on the lessons of World War II, created the Department of Defense (DOD, formerly the War Department), the Central Intelligence Agency (CIA) as well as the NSC. The NSC was designed to improve coordination of national security policy and to give the president better advice, but oftentimes it has been unable to overcome competition and conflict among the DOD, the State Department, and the White House.

The Cabinet (the oldest presidential institution dating back to George Washington) is another source of presidential coordination and advice. The Cabinet has long appealed to presidents because of tradition and the hope that they can effectively use the heads of the federal departments to manage the vast federal bureaucracy. However, the Cabinet has proven of limited value as an advisory body in recent times. Cabinet members have divided loyalty between their job as presidential advisors and their jobs as heads of large executive departments. Cabinet secretaries sometimes "go native"—begin to work more for the interests of the department than those of the president.

Nonetheless, the Cabinet remains an integral part of the institutionalized presidency. The composition of the Cabinet has symbolic importance, particularly sensitivity to minority concerns through the appointment of blacks, women, or Hispanics. Eisenhower's cabinet was unflatteringly characterized as "nine millionaires and a plumber."[32] Presidents choose between policy generalists and policy specialists associated with a particular constituency, such as farmers or veterans. To improve the effectiveness of the Cabinet as an advisory institution, some presidents have divided it into councils, similar to subcommittees, that included members of the White House staff. The vice president, whose role within the White House has increased in importance in all administrations since Carter, may also be part of Cabinet councils or work groups.

CENTRAL CLEARANCE AND LEGISLATIVE LIAISON

One of the most important changes in the legislative role of the presidency was the development of *central clearance*: White House review and approval of all agency legislative proposals before they are submitted to Congress. Central clearance of programs became institutionalized in the 1950s, helping formalize the president's role as "chief agenda setter."[33] Three separate but interrelated processes are included in program clearance: the approval of departmental legislative initiatives, submission of the president's package of legislative proposals, and the coordination of advice on whether the president should sign or veto legislation (called the "enrolled bill process").[34] Programs that used to originate within departments and agencies are sent through OMB, which coordinates with the White House staff and the president. This process increased presidential control of a diverse range of policy proposals from the bureaucracy, but it did not ensure greater success. Effective selling of the proposals on Capitol Hill is also needed.

The development of more formal legislative liaison operations corresponded with the growth of central clearance, beginning with the Eisenhower administration in the late 1950s. To a large extent, Larry O'Brien under Kennedy and Johnson fashioned the modern Office of Congressional Relations.[35] The liaison office coordinates the legislative efforts of the president, conveying information and carrying messages between the president and congressional leaders. The president's top lobbyists may engage in behind-the-scenes negotiations with key legislative leaders; other top staff people, such as the chief of staff or OMB director, may also be involved. Congressional liaison efforts help coordinate the president's lobbying efforts and most members of Congress perceive them as useful.[36] The experience and quality of the president's appointments to the Office of Congressional Relations influence the administration's legislative success. Jimmy Carter, in particular, suffered because of the inexperience and blunders by his liaison office.[37]

Richard Neustadt observes that, "All presidents wish that they could make Congress serve them as a rubber stamp, converting their agendas into prompt enactments, and most presidents will try to bring that miracle about, whenever and as best they can."[38] Nonetheless, direct personal involvement by the president varies considerably. Richard Nixon appointed a staff with extensive Capitol Hill experience and avoided much direct personal contact, since he found personally lobbying Congress distasteful. Ronald Reagan also relied heavily on staff to manage his legislative agenda on the Hill, but to a lesser extent than Nixon. Franklin Roosevelt, Johnson, Bush Sr., and Clinton took more active personal roles in lobbying with differing degrees of success. In 1990, Bush lobbied hard for enactment of the budget summit agreement, personally calling dozens of members. The proposal was defeated anyway. Kennedy, Eisenhower, Carter, and George W. Bush fall somewhere in the middle of the scale of personal involvement.

Presidential Leadership

In addition to the political environment and the institutions of the modern presidency, personal characteristics and the leadership abilities of the president influence legislative success. Presidents inherit essentially the same presidential institutions, and they have limited ability to shape the office and the policymaking process to their liking. Some presidents have greater management skills and may devise more effective means for coordinating policy. Others have more effective communication skills and may be better able to convince the public and Congress to support their programs. Political science sometimes minimizes presidential leadership because it is so difficult to measure objectively. However, it remains important, even from shared governance perspective that does not view all policy as originating from the White House.

Marcia Whicker and Raymond Moore developed a typology of presidential leadership based on two main criteria: management skills and selling skills.[39] Instead of focusing on psychological or personality characteristics, they identify the skills necessary for a president to succeed. A president who is a strong manager can set priorities, assemble qualified people, and take steps to achieve goals. The president who is a good salesperson can communicate, motivate, or even manipulate other leaders, the media, and the public. We consider both management and communication (selling) skills to be important in determining presidential leadership.

MANAGEMENT STYLE AND SKILLS

Within the parameters of the institutionalized presidency, presidents attempt to tailor decisionmaking to their own personal style. Two basic patterns have emerged since Franklin D. Roosevelt.[40] The first is a more formal, hierarchical organization of the presidency, resembling a pyramid. Directly below the president sits a powerful chief of staff who controls the access of people and information to the president. President Eisenhower best exemplified the pyramid management style. As in an army command, his chief of staff, Sherman Adams, served as a deputy president.[41] Adams summarized and initialed all memos going to the president and controlled access to him, even for Cabinet members. Richard Nixon also employed the pyramid style of management, having watched it in operation while he was Eisenhower's vice president. His powerful chief of staff, H. R. Haldeman, stood between Nixon and the rest of the political world. The advantages of the pyramid style is that it frees the president from the palace-guard politics that can occur in the White House, as well as protects the president's precious time. The danger is that the system can be inflexible and the president runs the risk of becoming isolated from diverse points of view and losing contact with people and problems.

The second approach is a much more open management style, with the president in the center, like the hub of a wheel. Openness and access to the president by a wide circle of advisors, individuals, and interests characterizes this approach. Franklin Roosevelt best exemplified the "hub-of-the-wheel" style, a wide open, freewheeling, conflict-ridden style with overlapping responsibility. John F. Kennedy also opted for this management style and was not averse to going around official channels, talking directly to officials at all levels of the bureaucracy. The advantages of the hub-of-the-wheel style include flexibility, the tendency to provide the president with widespread feedback from diverse constituencies, and the greater involvement of the president. The drawbacks are the confusion it can cause within the administration, leading to internal conflicts and wasting valuable presidential time.

Presidents may shift their management style over time. Carter initially opted for a more open administration, without a chief of staff. Two years later, he moved to a more hierarchical system and selected a chief of staff. Regardless of their management styles, every president since Lyndon Johnson thought it necessary to have a chief of staff. Carter tended to immerse himself with many of the details of policymaking and was accused of excessive micromanagement of the presidency. Ronald Reagan, in contrast, had a very detached management style, setting the general direction of policy and leaving it to his advisors to fill in the details and implement decisions. The Tower Commission, investigating the Iran-Contra scandal, concluded that the scandal was in part the fault of Reagan's overly detached management style.[42] Presidents Bush Sr. and Clinton, reacting to their immediate predecessors, adopted a more hands-on approach than Reagan, but without being swallowed up in detail like Carter.[43] Bill Clinton had some problems with the White House organization, which was somewhat disorganized and unfocused at times. George W. Bush adopted a management approach that appears less chaotic and more disciplined.

COMMUNICATION AND SELLING SKILLS

Presidents have varied in their ability to get their message across effectively since the days of George Washington and John Adams. Some, like President John Tyler (1841–45), were notorious for having poor relations with Congress and even with their own Cabinet. Others, like Franklin Roosevelt, had the reputation for communicating effectively with Congress. Today, communication and public relations are among the most important functions of the White House. A number of formal messages are delivered each year, including the State of the Union address, the budget message, and the economic report of the president. The president also issues special messages to Congress, letters, reports, and other documents. In addition, the president makes a number of speeches in various forums across the country, which usually makes the news. Clearly, formal communications between the White House and the Congress have increased over time.

Among recent presidents, Kennedy, Reagan, and Clinton had particularly good selling skills and were attractive media personalities. In contrast, Nixon and Carter had problems in communicating with the public and with Congress and were less attractive media personalities. George W. Bush entered office with a reputation as being warm but somewhat inarticulate. He seemed to do better than expected in terms of communication skills early in his term, particularly after the terrorist attacks. Selling skills include more than media skills, however. Johnson was not particularly effective on television, but behind the scenes he was a legendary salesman. Timing can be an important aspect of presidential success. A skillful president gauges the appropriate timing of actions or proposals in accordance with the domestic and international environment. George W. Bush seems a more savvy tactician than his father. All other things equal, it appears that presidents have a greater chance to see their legislative proposals enacted if they move relatively early in their administration. Several scholars argue that presidents must "move it or lose it," acting boldly to bring clear but limited priorities before Congress early in their terms.[44]

An important element combining management and communication skills is sometimes called the *administrative presidency*. Richard Nathan coined this term in describing the efforts by Richard Nixon and Ronald Reagan to adopt policy independently from Congress. Other recent scholars have also written of the utilization of administrative devices by presidents to further their policy preferences.[45] Presidents since George Washington have used executive orders as a means of facilitating their tasks as chief executive. However, modern presidents have found the device useful in broader policymaking. According to Gary King and Lyn Ragsdale, "Only with Franklin Roosevelt did the use of executive orders extend beyond administrative matters to include major presidential policy initiatives."[46] Although Nathan argues that this device is used to bypass Congress, one recent study observes that when presidents are successful with Congress, executive orders are used more.[47] Thus, administrative and legislative strategies have become intertwined. These and other presidential leadership skills are important in determining what pattern of policymaking emerges with Congress. One important device is supporting, changing, or altering the legislative agenda, our next topic.

The Legislative Records of Modern Presidents

"Support" versus "Success"

The political environment, presidential institutions, the president's leadership abilities, and policy agenda all help determine relations with Congress. This chapter has examined what the president brings to the equation of shared governance. We will now examine presidential legislative support and success to see how often Congress agrees with or goes along with the president.[48]

Presidential *success* with Congress measures the percent of presidential vote positions upheld. In contrast to success, *support* measures the percentage of legislators siding with presidential vote positions. Figure 3.2 reveals CQ's success and support scores on presidents' vote positions in the House. Note that success is nearly always greater than support until the mid-1980s. Reagan and Bush are the exceptions among modern presidents, receiving greater support than success. The figures for Clinton show dramatic differences in the two measures in his first term, with some recovery in the second term. One recent study finds support most influenced by the presidents' party margin in Congress, policy area, and the extent to which they take vote positions.[49]

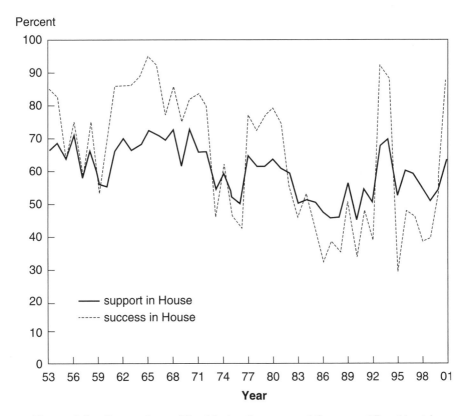

Figure 3.2 Comparison of Legislative Support and Success of Presidents' Vote Positions in the House, 1953–2001.
success = the percentage of presidential vote positions upheld;
support = the percentage of representatives siding with the president.

Source: *Congressional Quarterly Almanac* (Washington, D.C.: Congressional Quarterly, Inc.) annual. Updated by authors. Figure prepared by Brandon Prins.

THE VETO

When bargaining fails, veto threats, vetoes, and veto overrides characterize the competition to set the policy agenda. Congress had some success in overriding presidential vetoes of Nixon, Ford, and Reagan. George Bush Sr., who one observer calls "the veto king," and Clinton proved more able to resist overrides.[50] Despite substantial majorities in both houses, the Democratic Congress was unable to override a single Bush veto until near the end of his presidency. Clinton did not have to use the veto until Republicans took control of both chambers in 1995; even then, he was overturned just twice during his two terms in office, despite having Republicans in control of both chambers during six of his eight years in office. Table 3.2 compares recent administrations as to the number of vetoes and overrides and the percentage of vetoes overridden.

The veto is a formal mechanism that makes the president an effective participant in the legislative process. This tool provides presidents the opportunity to shape legislation and guarantees congressional consideration of presidential preferences. In terms of key institutional features in dealing with Congress, some argue that the presidential veto is the president's central domestic resource.[51] We believe the veto is a complex power, best understood by relating it to the other activities in adopting public policy. Understanding the use of the veto can help us uncover presidential influence over legislation and it is an important manifestation of presidential-congressional interactions. However, much of the research on the veto considers it largely in isolation.[52] Nevertheless, presidential vetoes provide a unique opportunity for directly examining presidential-congressional decisionmaking.

In January 1997, President Clinton obtained (for a brief time) a power available to three-fourths of the nation's governors but to none of the 41 previous presidents—the line-item veto. Long desired by presidents, the line-item veto allows an executive to eliminate part of a bill, not the entire bill as with the current presidential veto. Advocated in particular for spending bills, Congress passed a version of the line-item veto in 1996 by giving the president enhanced rescission authority. The law al-

Table 3.2 Presidential Vetoes and Congressional Overrides, 1961–2000

PRESIDENT	VETOES	VETOES OVERRIDDEN	PERCENTAGE OF VETOES OVERRIDDEN
Kennedy	12	0	0
Johnson	16	0	0
Nixon	26	7	27
Ford	48	12	25
Carter	13	2	15
Reagan	39	9	23
Bush	29	1	3
Clinton	30	2	7

Source: Office of the Clerk, U.S. House of Representatives, Historical Highlights.

lowed the president to rescind within five days individual items in appropriations bills not exempted by Congress.[53] President Clinton first used the line-item veto on August 11, 1997, to eliminate three tax or spending breaks from the fiscal 1998 budget. Later that same year, however, the Supreme Court ruled the line-item veto unconstitutional.

One final point to make about the president's legislative record is that during congressional recesses, the president is free to act with more impunity than when Congress is in session. A president can veto a bill by "putting it in his pocket," and since he does not have 10 days to sign the bill and Congress is in recess, he can effectively kill the legislation without a congressional override attempt. In addition to this "pocket veto," veto threats may also help modify legislation the president does not favor.

Another device presidents increasingly use during recesses are interim appointments. After Republicans in the Senate blocked Clinton's appointment of Bill Lann Lee, a California civil rights lawyer, to be head of the Civil Rights Division of the Justice Department, Clinton employed the seldom used constitutional mechanism of interim appointment. Lee served in this "temporary" position for several years. George W. Bush made several interim appointments in January 2002, for several nominees who were being blocked by the Democratic Senate.

Conclusion

When can the president set the agenda of government and dominate policymaking? The political environment must be conducive to presidential leadership in terms of domestic and international events, favorable public opinion, and generally supportive majorities in Congress. Presidential institutions must be used effectively—particularly the White House staff members who deal with Congress on a regular basis. Leadership qualities are also essential; the president must be able to communicate clear priorities, sell Congress and the public on their merits, and manage them effectively. Finally, the president's ability to play a leading role in shaping public policy depends on the presidential agenda: whether it is oriented to expanding, maintaining, or shrinking government; how congruent or divergent it is with relation to the congressional agenda; and how aggressively and quickly the president is willing or able to move it.

The conditions necessary for presidential dominance seem increasingly rare. The constraints on the presidency, both at home and abroad, have increased in recent years. Presidential resources are "at the margins" in influencing Congress, making the president a "facilitator rather than a director of change."[54] Yet when an event occurs of terrible magnitude such as the attacks on the World Trade Center and the Pentagon, the presidency can still dominate government and the nation. The country turns to the president in situations like this and has high expectations for presidential leadership. This environment does not last forever, however, and as George W. Bush discovered, presidential dominance in conducting a war against terrorism does not necessarily translate into domestic policy. In the long run, assuming success in the war against terrorism, the president's renewed dominance of foreign affairs after the September 11 attacks will likely revert to a more balanced relationship with Congress.

Notes

1. Richard E. Neustadt, "The White House and Whitehall," in Francis E. Rourke (ed.) *Bureaucratic Power in National Politics,* second edition (Boston: Little Brown, 1972): 172.
2. See, for example, Gary King and Lyn Ragsdale, *The Elusive Executive* (Washington, D.C.: CQ Press, 1988); Gregory L. Hager and Terry Sullivan. "President-Centered and Presidency-Centered Explanations of Presidential Public Activities," *American Journal of Political Science* 38 (1994): 1079–1103; Lyn Ragsdale and John J. Theiss III, "The Institutionalization of the American Presidency," *American Journal of Political Science* 41 (October 1997): 1280–1318.
3. Clinton Rossiter, *The American Presidency* (New York: New American Library, 1956): 3–24.
4. Bert Rockman, *The Leadership Question: Presidency and the American System* (New York: Praeger, 1984): 86.
5. Richard E. Neustadt, "Presidency and Legislation: Planning the President's Program," *American Political Science Review* 49 (December 1955): 980–1021.
6. Robert Declerico, *The American President* (Englewood Cliffs, NJ: Prentice-Hall, 1983): 277–278.
7. Richard Neustadt, *Presidential Power* (New York: Wiley, 1960).
8. George C. Edwards III, *The Public Presidency* (New York: St. Martin's, 1983).
9. Samuel Kernell, *Going Public*, third edition (Washington, D.C.: CQ Press, 1997).
10. Harold Barger, *The Impossible Presidency* (Glenview IL: Scott Foresman, 1984): 12.
11. Richard Rose, *The Postmodern President* (Chatham, NJ: Chatham House, 1988): 3.
12. Quoted in Thomas Cronin, *The State of the Presidency* (Boston: Little Brown, 1975): 233.
13. John W. Kingdon, *Agendas, Alternatives, and Public Policies* (Boston: Little Brown, 1984); Paul C. Light, *The President's Agenda* (Baltimore: Johns Hopkins University Press, 1982); Steven A. Shull, *Domestic Policy Formation* (Westport, CT: Greenwood Press, 1983).
14. Aaron Wildavsky, Steven A. Shull (ed.) "The Two Presidencies," in *The Two Presidencies: A Quarter Century Assessment,* (Chicago: Nelson Hall 1991); James A. Robinson, *Congress and Foreign Policymaking*, revised edition (Homewood, IL.: Dorsey Press, 1967).
15. Steven A. Shull, *American Civil Rights Policy from Truman to Clinton* (Armonk, NY: M.E. Sharpe, 1999).
16. Shull (1983), Chapter 2; Light (1982); Kingdon (1984).
17. Robert Spitzer, *The President's Veto* (Albany: State University of New York Press, 1988).
18. Harold Seidman and Robert S. Gilmour, *Politics, Position and Power*, fourth edition (New York: Oxford University Press, 1986).
19. Neustadt (1960).
20. George C. Edwards III, "Impact of Presidential Coattails on Outcomes in Congressional Elections," *American Politics Quarterly* 7 (January 1979); John A. Ferejohn and Morris P. Fiorina, "Incumbency and Realignment in Congressional Elections," in John E. Chubb and Paul E. Petersen (eds.), *The New Direction in American Politics* (Washington, D.C.: Brookings Institution, 1985): 99.
21. George C. Edwards III, "Presidential Electoral Performance as a Source of Presidential Power," *American Journal of Political Science* 22 (February 1978): 152–68.
22. John Mueller, *War, Presidents, and Public Opinion* (New York: Wiley, 1973).
23. Hodding Carter III. Remarks made at Washington University, St. Louis, MO, March 23, 1988.
24. George C. Edwards III, *At the Margins: Presidential Leadership of Congress* (New Haven: Yale University Press, 1989): 152–168.
25. Ibid., 118.

26. Jon Bond and Richard Fleisher, *The President in the Legislative Arena* (Chicago: University of Chicago Press, 1990); Dennis W. Gleiber and Steven A. Shull, "Presidential Influence in Policymaking," *Western Political Quarterly* 45 (1992): 441–467; Paul Brace and Barbara Hinckley, *Follow the Leader* (New York: Basic Books, 1992); Ken Collier and Terry Sullivan, "New Evidence Undercutting the Linkage of Approval with Support and Influence" *Journal of Politics* 57 (1995): 197–209; Steven A. Shull and Thomas C. Shaw, *Explaining Congressional-Presidential Relations* (Albany, NY: SUNY Press, 1999): 90.

27. John E. Schwartz and L. Earl Shaw, *U.S. Congress in Comparative Perspectives* (Hinsdale, IL: Dryden Press, 1976): 307.

28. *Roll Call* (Washington, D.C.: Congressional Quarterly Inc., 1990): 35b.

29. *New Orleans Times-Picayune*, January 1, 1995: A-10.

30. Charles E. Jacob, "The Congressional Elections and Outlook," in Gerald Pomper (ed.), *The Election of 1976* (New York: David McKay, 1977): 101.

31. Bond and Fleisher (1990); Edwards (1989); Steven A. Shull, *Presidential-Congressional Relations* (Ann Arbor: University of Michigan Press, 1997); Shull and Shaw (1999): 90.

32. Nelson Polsby, "Presidential Cabinet Making: Lessons for the Political System," in Steven A. Shull and Lance T. LeLoup (eds.), *The Presidency: Studies in Policymaking* (Brunswick, OH: Kings Court, 1979): 83.

33. Richard E. Neustadt, "The Presidency and Legislation: The Growth of Central Clearance," *American Political Science Review* 48 (September 1954): 646.

34. James F. Hyde and Stephen J. Wayne, "White House-OMB Legislative Relations," in Shull and LeLoup (1979).

35. Stephen J. Wayne, *The Legislative Presidency* (New York: Harper & Row, 1978), Chapter 5.

36. Abraham Holtzman, *Legislative Liaison: Executive Leadership in Congress* (Chicago: Rand McNally, 1970): 284; Ralph K. Huitt, "White House Channels to the Hill," in Harvey C. Mansfield (ed.), *Congress Against the President* (New York: Praeger, 1975): 83.

37. Ken Collier, *Between the Branches: The White House Office of Legislative Affairs* (Pittsburgh: University of Pittsburgh Press, 1997).

38. Richard E. Neustadt, "Politicians and Bureaucrats," in David Truman (ed.), *Congress and America's Future*, second edition (Englewood Cliffs, NJ: Prentice-Hall, 1973): 136.

39. Marcia Whicker and Raymond Moore, *When Presidents Are Great* (Englewood Cliffs, NJ: Prentice-Hall, 1988).

40. Steven Hess, *Organizing the Presidency* (Washington, D.C.: Brookings Institution, 1976).

41. Frank Kessler, *The Dilemma of Presidential Leadership* (Englewood Cliffs, NJ: Prentice-Hall, 1982): 59.

42. *Congressional Quarterly Weekly Reports* (February 28, 1987): 339.

43. William Safire, "Bush's Cabinet" *New York Times Magazine* (March 25, 1990): 32.

44. Light, (1982); James Pfiffner, *Strategic Presidency,* revised edition (Lawrence, KS: University Press of KS, 1996); Shull and Shaw (1999).

45. Richard P. Nathan, *The Administrative Presidency*, second edition (New York: John Wiley); Richard A. Waterman, *Presidential Influence and the Administrative State* (Knoxville: University of Tennessee Press, 1989); Robert F. Durant, *The Administrative Presidency Revisited* (Albany: SUNY Press, 1992).

46. Gary King and Lyn Ragsdale, *The Elusive Executive* (Washington, D.C.: CQ Press, 1988): 122.

47. Brad T. Gomez and Steven A. Shull, "Presidential Decisionmaking: Explaining the Use of Executive Orders," presented at the Southern Political Science Association, Tampa, FL., November 2–5, 1995; Shull, (1997): Chapter 7.

48. The CQ measures do not distinguish between major and minor proposals and qualitative measures may be just as important. See Steven A. Shull, *Domestic Policy Formation: Presidential-Congressional Partnership* (Westport, CT.: Greenwood Press, 1983): 195–199; Shull (1997), Chapter 6; John Bond, Richard Fleisher, and Glen S. Krutz, "Empirical Findings on Presidential-Congressional Relations," in *Rivals for Power*, James A. Thurber (ed.) (Washington, D.C.: CQ Press, 1996).

49. Shull and Shaw (1999); Brandon C. Prins and Steven A. Shull, "Thinking About Time and Space: Does Aggregation Affect Our Understanding of Presidential Legislative Success?" delivered at the American Political Science Convention, San Francisco (August 30–September 2, 2001).

50. Robert Spitzer "The Veto King," Paper presented at the Conference on the Presidency of George Bush, Hofstra University, Hempstead, NY April 17–19, 1997.

51. Spitzer (1988): 25.

52. Richard A. Watson, *The President's Veto Power* (Lawrence: University Press of Kansas, 1993); David W. Rohde and Dennis M. Simon, "Presidential Vetoes and Congressional Response," *American Journal of Political Science* 29 (1985): 397–427; Sam B. Hoff, "Presidential Support and Veto Overrides," *Midsouth Journal of Political Science* 13 (Summer 1992): 173–190; Charles Cameron, *Veto Bargaining* (New York: Cambridge University Press, 1999). For an exception to examining only the veto, see Shull and Shaw (2000).

53. Lance T. LeLoup et al., "President Clinton's Fiscal 1998 Budget: Political and Constitutional Paths to Balance," *Public Budgeting and Finance*, Vol. 18, No. 1 (Spring 1998): 3–32.

54. Edwards (1989): 223

CHAPTER 4

Congress and Policymaking

Congress has the strength of the free enterprise system; it multiplies the decisionmakers, the points of access to influence and power, and the creative moving agents. It is hard to believe that a small group of leaders could do better. What would be gained in orderliness might well be lost in vitality and sensitiveness to the pressures for change.

—RALPH K. HUITT (1964)

When can Congress set the agenda and lead government? Under what circumstances does Congress cooperate with or follow the president? According to many experts, the world's most powerful legislative body sits at the U.S. Capitol end of Pennsylvania Avenue. Yet Congress is popularly perceived as disorganized and fragmented—and often as an obstacle to effective policymaking. This is not a misperception or a contradiction, but rather reflects the fact that *Congress has multiple personalities as a policymaker.*

This chapter explores several important questions about Congress's role as a partner in national policymaking. First, what is the potential for congressional leadership? What are its resources and strengths as well as its limitations and constraints? How do election results determine the membership, define the policy agenda, and establish the parameters and environment for executive-legislative relations? How has Congress evolved as an institution? How have recent institutional changes in the legislative process, committees, and rules and procedures affected Congress's decisionmaking capacity and influence in government? Can congressional leaders actually lead senators and representatives? Finally, in the face of increased institutional conflict, how does Congress attempt to achieve its own policy agenda? The answers to these questions will help us to better understand policymaking on Capitol Hill.

The Potential for Congressional Leadership

Congress was the dominant institution of government throughout the early years of the Republic. As we saw in Chapter 2, the president only rarely dominated Congress during the nineteenth century. The transition to the modern era strengthened the president and ushered in a period of presidential government. Yet even the most powerful presidents, from Franklin D. Roosevelt to Lyndon B. Johnson, had to confront a legislative branch that was sometimes assertive. The war in Vietnam and Watergate triggered a resurgence in congressional power as the House and Senate attempted to restore a more favorable balance with the president. Spurred by the globalization of the economy, the end of the cold war, and the reduced ability of the president to control world events, the role of Congress appears to be growing rather than shrinking.[1] The assertive 104th Republican Congress in 1995 to 1996, the first GOP majority in 40 years, proved that the legislative branch could dominate the government agenda, at least for a period. It also proved that the legislative branch, just like the president, could overreach and make political mistakes.

POLITICAL RESOURCES AND SOURCES OF CONGRESSIONAL POWER

The Constitution remains the wellspring of congressional power in national government. By any measure, the "First Branch" of government detailed in Article I has formal powers that are superior to the presidency. Article I, Section 8, gives Congress the power to raise revenues, borrow money, regulate commerce, coin money, establish the post office, create courts, raise and support the armed forces, declare war, and make laws that are necessary and proper to carry out the Constitution. Under the system of checks and balances, many of Congress's formal powers are "negative" in the sense that they impinge on executive prerogatives: veto overrides, confirmation of appointees, oversight, ratification, and investigation. Yet constitutional powers alone cannot explain the ebb and flow of congressional power or variations in the effectiveness of the policymaking process.

The seniority system and the relative stability of membership is also a source of congressional strength. Traditionally, committee chairmanships were awarded to the member of the majority party with the longest service on the committee. That tended to reward members from safe seats. Chairs of powerful committees such as Appropriations or Ways and Means often had to wait decades to earn their posts. Compared to a member with decades of service, presidents and their appointees often were seen as mere transients in Washington. The Republicans changed the seniority system after 1995, term-limiting committee chairs as well as the Speaker. Today, policy leadership in Congress may come from committees and subcommittees (policy specialists) or from the party leaders (policy generalists) with a perspective more comparable to the president's.

Congress also possesses institutional resources that enhance its policymaking role. Despite cuts in congressional staff under the Republicans in the 1990s, the legislative branch still spends billions of dollars on staff and agencies that support its policymaking capability.[2] Congress has thousands of employees working for members in their home districts and Washington, committee staff, and agencies such as the Congressional Budget Office, the Legislative Research Service, and the General Accounting Office. This gives Congress information capabilities that allow it to compete with the presidency.

In recent years, expanded party leadership organizations and strengthened party leaders have facilitated congressional policymaking. In some ways, congressional leaders have adopted some of the techniques of the presidency, using national media campaigns to push their policy positions. More visible, activist leaders, such as former House Speaker Newt Gingrich (R-Ga.) and Senate Majority Leader Tom Daschle (D-S.Dak.), appear on television and radio programs, promoting the congressional agenda. Increasingly "message politics" dominates the calculations of party leaders trying to gain political advantage with the American people.[3]

Congressional rules and procedures that foster collective decisionmaking increased notably in the 1980s and 1990s, providing additional capacity for a more assertive congressional leadership. The congressional budget process, particularly reconciliation, has enhanced the power of congressional majorities to act decisively and comprehensively.[4] Compared to the domination of subcommittees and the fragmentation of power in the 1970s, by the late 1980s and 1990s, more congressional policy responses and strategies were developed centrally by the party leaders. Under the Democrats in the 1980s, party task forces wrote important bills that bypassed the committee system. Under the Republicans in the 1990s, the Speaker and party leaders formulated many of the party's most important legislative initiatives. Although committees regained influence after Republicans maintained control of Congress for four consecutive elections, the experience of recent years has proven that, given the right political conditions, Congress can overcome its political fragmentation and move with decisiveness.

THE LIMITS OF CONGRESSIONAL POWER

Factors that empower the president or constraints that reduce the potential for congressional leadership tend to restrict congressional policymaking. Both the president's constitutional powers and informal powers, greatly enhanced in the twentieth century, check the exercise of congressional leadership. The veto power, when legislative and executive branches are in direct conflict, requires a two-thirds majority for Congress to exercise its will. Despite the end of the cold war, war powers still favor the president in times of crisis, which the September 11, 2001, attacks so vividly demonstrated.

Perhaps the greatest constraint on congressional leadership in national policymaking is the individualistic and fragmented nature of Congress. The House and Senate remain a cross section of 435 individuals, each with his or her own motives, interests, and goals. Despite the increase in partisanship, they remain largely self-selected and responsible for their own election to Congress. Their allegiance is to the voters who elected them first, not their political party. The committee system fragments power by dividing up the political turf, creating independent sources of expertise and legislative authority. The devolution of power to subcommittees in the 1970s further fragmented congressional power.[5] With weaker rules than the House of Representatives and more opportunities for obstruction, the Senate is particularly decentralized and difficult for anyone—inside or outside of the legislature—to lead.[6] Regionalism and competing sectional interests often make collective decisionmaking difficult. Despite apparent electoral security, members seem to be increasingly timid and reluctant to confront controversial issues and face up to tough policy choices.[7] To foster their reelection, members tend to emphasize noncontroversial district service, pork-barrel projects, and "credit-taking."[8]

The fact that the public holds Congress's members and leaders in low esteem also constrains its ability to lead government. Except during the Watergate scandal in the early 1970s, the public has consistently evaluated the presidency and other elements of the government more highly than Congress. Figure 4.1 compares approval

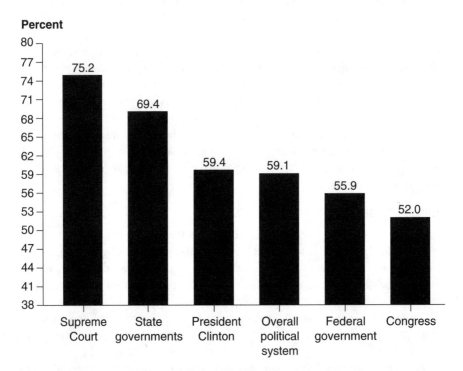

Percent

Figure 4.1 Comparison of Public Approval of Congress with Other Elements of Government.

Source: Gallup Poll, 1998, reported in John R. Hibbing and James T. Smith, "What the American People Want Congress to Be," in Lawrence C. Dodd and Bruce I. Oppenheimer (eds.), *Congress Reconsidered,* seventh edition (Washington, D.C.: CQ Press, 2001): 50.

of Congress to other institutions. Congress ranks below the Supreme Court, the president, and even the federal government as a whole. Members often contribute to this problem by running against Congress, criticizing and ridiculing the very institution to which they are trying to get elected.[9]

What can we conclude about the potential for congressional leadership in the policy process? Congress has a number of resources and traditions upon which to draw in making national policy. At the same time, its influence is limited by its very nature as a representative assembly, as well as by other political constraints. To better understand congressional policymaking, we look at congressional elections and the political environment, congressional institutions including rules and procedures, and congressional leadership.

Elections and the Political Environment

ARE CONGRESSIONAL ELECTIONS RESPONSIVE TO CITIZENS?

Congressional elections determine the membership of the House and Senate, which creates the context for policymaking. Many critics of congressional elections argue that elections are not particularly responsive to citizens because of several factors: low turnout, low levels of voter information, the advantages of incumbency and high reelection rates, and the power of special interests that finance campaigns. Voter turnout in midterm elections is low, usually around 35 percent nationally (compared to 50 percent when Congress is elected in a presidential election year). Numerous surveys prove that on many issues, voter information and interest is low. Do these facts in themselves mean that Congress is unresponsive to the policy preferences of the public? Not necessarily.

Incumbency is a critical factor in congressional elections. Following World War II, competition in congressional elections began to decline. Incumbents won reelection more frequently and by larger and larger margins. Traditionally, certain congressional districts were regarded as "swing seats" that reflected national political sentiments and presidential election results, not just local concerns. In 1948, one in five congressional districts were considered marginal swing seats (defined as the winner receiving 55 percent of the vote or less). By 1970, the number of swing seats had declined to one in 13 districts, a phenomena referred to as "declining marginals."[10] Incumbent success was attributed to changes in the behavior of members, who expanded their salaries, increased their staff located in the district, enhanced travel allowances, and gave themselves perquisites of office worth more than a million dollars.[11] Incumbents emphasized casework, helping constituents deal with various problems. They "brought home the bacon," providing a host of pork-barrel projects in their districts, such as hospitals, military bases, dams, and other spending that boosts the local economy. This trend continued through the 1980s. In 1988, a record 98 percent of members seeking reelection to the House of Representatives were returned to office, with 96 percent reelected in 1990. Only one Senate incumbent was defeated in 1990. These trends led to a national movement for term limits in the early 1990s which has since dissipated. Have high reelection rates made Congress immune to change? Not necessarily.

The cost of getting reelected has grown astronomically in recent decades, to an average of over $1 million every two years for a House election and several times as much for a Senate seat. Expensive races in either body can far exceed these averages. In 2000, Democrat Jon Corzine spent over $60 million mostly out of his own pocket, to win an open Senate seat from New Jersey. As both parties and interest groups found ways around limits established by the 1974 Federal Election Campaign Finance Act (FECA), one observer concludes, "the system essentially collapsed in 2000" because of unregulated funds.[12] So-called soft money (not covered by federal law) and independent expenditures reached new records.

The growing cost of campaigns for Congress has several important consequences. First, legislators spend more and more of their time "dialing for dollars," reducing the time spent legislating or talking to regular constituents. Second, members are more cautious about what they say and do, fearing negative attack ads from their opponents or groups making independent expenditures. Third, the money chase can affect how party leaders are selected. Members now consider a potential leader's fund-raising abilities along with leadership skills and media presence.[13] Finally, the unwillingness of the two parties to give up their own particular fund-raising advantages for the sake of campaign finance reform has fueled continued public cynicism about Congress and undermined its public approval as an institution. A major campaign finance reform bill banning soft money passed in 2002, but it was immediately challenged in court.

Low turnout, low voter interest and information, incumbency success, and campaign finance problems give rise to a cynical view of congressional elections and their responsiveness to voters. However, despite these problems, the congressional membership underwent significant change in the last decade, and congressional elections *do* provide an important measure of responsiveness to voters' policy preferences. Even with high reelection rates, turnover increased in the 1990s. Reapportionment and redistricting, higher rates of voluntary retirement (often in anticipation of defeat), and increased electoral competition combined to create significant changes in the composition of the Congress. In 1992, 110 new members were elected to the House and 14 to the Senate. In the 1994 Republican sweep, 86 new representatives and 11 new senators were elected. In 1996, 1998, and 2000, the Democrats made modest gains, but Republicans maintained control. Congress today is more diverse, with a higher proportion of women, blacks, and Hispanics. Despite the reputed lack of turnover, a majority of current members of the House and Senate were elected in the last five elections.[14]

Campaign financing abuses and the high costs of elections have not meant that congressional races are less competitive. On the contrary, since both political parties engage in the same fund-raising practices, parties can run stronger candidates in virtually all open seats, and stronger challengers against incumbents. Perhaps the most important change is how elections have changed the ideology of members of Congress, Republican members are now more conservative and Democrats more liberal, reducing the number of moderates in both parties. As a result, Congress is more contentious and divided along party lines. At the same time, Congress is more responsive to national trends than a generation earlier.

NATIONAL ISSUES AND THE PARTISAN AND IDEOLOGICAL COMPOSITION OF CONGRESS

One of the most notable changes since 1990 is the increased nationalization of elections. After years of emphasis on local issues and noncontroversial district service, the 1994 Republican "Contract with America" articulated a national agenda for congressional candidates. Although fewer than half of the voters had even heard of the "Contract," it may have resonated with enough voters to shift the two-party vote nationally. That trend continues into the 2000s. In comparison to congressional elections before 1994, recent elections reflect greater attention to national issues and party differences.

Congressional elections not only determine which party controls the legislative branches of government, it determines the ideological composition of the House and Senate. Party and ideology are related, of course, but their relationship can vary. At some points in time, parties can be highly unified or cohesive, sharing a common ideology. At other times, members of the legislative party can have quite divergent views and lack intraparty cohesion. That was true of the Democratic party for many years because of the split between a conservative southern wing and northern liberals. Some scholars argue that the distribution of policy preferences is more important than party label.[15] Equally important to intraparty cohesion is interparty conflict: the degree that the policy agenda of the two parties varies. Hence, elections determine both party and ideology, which helps define how Congress and the president work together.

Recent elections have produced Republicans and Democrats with divergent priorities who are willing to fight hard for those differences. Figure 4.2 shows some of the major policy differences between candidates of the two major parties. Republican and Democratic candidates differ markedly in their stands on school prayer, taxes, term limits, free trade, and constitutional amendments dealing with the budget.[16] The parties also differ in their preferences for government spending in areas such as the arts, the environment, welfare, and housing (not shown). Republican candidates are increasingly more conservative while Democrats are increasingly more liberal. In the congresses of 1970s, policy preferences were spread out more evenly between parties. That is to say, there were more conservative Democrats and moderate to liberal Republicans. By 2000, however, ideological differences between the parties were sharper. Based on studies of roll call voting, the most liberal Republican is to the right of the most conservative Democrat.[17] Aldrich and Rohde conclude, "The separation of each party from the other is almost the maximum possible."[18]

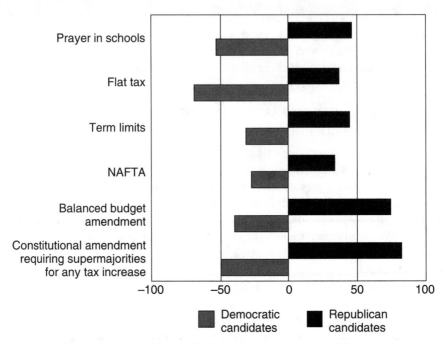

Figure 4.2   Ideological Differences Between Republican and
Democratic House Candidates.

Source: Data from Project Vote Smart National Political Awareness Test (1998), reported in Robert S. Erickson and Gerald
C. Wright, "Voters, Candidates, and Issues in Congressional Elections," in Lawrence C. Dodd and Bruce I. Oppenheimer
(eds.), *Congress Reconsidered,* seventh edition (Washington, D.C.: CQ Press, 2001): 75.
Note: Each bar represents the percentage of candidates favoring minus the percentage opposed to each issue.

This is very important for understanding the increased partisanship and, as we
will see below, the increased power of party leaders. It also relates to deadlock in
government. Congressional elections are now less about local issues and more about
national issues. Erickson and Wright summarize some of the consequences of the
changes in recent years:

> The average voter knows little about his or her representative and only a bit
> more about his or her senators. . . . Nevertheless, the electorates that candi-
> dates and parties face are smart and discerning, and they reward faithful
> representation. . . . Elections bring about much higher levels of policy rep-
> resentation than most observers would expect based on the low levels of
> citizen awareness.[19]

Congressional elections have changed the composition of Congress and the
environment for presidential-congressional policymaking. The growing conflict between the parties has led to important changes in the legislative process, committee

system, and party leaders. Before turning to those changes, we look at the way Congress actually makes laws.

Congressional Institutions

AN OVERVIEW OF THE LEGISLATIVE PROCESS

Congress makes policy in a very different manner from the president. The most familiar congressional "product" is public laws, but its policy outputs also include private bills; simple, concurrent, or joint resolutions; confirmation of presidential nominees; ratification of treaties; instructions to agencies; oversight; and a variety of other actions. Since we limit our case studies to legislation, the following concentrates on how Congresses enacts bills into law.

Introduction of Legislation. A member of Congress must introduce bills even if they are drawn up in the executive branch. The number of bills introduced in a Congress varies considerably and has declined significantly over the past two decades. In the mid-1970s for example, 24,283 bills were introduced in a two-year period, 2,870 were reported by committee, and 588 passed. In the 106th Congress of 1999 to 2001, 9,158 bills were introduced, and 580 were enacted into law.[20] Some of this decline reflects change in cosponsorship rules, but clearly, legislators today simply find it less useful to introduce a lot of bills than they did a generation ago.[21] Fewer bills are passing as well. This does not mean that Congress is less powerful, but rather, that it is concentrating on more important legislation that sometimes encompasses several different bills at the same time.

Referral to Committee. Most bills are referred to committee in the House and the Senate by their respective parliamentarians. This process is now largely automatic compared to earlier times when sending a bill to a favorable or unfavorable committee made the difference between success or failure. Multiple referrals of House bills became more common in the 1980s, but was eliminated by the Republicans in 1995. Committee chairs refer bills to subcommittees, which do most of the work of holding hearings and writing legislation. In the 1991–1992 Democratic Congress, the House had 22 standing committees with 138 subcommittees, compared to 16 standing committees and 86 subcommittees in the Senate. Republicans streamlined and reduced the independence of committees after taking control of Congress. In 2001 to 2003, the 107th Congress, the House had 19 standing committees with 88 subcommittees, compared to 16 standing committees and 68 subcommittees in the Senate.

Committee Review and Markup. Committees vary considerably in terms of their power and prestige, internal rules and procedures, reliance on subcommittee or full committee markup, and the role of minority party members.[22] Committee chairs help shape the agenda, determining which bills will be heard, although this is less true today in the case of major legislation. The committee or subcommittee process begins with public hearings, where testimony is taken from a variety of witnesses, particularly proponents. Administration officials play an active role in testifying for and against legislation whether it was initiated in the executive branch or in Congress. Hearings are designed to build support for legislation as much as to provide new information. *Markup* is the process of amending a bill line by line; it is characterized by the active participation of legislative staff. Markup can be exceedingly complex with legislation such as tax reform bill or a crime bill that can encompass thousands of pages. The president's congressional liaison office monitors the markup process carefully, attempting to clarify the president's stance and intentions. Once markup is complete, a bill must be reported by a vote of the full committee. The full committee occasionally makes substantial changes in the subcommittee version, or may simply decline to send it to the floor at all. The margin of passage and the partisan or regional split on a committee vote send an important signal and can influence the outcome on the subsequent floor vote.

Rules and Floor Consideration.   In the House, bills reported by committees go to the Rules committee, a panel appointed by and loyal to the Speaker.[23] The majority party leadership controls the House agenda, determining which legislation will be heard at what time. In the Senate, bills are scheduled for floor consideration by *unanimous consent agreements* between the majority and minority leaders. Rules for floor consideration are much more restrictive in the House than in the Senate. Time for debate is strictly allocated between supporters and opponents, and amendments are often limited by the use of *closed* and *modified-closed* rules. Debate is unlimited in the Senate but a filibuster can be broken by a cloture (a closing of debate) vote of 60 members. In the House, legislation may be subject to an up or down vote with no amendments allowed, it may be changed significantly through amendments offered on the floor, or it may be replaced completely by a substitute version of the bill. Floor debate provides an opportunity to make a public record and clarify legislative intent, but it is rarely instrumental in determining the outcome of the vote.

Voting. Members of the House vote by "electronic device" and can watch the progress of the vote on a large tote board during the voting period, usually 15 minutes. The Senate still conducts its recorded votes by calling the roll. Although many minor issues are approved by voice vote in both houses, major votes, particularly in the House, are usually recorded. Members sometimes hold back their vote to watch patterns unfold. Attempts by party leaders and administration lobbyists to shape the outcome begin long before the vote and continue through the waning minutes as the vote is completed. Leaders use their party whips and whip organization to get approximate head counts beforehand and may delay a vote until they can generate more support. Senators tend to be more independent, less influenced by leadership pressure, and the Senate is more informal and consensus-oriented in procedures. In the House, party leadership is more powerful, rules are more formal, and the minority party plays a lesser role than in the Senate.

Party leaders in both chambers are somewhat limited in the rewards and sanctions that are available to them to generate support. Even when the leadership pulls out all the stops and makes a vote a test of party loyalty, success is not guaranteed. Nonetheless, *party remains the most important single predictor of floor voting.* Although party discipline is less rigid in Congress than in most parliaments, party voting is increasing in recent years. The 1995–1996 Republican Congress was extremely partisan and witnessed a degree of party leadership and discipline that had not been seen in the United States in many decades. Yet even during sharply partisan legislative periods, regional splits that cut across party lines can occur. This is true with issues such as agriculture, energy, or natural resources.

In certain circumstances, the process described above is not followed. In passing the antiterrorism bill in October of 2001, for example, the bill skipped the committee stage in the Senate altogether and the House committee's work was simply discarded. The growing extraordinary resolution of policy deadlocks by definition alters or goes outside the normal legislative process. The policymaking process in Congress is complex, confusing, messy, often chaotic. Coalitions shift, key leaders change, and the influence of the president waxes and wanes. As Huitt suggests in the quotation that opens this chapter, certain benefits are derived from an open legislative process. However, to participate fully with the president in the policy process, Congress must not only represent various interests but must be capable of clarifying an agenda and acting collectively in a timely fashion.

IMPORTANT INSTITUTIONS THAT AFFECT POLICYMAKING

Supermajority Institutions. Margins greater than simple (50 percent plus one) majorities are called supermajorities. The two most important supermajority institutions that help shape the dynamics of presidential-congressional policymaking are the 60-vote majority (three-fifths of membership) needed to invoke cloture (cut off debate) during a Senate filibuster, and the two-thirds majority in both houses needed to override a presidential veto. Recent research suggests that gridlock between Congress and the president has increased because of these supermajority institutions and the changing policy preferences of members. As elections change the ideology of members, a "revolving gridlock" of sorts takes place.[24] When views are sharply divided and strongly held, it becomes more difficult to pass legislation in the Senate because, in effect, 41 senators can prevent a bill from passing. An example of this is the economic stimulus package that deadlocked in Congress in late 2001. Despite the urgency following the terrorist attacks, opponents threatened a filibuster and negotiators could not come up with a compromise that could get 60 votes in the Senate, even though a simple majority of senators would have voted for the bipartisan compromise.[25] A watered down stimulus bill finally passed in 2002.

Bicameralism. In addition to supermajority rules, the fact that Congress has two separate houses (bicameralism) affects the legislative process and relations with the president. Sarah Binder's study suggests that bicameralism is central to understanding gridlock and the dynamics of policy change.[26] She finds that differences between the House and Senate have a major impact on legislative gridlock. This phenomenon is even more pronounced when different parties control the House and Senate, as they did throughout 1981 to 1987 and 2001 to 2002.

The Budget Process and Rules. One of the most important congressional reforms was the enactment of the Budget and Impoundment Control Act of 1974. Commonly known as the Congressional Budget Act, it put restrictions on the president's ability to withhold funds appropriated by Congress. More importantly, it created a new set of institutions that allowed Congress to enact its own budget and challenge the president's priorities and numbers. The budget process changed the legislative process in several important ways. First, it allowed party leaders to have more control of the legislative process. Second, it reduced the number of bills and increased their length—more and more legislation was passed through "omnibus" bills (multiple bills and topics included in the same package). Third, legislation coming to the floor of the House had more restrictive rules limiting amendments. Fourth, deadlock between the Congress and the presidency over budget issues increasingly required the use of extraordinary resolution such as summits. The more centralized control afforded by the budget process allowed congressional leaders to negotiate more authoritatively with the president.

A key element of the budget process is *reconciliation*—a procedure from the 1974 act that instructs committees to make changes in taxes and spending. Reconciliation provides a means to shape the budget from the top down in a single bill.[27] Because of interbranch and interparty conflicts, fewer and fewer spending bills passed on time. As a result, more bills were lumped together in huge omnibus packages, usually reconciliation bills.[28] The Senate was also drawn into the process of relying on megabills, both under Republican and Democratic majorities. As more and more legislative time was devoted to the budget, the number of roll calls and bills passed declined. At the same time, the bills that passed were longer, tripling in average page length between the early 1970s and the late 1980s. Those bills came to the floor with more restrictive rules either limiting amendments (restrictive or modified-closed rules) or prohibiting all amendments (closed rules).

Changes in the budget process since 1974 have strengthened congressional majorities.[29] Totals in the congressional budget resolution were made binding, placing stricter limits on the actions of committees and subcommittees. Bills that violated the targets were subject to points of order on the floor, requiring supermajorities to waive the budget rules. These new rules placed restrictions never seen before in Congress. In the Senate, for example, the enforcement provisions provided time limits on debate and restrictions on amendments on a regular basis for the first time in the chamber's 200-year history.

The strengthening of the congressional budget process removed many obstacles to majority rule. John Gilmour summarizes the result:

> The budget reforms adopted since 1974 have increased the power of congressional majorities: helping overcome a lack of coordination in budgeting that weakened Congress *vis-à-vis* the executive; providing Congress with procedures that permit adopting a far more coherent budget policy than previously possible; and enabling Congress to exercise more deliberate control over the budget and deficit. Now, what majorities want to accomplish in the budget, they can.[30]

Committees, Party Leaders, and the Policy Agenda

COMMITTEES

Centralization versus Decentralization in the Legislative Process. The distribution of power within the House and Senate is a critical determinant of how effectively Congress makes policy and shares leadership of government. Throughout history, Congress has gone through cycles of relative centralization or decentralization. The distribution of power within Congress has varied among committees and their chairs, party leaders, and rank-and-file members. Greater centralized power is normally associated with the ability to make policy decisions more quickly and decisively. Decentralized, fragmented power is associated with deliberation rather than speed or decisiveness. Writing in the 1880s, Woodrow Wilson lamented the great power—what he called the "impervious authority"—of standing committees that dominated Congress.[31] Two decades later, in the early twentieth century, party leaders had grown more powerful, particularly the Speaker of the House. The House finally revolted against the excesses of "Czar" Joseph Cannon in 1910, stripping the Speaker of many powers.[32] In the decades that followed, the entrenchment of the seniority system—giving committee chairmanships to majority party members who had been on committees the longest—led to a Congress again dominated by powerful committees.[33] Before looking at recent trends, we consider different theories of committees.

The Committee and Subcommittee System. Political scientists have different theories of the role committees play in the legislative process. The *informational theory* focuses on committees as servants of the larger chamber whose main function is to provide information and specialized expertise in a complex environment.[34] The *distributive benefits theory* focuses on the role that committees and subcommittees play in fostering reelection by allowing members to "bring home the bacon."[35] The *party dominance theory* views committees and subcommittees as subservient to the majority party leaders, with their main function to support party programs.[36] Evidence supporting these theories is mixed, but it may be that different theories are more appropriate at various times. The distributive benefits theory seems to fit the Congress of the 1970s with its declining marginals and emphasis on district service. On the other hand, the party dominance theory may be a better fit for the 1990s and 2000s because of the strengthening of the budget process and party leaders. The dominance of committees by party leaders reached its zenith in 1995 after the Republican takeover. We look at these changes in more detail.

Subcommittee Dominance. By the 1970s, power had become more decentralized in Congress and increasingly dominated by subcommittees.[37] Congress adopted a "subcommittee bill of rights": New rules limited the discretion of the committee chair in assigning bills to subcommittees and in delaying referral. Subcommittees were given the right to select their own chairmen, write their own rules, hire their own staff, schedule their own sessions, and have complete control of their own budgets. In 1974, the House Ways and Means Committee, which had not used subcommittees, was forced to organize and use them. These reforms had a profound impact in just a few short years, democratizing the House, and to a lesser extent, the Senate. Congress was no longer dominated by a few powerful "whales" who chaired major committees, but instead was dominated by a large school of "minnows" who chaired subcommittees. In 1970, only 35 percent of all bills were initially heard in subcommittee. By 1980, 80 percent of all initial hearings were in subcommittee.[38] For individual members, the benefits were immense and they gained obvious advantages for securing reelection. Power became more fragmented and greater interest group access made the task of coalition-building more difficult. Lawrence Dodd and Bruce Oppenheimer summarize the impact:

> Subcommittee government created a crisis of interest aggregation. It largely removed committees as arenas in which interests would be compromised, brokered, and mediated; and it led to increased dominance of committee decisionmaking by clientele groups, to narrowly focused policy leadership, and to confusion in policy jurisdictions.[39]

Weakening Committee Power. Despite the decentralization of power to committees and subcommittees, other reforms were adopted at the same time that would eventually strengthen party leaders. The goal of these reforms was to streamline legislation, enhance majority rule, and reduce opportunities for minorities to block or dilute legislation. The Democratic caucus became an agent of a more disciplined party apparatus in the House of Representatives. In 1973, the Democrats established the Policy and Steering Committee to take control over the process of making committee assignments. The caucus also attempted to strengthen the Speaker of the House in addition to giving him an important role on the Policy and Steering committee. The Speaker was given the right to nominate Democratic members of the Rules

Committee subject to caucus approval. The objective was to make the crucial Rules panel, with its control over the House agenda and rules for debate and amendment, loyal to the leadership. The Speaker was also given greater influence in determining the referral of bills to committees (including multiple referrals), in creating special ad hoc committees, and in setting time limits on consideration.

The trend toward strengthening party leaders at the expense of committees culminated in the 104th Congress in 1995. Speaker Newt Gingrich served notice that committees would be servants of the majority party, not vice versa. The Speaker had such strong initial support that the Republicans allowed him to handpick committee chairs, sometimes completely disregarding seniority. Major House committee reforms adopted in the 104th Congress included the following:[40]

- limiting committee and subcommittee chairs to one six-year term
- reducing committee staff by one-third
- limiting members to two committees and four subcommittee assignments
- limiting members to chairing one committee or subcommittee
- giving chairs the power to appoint subcommittee chairs
- limiting most committees to five subcommittees
- abolishing three committees and transferring their jurisdiction
- eliminating joint referral of bills to committees
- prohibiting proxy voting (members must be present to vote)
- opening all committee sessions to media

Such reforms would have been unthinkable for the powerful committee chairs—the "old bulls"—of an earlier generation. Robert Walker (R-Pa.), one of Gingrich's lieutenants, expressed the philosophy of the Republican leadership: "We're trying to get away from the idea that all these committees are fiefdoms over which the chairmen have complete control and are jealous of each other's prerogatives."[41] This imbalance between the leadership and committee chairs did not last for long. After Gingrich left the speakership in 1999, committees regained some measure of their influence and autonomy, although nothing like they had enjoyed in earlier generations.

Committees are traditionally weaker in the more individualistic Senate than the House. But even the Senate adopted some major committee reforms under Republican rule. Six-year term limits for committee chairs were adopted as well as secret balloting for chairs, and limits on the number of committees a senator could chair. Even with Republican reforms, committee chairs could sometimes still exercise considerable power.

Party Leadership

House Leadership. The ability to set the agenda and share governance with the president means Congress must be able to consistently forge majority coalitions. This is achieved primarily through the party leaders, although it does not mean that majorities necessarily pit Republicans against Democrats. The chief party leader of the

House is the Speaker, who is elected by the 435 members. He is supported by the majority leader, majority whips, and several assistants. The minority leader, assisted by minority whips, leads the minority party. The 40-year string of Democratic Speakers began in the 1950s with Sam Rayburn (Tex.) and continued through Mike McCormack (Mass.), Carl Albert (Okla.), Tip O'Neill (Mass.), Jim Wright (Texas), and ended with Tom Foley (Wash.), who was defeated in November 1994. These Speakers differed considerably in their personal leadership style, from the reserved, conciliatory style of Tom Foley to the aggressive, partisan style of Jim Wright. After the Republicans captured the Congress in 1994, Richard Gephardt (D-Mo.) was elected minority leader.

Newt Gingrich was the first Republican Speaker since the 1950s and perhaps the most powerful Speaker of either party since Joseph Cannon, just after the turn of the century. Beginning in the late 1980s, Gingrich led a group of younger, more conservative Republican members—frustrated with years out of power—who rebelled against their own leaders and pushed for a more confrontational style. Gingrich and his allies were considered "bomb throwers" by the majority Democrats and contributed to the growing partisanship in Congress. Gingrich led the ethics probe that eventually toppled Speaker Jim Wright in 1988, and he has remained anathema to many Democrats ever since. His reign lasted only four years—a period punctuated by a failed revolt by members of his own party during the 105th Congress. After Republicans lost seats in the 1998 midterm elections, he resigned as Speaker and from the House before Republicans replaced him. Robert Livingston of Louisana was chosen to succeed Gingrich but never had the chance. In an environment poisoned by the partisanship associated with the House impeachment of Bill Clinton, revelations of Livingston's own extramarital affairs led to his resignation as well. Finally, Republicans turned to a less-confrontational, behind-the-scenes party loyalist, Dennis Hastert of Illinois for Speaker. A former wrestling coach, Hastert served as speaker in the 106th and 107th Congresses. He was instrumental in restoring some of the prerogatives for committees in terms of making policy that they had lost in the 104th and 105th Congresses.

Senate Leadership. Party leaders in the Senate tend to be weaker than their House counterparts. The chief party leader of the Senate is the majority leader who is elected by the majority party. He has the responsibility for setting the Senate agenda and building majority coalitions. After the 1994 elections, Senator Bob Dole (R-Kan.) was chosen as majority leader. He had also served as majority leader in the last prior Republican Senate from 1985 to 1986. Dole resigned in May 1996 to devote full time to his campaign for president, which he lost to President Clinton. Trent Lott (R-Miss.) was elected majority leader after Dole's resignation; he was reelected in the 105th and 106th Congress. Tom Daschle (D-S.D.) served as minority leader in the 104th through 107th Congresses. Midway through 2001, Daschle became majority leader after the Democrats took over control as a result of Senator Jeffords' party switch. Senator Lott became minority leader.

Congressional leaders of both parties must work constantly to build or maintain successful coalitions. Unlike parliamentary systems, leaders cannot simply count on party discipline although more and more, House and Senate votes follow party lines. The Speaker has a number of formal and informal powers to help lead: He presides over sessions, recognizes members to speak during debate, has influence on committee assignments, can direct reelection campaign funds to certain members and chooses members to take trips and to serve on conference committees. Party leaders can help a member get a bill on the calendar, or conversely, block it. Yet leadership is more than using formal powers. It also depends on personal leadership skills and the existence of common policy preferences within a party and how effectively a leader can respond to those preferences.

Leadership is more informal in the Senate where power is more equally divided. There, leaders have fewer formal powers, and must rely on persuasion. Majority leaders Dole and Lott had a more difficult time than Speaker Gingrich in maintaining party discipline. That was reflected in the fact that from 1995 to 1996, the Senate derailed many of the House-passed elements of the Contract with America. Nonetheless, the agenda set by the House put pressure on the Senate, which also showed record levels of party voting. Figure 4.3 shows the increase in party loyalty in voting in the House and Senate from 1954 to 2000. Note that in 1995 an average of 90 percent of Republicans voted with their party on votes that divided the two parties.

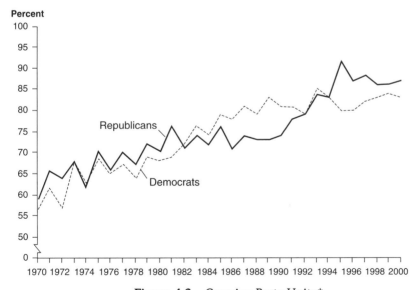

Figure 4.3 Growing Party Unity*

* percentage of members voting with their own party on votes where a majority of Republicans vote against a majority of Democrats
Source: Computed from figures reported by *Congressional Quarterly Weekly Reports/CQ Weekly* (1990–2001). Reported by Roger H. Davidson and Walter J. Oleszek, *Congress and Its Members* (CQ Press, 2002): 276.

Conditional Party Government. Many factors are at work in determining the strength of party leadership in Congress: election results, rules and procedures, and the influence of committees. In terms of election results, we noted the change in the party composition of Congress in recent years, bringing in more liberal Democrats and more conservative Republicans. We also saw changes in the congressional budget process that allowed majorities to act more effectively after the extreme fragmentation of power and "subcommittee government" of the 1970s. Finally, we saw how Republican party leaders assumed much greater power following their takeover of Congress in the 1994 elections.

These developments seem to fit a theory of congressional policymaking articulated by David Rohde called *conditional party government.*[42] This theory argues that assertive, powerful, more centralized party leadership exists when two conditions are met: intraparty cohesion and interparty polarization. Intraparty cohesion has increased since the 1960s, particularly for the Democratic party. At that time, the party was divided between southern conservatives and northern liberals. Following a southern realignment toward the Republicans, the Democrats today tend to be more uniform in their ideology. Votes in Congress that find a majority of one party voting against a majority of the other have increased from 30 percent of all votes in the 1960s to 70 percent of all votes in the 1990s, reflecting this increase in interparty conflict. Rohde argues that strong majority party leadership goes beyond party cohesiveness—that assertive party leaders help in "shaping members' preferences, the character of the issues on the agenda, the nature of legislative alternatives, and ultimate political outcomes."[43] This suggests that as party leadership grows stronger, Congress is more assertive is trying to set the policy agenda of government.

Congress and the Policy Agenda. The case of Newt Gingrich and the Contract with America is revealing in terms of how far Congress can go in driving the government agenda and of how quickly the balance of power with the president can change. On September 27, 1994, on the steps of the Capitol, 367 Republican incumbents and challengers for seats in the House signed the Contract with America.[44] It was a set of promises stating that if Republicans gained control of the House, 10 major pieces of legislation would come to a vote within the first 100 days of the 104th Congress. It was a carefully crafted agenda designed to appeal to disaffected voters, giving Republican candidates a national platform. Promises in the Contract included term limits, a balanced budget amendment, welfare reform, crime control, tax cuts, tort reform, and other issues.

After winning the election and capturing the House of Representatives for the first time in 40 years, Gingrich claimed an unprecedented mandate for Congress. House Republicans kept their promise by voting on all major provisions within 100 days. These were heady times for the Republicans: the House was in session for 487 hours during the first three months compared to an average of 123 hours over the prior 20 years. The Senate was another matter, though. Only one and part of another provision of the Contract passed both houses in 1995. Congressional dominance of the agenda, however, barely lasted the year. The most protracted battle of 1995 was with President Clinton over the Republicans' balanced budget plan (this case is profiled in Chapter 7). Democrats attacked the Republicans on their planned Medicare cuts, and refused to give in to Republican demands on the budget. Clinton threatened and used the veto, and a budget stalemate ensued, marked by two separate government shutdowns. The Democrats won the public relations battle if not the policy battle: Voters largely blamed the Republicans for the shutdowns. Clinton's approval rating climbed while Gingrich's sank. The Democrats carried those winning issues with them to the 1996 elections, getting Clinton reelected and reducing the Republican majorities.

The Contract with America showed that under certain extraordinary political conditions, Congress can dominate the policy agenda. But those conditions can change quickly and power relationships between the branches remain very fluid. Because of Republican miscalculations, it took the presidency less than a year to recover from the devastating 1994 elections and effectively counter congressional attempts to dominate government. Under the Republican Congress, the institutional changes in terms of the balance of power between committees and party leaders was profound, but not necessarily transforming and permanent. By 2001, committees had moved back toward their more traditional important role in the legislative process. However, as long as rules on committee chair term limits stay in place under the Republicans, the committees are not likely to achieve their former levels of power.

Conclusion

Congress has emerged as a coequal with the presidency, yet there are numerous, often contradictory patterns of policymaking. As an institution, Congress continues to strengthen its ability to pursue its own agenda while checking the prerogatives of the executive branch. It has bolstered its own agencies such as the Congressional Budget Office and the General Accounting Office. In 2002, the GAO sued the Bush administration to release documents surrounding their energy policy. This marked the first suit ever brought by GAO against the White House. Increasingly detailed statutes constrain agency discretion and enhance legislative influence. Congressional investigations are mounted to discredit and blunt presidential policies. Congress is now more assertive in foreign policy as well as domestic policy. Legislation like the Helms-Burton Act concerning trade with Cuba (profiled in Chapter 5) shows a Congress determined to pursue its own policy objectives, even in foreign policy.

Despite efforts on both sides, *neither branch can govern autonomously*. When can Congress set the agenda and take a leading role in shaping public policy? For major policy initiatives, it can rarely govern alone except in cases of presidential acquiescence or veto-proof majorities. Only in rare cases can Congress override a presidential veto. But even if it can rarely dominate, Congress shares governance with the presidency and plays an increasingly important role in defining issues and shaping policies. Congressional majorities today are better equipped to challenge and confront the president when they so desire. Even the tragic terrorist attacks of September 11, 2001, only temporarily diminished interbranch competition, and then primarily in the area of foreign affairs. In the subsequent chapters, we will explore a number of case studies that show the many different patterns of presidential-congressional policymaking that can take place today.

Notes

1. See, for example, L. Gordon Crovitz and Jeremy A Rabkin (eds.), *The Fettered Presidency* (Washington, D.C.: American Enterprise Institute, 1989).
2. For a discussion of the growth of staff, see Michael J. Malabin, *Unelected Representatives: Congressional Staff and the Future of Representative Government* (New York: Basic Books, 1980).
3. C. Lawrence Evans, "Committees, Leaders, and Message Politics," in Lawrence C. Dodd and Bruce I. Oppenheimer, *Congress Reconsidered,* seventh edition (Washington D.C.: CQ Press, 2001): 217–243.
4. John Gilmour, *Reconcilable Differences?* (Berkeley, CA.: University of California Press, 1990).
5. Lawrence C. Dodd and Bruce I. Oppenheimer, "The House in Transition: Partisanship and Opposition," in Dodd and Oppenheimer (eds.), *Congress Reconsidered*, third edition (Washington, D.C.: Congressional Quarterly Inc., 1985): 43–46.
6. Norman J. Ornstein, Robert L. Peabody, and David W. Rohde, "Change in the Senate: Toward the 1990s," in Dodd and Oppenheimer (eds.), *Congress Reconsidered,* fourth edition (Washington, D.C.: Congressional Quarterly Inc., 1989): 13–38.
7. See Morris P. Fiorina, *Congress: Keystone of the Washington Establishment* (New Haven, CT.: Yale University Press, 1974). For a critique of congressional "timidity" in the 1988 elections, see *New York Times* (March 18, 1990): 16.
8. See David R. Mayhew, *Congress: The Electoral Connection* (New Haven, CT.: Yale University Press, 1974), for a discussion of "credit taking."
9. For a detailed look at public attitudes toward Congress see John R. Hibbing and James T. Smith, "What the American Public Wants Congress to Be," in Dodd and Oppenheimer (2001): 45–65.
10. Mayhew (1974).
11. Roger H. Davidson and Walter J. Oleszek, *Congress and Its Members* (Washington, D.C.: Congressional Quarterly Inc., 1981): 123–124.
12. Anthony Corrado, "Financing the 2000 Elections," in Gerald M. Pomper (ed.), *The Election of 2000* (New York: Chatham House, 2001): 93.
13. Walter J. Oleszek, "The New Era of Congressional Policymaking," in James Thurber (ed.) *Rivals for Power: Presidential–Congressional Relations* (Washington D.C.: CQ Press, 1996): 53.
14. Roger H. Davidson and Walter J. Oleszek, *Congress and Its Members*, eighth edition (Washington, D.C.: CQ Press, 2002): 120.
15. David W. Brady and Craig Volden, *Revolving Gridlock* (Boulder, CO.: Westview, 1998): 3.
16. Robert S. Erickson and Gerald C. Wright, "Voters, Canidates, and Issues in Congressional Elections," in Dodd and Oppenheimer (2001): 75.
17. John H. Aldrich and David W. Rohde, "The Logic of Conditional Party Government," in Dodd and Oppenheimer (2001): 280–282.
18. Ibid., 282.
19. Erickson and Wright (2001): 90.
20. Davidson and Oleszek (2002): 238.
21. Roger H. Davidson, "The Presidency and Three Eras of the Modern Congress," in Thurber (1996): 23
22. See Richard F. Fenno Jr., *Congressmen in Committees* (Boston: Little, Brown, 1973).

23. See Walter J. Oleszek, *Congressional Procedures and the Policy Process,* third edition (Washington, D.C.: CQ Press, 1989), for an overview.

24. Keith Krehbiel, *Pivotal Politics* (Chicago: University of Chicago Press, 1998).

25. Comments of Senate Majority Leader, Tom Daschle, on the News Hour with Jim McNeil, PBS, December 20, 2001.

26. Sarah A. Binder, "The Dynamics of Legislative Gridlock 1947–96," *American Political Science Review,* 93 (September 1999): 519–533.

27. See Lance T. LeLoup, "After the Blitz: Reagan and the U.S. Congressional Budget Process," *Legislative Studies Quarterly* 7 (August 1982): 321–339.

28. Lawrence C. Dodd and Bruce I. Oppenheimer, "Consolidating Power in the House," in Lawrence D. Dodd and Bruce I Oppenheimer, *Congress Reconsidered sixth edition* (Washington D.C.: CQ Press, 1997): 48.

29. Lance T. LeLoup, Barbara L. Graham, and Stacey Barwick, "Deficit Politics and Constitutional Government: The Causes and Consequences of Gramm-Rudman-Hollings," *Public Budgeting and Finance* 7 (Spring 1987): 83–103.

30. Gilmour (1990): 224.

31. Woodrow Wilson, *Congressional Government* (Boston: Houghton Mifflin, 1885): 318.

32. White L. Busby, *Uncle Joe Cannon* (New York: Henry Holt, 1927).

33. Davidson, (1996): 66.

34. Keith Krehbiel, *Information and Legislative Organization,* 81 (Ann Arbor: University of Michigan Press, 1991).

35. Kenneth A. Shepsle and Barry R. Weingast, "The Institutional Foundations of Committee Power," *American Political Science Review* (March 1987): 85–104.

36. Gary W. Cox and Mathew D. McCubbins, *Legislative Leviathan: Party Government in the House* (Berkeley, CA.: University of California Press, 1993).

37. Norman J. Ornstein, "Causes and Consequences of Congressional Change: Subcommittee Reforms in the House of Representatives," in Norman Ornstein (ed.), *Congress in Change* (New York: Praeger, 1975): 88–114.

38. Ibid., 82.

39. Dodd and Oppenheimer (1985): 47.

40. C. Lawrence Evans and Walter J. Oleszek, "Congressional Tsunami? The Politics of Committee Reform," in Dodd and Oppenheimer (1997): 193–211.

41. Representative Robert Walker (R-Pa.) quoted in *Congressional Quarterly Weekly Report,* Supplement to No. 12 (March 25, 1995): 10.

42. David W. Rohde, *Parties and Leaders in the Post-Reform House* (Chicago: University of Chicago Press, 1991).

43. Ibid., 192.

44. James G. Gimpel, *Fulfilling the Contract* (Boston: Allyn and Bacon, 1996)

CHAPTER 5

Foreign Policy

I make American foreign policy.

—PRESIDENT HARRY S TRUMAN

*If you want us (Congress) in on the landings,
you have to have us in on the takeoffs.*

—SENATOR ARTHUR VANDENBERG TO PRESIDENT HARRY TRUMAN

After World War II, in the dawn of the nuclear age, amid the
tensions of the cold war, many scholars and political leaders argued persuasively
for presidential dominance in foreign affairs.[1] In addition, most presidents preferred foreign policy. There was less competition, and they could deal with lofty issues such as world peace rather than welfare checks. This led Aaron Wildavsky to
assert that there were two presidencies in the United States: one for foreign policy
and one for domestic policy.[2] British scholar Marcus Cunliffe wrote of this imbalance that "the presidency works badly. . . there is not enough leeway in domestic
affairs . . . . and in foreign affairs he possesses too much capacity to commit the nation to disaster."[3]

More than any other single event, the Vietnam War caused a reassessment of the
presumption of presidential superiority and led Congress to reassert an independent,
substantive role in foreign policy. Numerous studies confirm and support the expanded
role of Congress; while others question whether Congress has increased its influence
substantially.[4] Constitutional ambiguity with regard to congressional war powers and
the president's power as commander in chief became an "invitation to struggle" over
control of foreign policy in the post-Vietnam era. The past two decades have witnessed
a search for an appropriate balance between the two branches.[5]

No search for balance was necessary after September 11, 2001. Three days after
the terrorist attacks, both houses of Congress adopted a broad resolution authorizing

President George W. Bush "to use all necessary and appropriate force against those nations, organizations, or persons he determined planned, authorized, committed, or aided" the terrorist attacks.[6] The resolution passed 98–0 in the Senate and 420–1 in the House with relatively little debate, unlike the long debate and closely contested congressional vote to allow Bush's father in 1991 to use force against Iraq. Congress reacted to the terrorist attacks similarly to how it acted following the Japanese attack on Pearl Harbor on December 7, 1941. Despite the new balance in presidential-congressional relations in foreign policy, the reaction to September 11 clarified for a new generation that in time of grave national crisis, the nation looks to the president for leadership.

Barring more attacks or comparable crises, in the coming years the relationship will likely regain its traditional balance. Compared to parliamentary systems, the legislative branch in the United States has much more influence. When asked what struck him most about the American political system, a former British ambassador pointed to the "extraordinary power of Congress over foreign policy."[7] Congress plays a significant role in shaping the defense budget and deciding issues related to foreign aid, weapons systems, base locations, and other aspects of military policy that have local and regional implications.[8] In the post-Vietnam era, however, congressional influence extended into numerous other areas. Critics argue that Congress is guilty of excessive micromanagement, which makes American foreign policy less coherent than the policies emerging from unified parliamentary democracies. Divided government and conflict between the president and Congress affects foreign policy as well. Elliot Abrams observes:

> What makes the system not only different but much worse is the infusion of ideology and partisan politics into the struggles between the branches. . . . This ideological venom in the relations between Congress and the executive makes it particularly difficult to conduct a sensible foreign policy.[9]

How has U.S. foreign policy evolved in the postwar era? Absent a crisis, is the president still more capable of leadership in foreign affairs? Can the United States make coherent policy under separation of powers and divided government? How does the changing domestic and international environment affect the patterns and results of making foreign policy? This chapter explores these questions and examines recent cases that exemplify the four patterns of presidential-congressional policy-making. We begin by considering in more detail how U.S. strategies for foreign policy and national defense have evolved since the end of World War II.

The Evolution of U.S. Foreign Policy

From its earliest years as a nation, the United States attempted to avoid what George Washington called "foreign entanglements." Located on a continent distant from their European ancestors, Americans attempted to stay out of European affairs if European nations, in turn, would not meddle in the Western Hemisphere. Although the United States participated in World War I, American isolationism remained strong until the bombing of Pearl Harbor by Japan. After World War II, isolationism was seen as no longer possible or desirable in American foreign policy. After World War II until the late 1960s, surveys revealed that foreign policy competed about equally with domestic policy as the American public's "most important problem."

THE COLD WAR AND CONTAINMENT OF COMMUNISM

Although the United States and the Soviet Union had fought as allies to defeat Germany and Japan, the alliance was one of necessity. American leaders felt a strong distaste for communism, and once victory was assured, the alliance collapsed. The nation derived an important lesson from World War II: Never again would the United States be a passive bystander in the international arena in the face of massive aggression.[10] The nation's worst fears were realized when Soviet troops occupied Eastern Europe, setting up puppet communist regimes loyal to Moscow. Former British Prime Minister Winston Churchill warned that the Soviets had built an "iron curtain" across Europe. Cold war tensions divided the world in two. This bipolar international system dominated the world order for nearly 50 years until the collapse of the Soviet Union.

President Harry S Truman played an important role in defining postwar foreign policy, announcing that the United States would "support free peoples who are resisting attempted subjugation."[11] The economy of a devastated Europe was of great concern: Economic chaos and poverty bred unrest, which American leaders feared would open the door to communist disruption. In addition, economically weak nations would be unable to defend themselves from an attack by the Soviet Union. To prevent these eventualities, Secretary of State George Marshall proposed a plan for rebuilding Europe. The Marshall Plan poured billions of dollars of aid into Europe to achieve the "revival of a working economy in the world so as to permit the emergence of political and social conditions in which free institutions can exist."[12]

The cornerstone of postwar foreign policy was articulated within weeks of the announcement of the Marshall Plan. State Department Soviet affairs expert George Kennan described the doctrine of containment: "The main element of any United States policy toward the Soviet Union must be that of a long-term, vigilant containment of Russian expansive tendencies."[13] In 1949, the United States finalized its first modern peacetime military alliance with the nations of Western Europe. The North Atlantic Treaty Organization (NATO) committed the United States to stationing troops abroad and protecting the nations of Western Europe with its nuclear weapons. In response, the nations of Eastern Europe and the Soviet Union formed their own military defense treaty, the Warsaw Pact.

The first major application of the containment doctrine came in Korea in 1950, when communist North Korea invaded South Korea. Even though Korea had not earlier been defined as within the network of U.S. security interests, the Truman administration saw it as a test of the nation's will to stand up to communist aggression. Fighting under the banner of the United Nations, U.S. forces initially achieved military successes. This encouraged them to expand the aims of the war by entering North Korea, with the objective of reuniting it with the south. The United States ignored warnings from China, which had been under communist rule since 1949, not to invade North Korea.[14] The Chinese surprised American forces, driving them back. There followed a bloody stalemate.

President Dwight Eisenhower forced a settlement in the Korean War by threatening to use nuclear weapons against North Korea. He used the doctrine of "massive retaliation" to back up the strategy of containment. U.S. foreign policy had important domestic consequences. During the 1950s, anticommunist hysteria swept the country, fanned by demagogues like Wisconsin Senator Joseph McCarthy. Billions were spent to build an interstate highway system designed for the rapid transportation of troops and equipment. The success of the Soviet's earth-orbit satellite, *Sputnik*, prompted the United States to increase spending for education and scientific research. More money went to defense after the Soviet Union developed long-range intercontinental ballistic missiles (ICBMs). The success of communism in appealing to newly independent Third World nations also caused growing concern in the United States. The most troublesome such development was the 1959 Cuban revolution that brought to power Fidel Castro, who installed a communist regime only 90 miles off the U.S. coast.

President John F. Kennedy made few changes in the containment doctrine. Early in his administration, the CIA persuaded Kennedy to approve a clandestine invasion to liberate Cuba, named for its landing spot, the "Bay of Pigs Invasion." The operation was a fiasco, not only failing but also embarrassing the administration at home and around the world.[15] A more serious crisis developed in 1962 during the 13-day Cuban missile crisis, when the world came closer to nuclear war than ever before. In the words of Graham Allison, "There was a higher probability that more human lives would end suddenly than ever before in history."[16] The Soviet Union had placed offensive nuclear missiles in Cuba, and a confrontation was averted only after Premier Nikita Khrushchev backed down and agreed to remove the missiles. The event had a chilling effect on Kennedy, who later softened his rhetoric and favored detente—normalization of relations between the superpowers and reduction of world tensions.

By the 1960s, the Soviet Union had reached nuclear parity with the United States. In the continuing arms race, both sides possessed massive arsenals of nuclear weapons, capable of destroying the world many times over. If containment was the cornerstone of postwar foreign policy, the doctrine of deterrence was the cornerstone of U.S. strategic defense policy. The premise was that if neither superpower can destroy the other in a first-strike nuclear attack without suffering unacceptable damage itself, both sides will be deterred from attacking. The doctrine is also known as *mutually assured destruction* or MAD. Throughout this period, containing communism and managing nuclear weapons fell largely to the president. When South Vietnam was threatened by the communist regime in North Vietnam, it was the president who took action.

THE VIETNAM WAR AND ITS AFTERMATH

In 1964, based on a disputed incident involving U.S. and North Vietnamese ships in the Gulf of Tonkin, Congress passed a resolution giving President Johnson the go-ahead to use military force against the Vietnamese communists. Although Johnson promised in the 1964 presidential campaign not to expand U.S. participation in Vietnam, he used the Gulf of Tonkin Resolution to justify sending thousands of Americans to fight for South Vietnam: 550,000 troops by 1967. The Johnson administration rationalized U.S. intervention using the "domino theory": If Vietnam were to come under communist rule, the other nations of Southeast Asia would fall as well. Although most Americans supported the war at first, a large and vocal segment of society vehemently opposed U.S. involvement. Opposition grew as the war dragged on. A growing coalition in Congress tried to end the war by cutting off funds and withdrawing U.S. troops. Under siege, Johnson withdrew from the 1968 presidential election, paving the way for the election of Republican Richard Nixon.

Two dimensions emerged in Nixon's foreign policy. The first conformed to the containment doctrine that dominated the postwar period, but the second was a reaction to Vietnam, based on a more pragmatic view of America's role in the world. Nixon first attempted to gain a military victory in Vietnam, secretly bombing Cambodia and escalating the war. When it became clear that military victory would not occur, the administration began turning over responsibility to the South Vietnamese and withdrawing U.S. troops. Nixon and Secretary of State Henry Kissinger recognized that the Vietnam War had been a tactical disaster, even though they supported its aims.

Although they did not challenge the basic doctrine of containment, they did question the best strategy to achieve it. What emerged was the Nixon doctrine, which stressed indirect military assistance to friendly governments rather than direct intervention with American troops. Nixon announced that:

> . . . the postwar period in international relations has ended. The United States will participate in the defense and development of allies and friends but. . . . America cannot—and will not—conceive all the plans, design all the programs, execute all the defense of the free nations of the world.[17]

Nixon also pursued a policy of detente with the Soviet Union and China, opening up and improving relations. Despite detente, a restive Congress took a much closer look at foreign policy, national security, intelligence gathering, and arms control. Hostility between Congress and Nixon spilled into the realm of foreign policy.

The bipartisanship and interbranch cooperation that had characterized the making of foreign policy through the late 1960s declined notably. The change in strategies in applying containment may have begun to reduce international tensions, but Democratic President Jimmy Carter hoped to go further and eliminate the containment doctrine altogether.

Carter believed that the containment era was at an end, and that U.S. foreign policy should be based on greater international cooperation, arms reduction, and an emphasis on human rights.[18] U.S. foreign policy goals during the Carter administration included promoting peace in the Middle East through the Camp David agreements and negotiating the Panama Canal treaties. However, his human rights policy proved difficult to apply fairly, particularly in cases of abuses by important allies. The feeling of U.S. weakness in the world was further exacerbated by the Islamic fundamentalist revolution in Iran and the seizure of American hostages in the U.S. embassy in Tehran.

Ronald Reagan capitalized on this feeling of weakness in U.S. foreign policy in the 1980 presidential campaign, promising a massive defense buildup and a tougher stance toward the Soviet Union, which he called the "evil empire." The rhetoric of U.S. foreign policy sounded much like it had in the 1950s. The United States invaded the tiny Caribbean nation of Grenada in 1983 after a left-wing coup. Marines were sent to Lebanon. Containment was applied in Central America by assisting the Contra rebels in Nicaragua against the Marxist Sandinista regime. By the mid-1980s, the United States had rapidly expanded its military capability, and U.S. foreign policy looked much as it had 40 years before. However, when Mikhail Gorbachev assumed power in the Soviet Union in 1985, events unfolded that would end the cold war, permanently altering the international system and U.S. foreign policy. George Bush Sr. became the first post-cold war president, and the United States attempted to provide leadership in a transformed world.

The New International Environment

THE END OF THE COLD WAR

Mikhail Gorbachev served as president of the Soviet Union from 1985 until December 1991, when the USSR broke up into separate republics. The reform process began slowly. Gorbachev launched a gradual campaign to restructure the Soviet economy, called *perestroika,* and a policy of greater openness, called *glasnost.* The Reagan administration was cautious but began to see that the changes were real. A tide of reform swept through Eastern Europe, toppling the old guard and undertaking experiments in democracy and market capitalism. The end of the cold war and demise of the Soviet empire had dramatic implications for U.S. foreign policy. After years of confrontation in the Mideast, for example, the U.S. and Russia found themselves on the same side in opposing Iraq's invasion of Kuwait, led by Saddam Hussein. In the new world order, multilateralism and the United Nations played a much more important role. President George Bush Sr. was the first president to maneuver in this new world order and it represented new challenges to the United States. Indicative of the new approach was the Gulf War (see case that follows) where an unprecedented international coalition was assembled and the war was financed by foreign contribution, primarily wealthy Gulf oil states.

Clinton inherited several pressing international problems from the Bush administration, which led to military involvement in Somalia, Haiti, and Bosnia. Further evidence of the end of the cold war was Clinton's recognition of the communist government of Vietnam, and U.S. approval of NATO expansion to include three former eastern bloc nations (Poland, Hungary, and the Czech Republic). A former governor like Clinton, George W. Bush came into office in 2001 with little experience in foreign policy. He also inherited unresolved problems such as the conflict between Israel and the Palestinians. He chose a highly experienced team to assist him, including Colin Powell as secretary of state, Condoleezza Rice as national security advisor, and Donald Rumsfeld as secretary of defense.

Bush's initial foreign policy stands raised concerns among European allies that he would be more unilateralist in approach, content to let the United States go it alone. Of particular concern were his decisions to abandon the 1972 Antiballistic Missile Treaty and push for a missile defense system, and to disavow the Kyoto treaty on global warming. Bush also sought to increase defense spending. The United States had entered the 1990s with defense spending at record levels for peacetime, along with huge budget deficits. The end of the cold war increased the pressure for cuts in defense spending to produce a "peace dividend" to finance deficit reduction, domestic programs, and tax relief. By the end of the 1990s, military spending declined significantly and pressures to increase spending were building. The events of September 11, 2001, helped crystallize these sentiments and ushered in a new era of increased defense spending.

THE WAR AGAINST TERRORISM

The terrorist attacks of September 11, 2001, profoundly changed the environment for foreign policy in the United States and the rest of the world. The United States attempted to assemble an international coalition to support its war in Afghanistan against Al Queda, the international terrorist organization headed by Osama bin Laden, and the radical Islamic Taliban who ran the country. As the target of the attack, the United States was willing to go it alone, although policymakers realized it was better in the long run to get support not only from NATO allies, but also from Middle East nations. While the United States and nations in the West were aware of the terrorist threat before September 11, those events produced a dramatic shift. With some 3,000 killed in attacks on the U.S. mainland, homeland defense and a worldwide effort to find and destroy terrorist networks became the overriding goal of foreign policy. On the domestic front, the war against terrorism changed how Americans travel, altered civil rights (see Chapter 6), and prompted the creation of the Office of Homeland Security. It is still to early to predict how this element of the political environment will evolve, but it initially seemed to tip the balance of presidential-congressional power toward the president.

FREE TRADE ISSUES

As globalization progressed in the last decade, the environment for foreign policy increasingly concerned trade liberalization.[19] Bill Clinton and George W. Bush were more interested in trade matters within the realm of foreign policy than their predecessors. In 1993, Clinton won a major victory with Congress in gaining congressional approval of NAFTA (the North American Free Trade Agreement). In an unusual presidential-congressional alliance, Clinton received support from a majority of Republicans and convinced enough Democrats to support NAFTA to win. In 1997, Clinton requested expanded authority to make so-called "fast-track" trade agreements that restricted Congress's ability to amend. Clinton argued, "It will promote peace; it will promote freedom; it will promote stability; it will raise the level of living standards in other parts of the world even as it maintains America as the world's most prosperous nation."[20] Led by legislators of Clinton's own party, such as House majority leader Dick Gephardt (D-Mo.) and Senate minority leader Tom Daschle (D-S.Dak.), Congress denied his request. George W. Bush had more success with the same request four years later. Strengthened by his post-September 11 support, the House voted to give Bush fast-track authority. Despite his advocacy of free trade, Bush imposed tariffs on imported steel in 2002 to protect U.S. steel companies and workers. It resulted in retaliatory tariffs imposed on U.S. goods by Russia and the European Union.

Making Foreign Policy

EXECUTIVE BRANCH INSTITUTIONS

The executive branch's system for foreign policy, defense, and national security was designed to meet the needs of the cold war era. The State Department and the Department of Defense (originally the War Department) were two of the first four federal departments, dating back to George Washington's first Cabinet. After World War II, several changes in the executive branch were adopted. The National Security Act of 1947 created the Department of Defense (DOD), the National Security Council (NSC), the Central Intelligence Agency (CIA), and the Joint Chiefs of Staff. Despite efforts to avoid conflict and duplication, bureaucratic infighting and competition has often plagued the making of foreign policy in the executive branch. If the president does not manage them effectively, the national security staff can get out of control, as Reagan's NSC did in the Iran-Contra scandal. These formal institutions have not always suited the needs of presidents in making foreign policy decisions. Thus, the roles of the secretary of state, national security adviser, and secretary of defense have fluctuated markedly in different administrations. For example,

National Security Adviser Henry Kissinger dominated foreign policymaking in Nixon's first term. Eisenhower, Bush, and Clinton, in contrast, relied heavily on their secretaries of state. Yet Secretary of State Colin Powell seemed frozen out of George W. Bush's inner circle until after September 11, when he regained stature within the administration.[21]

In crisis situations, when presidential power is greatest, presidents often rely on ad hoc decisionmaking groups rather than formal entities such as the NSC. Presidents are most comfortable with manageable groups that include advisors in whom they have personal trust. In making routine, noncrisis foreign policy decisions, the State Department is usually in charge. However, presidents have often been critical of State for its rigid hierarchy, caution, inefficiency, and traditionalism.[22] Rivalries periodically arise between Defense and State over diplomatic or military solutions to problems. Some argue that the DOD is more pragmatic and adaptable to a president's needs.[23]

LEGISLATIVE BRANCH INSTITUTIONS

The Senate, with its constitutional powers to ratify treaties and confirm ambassadors, has been more prominent traditionally in foreign policy than the House of Representatives. In recent years, however, House members have actively sought more input into foreign policy, while the Senate Foreign Relations Committee has declined in effectiveness and prestige. As some of the cases that follow suggest, greater congressional participation in foreign policy is part of the general assertiveness of Congress and reflects many of the institutional changes of the 1970s and 1980s. As policy differences with the White House became more pronounced, the Democratic Congresses in the 1980s used whatever techniques were available to contest presidential policy. For example, the Reagan administration's policy in Nicaragua was checked by the enactment of the Boland amendments, which restricted assistance to the Contra rebels.

House Speaker Jim Wright (D-Tex.) asserted himself in foreign policy to a greater extent than previous congressional leaders, traveling around the world. His independent peace initiatives in Central America and use of the media to highlight policy differences infuriated the Reagan administration. His successor, Speaker Tom Foley, (D-Wash.) did not follow Wright's lead, nor did Speaker Newt Gingrich (R-Ga.), who focused more on domestic matters. Nor did the Senate under Majority Leader Trent Lott (R-Miss.) seek to wield much foreign policy authority in a relatively peaceful international environment. Apart from congressional party leaders, Senate Republican committee chairs, such as Jesse Helms (R-N.C.), exerted considerable influence in foreign policy. Thus, if world tensions ease and foreign policy increasingly affects the domestic economy, Congress is likely to become even more involved. If world tensions increase, and terrorism becomes more of a problem, Congress will probably continue to defer to the president. Will the September 11 terrorist attacks permanently tilt the legislative-executive balance?

IS THE PRESIDENT STILL DOMINANT IN FOREIGN AFFAIRS?

Despite the reassertion of congressional power after the Vietnam War and the continuing struggle between branches, the president retains certain advantages over Congress. This remains true despite the 1973 War Powers Resolution and other restrictive legislation. Presidents can shape foreign policy by recognizing foreign governments, by making international agreements and negotiating treaties, by appointing key personnel to conduct foreign policy, and by using military force when necessary.[24] Many aspects of presidential power in foreign affairs go beyond votes in Congress.[25] Also, one or two critical votes—such as the 1991 vote to authorize the use of force in the Persian Gulf—may be far more important than half a dozen lesser measures that a president loses. Acting as commanders in chief of the armed forces, President Reagan invaded Grenada in 1983 and President Bush invaded Panama in 1989, both without prior congressional approval. Although he sought House and Senate approval before launching Operation Desert Storm in 1991, Bush asserted his right to use force against Iraq even without it. Clinton also asserted his role as commander in chief in Haiti and Bosnia despite some opposition in Congress. And George W. Bush was given vast discretion by the Congress to pursue the war on terrorism.

The U.S. response to the terrorist attacks leads us to question again just how different presidential influence is in domestic and foreign policy. Do "two presidencies" still exist? What evidence can help us clarify the relative power of Congress and the president in foreign affairs? Wildavsky argued in 1966 that presidents rarely lost on any major initiatives in foreign affairs and defense. In looking at presidential initiatives, he found that Congress approved 70 percent of foreign policy proposals compared to only 40 percent of domestic proposals.[26] These differences seemed to decline over the next decade, when foreign policy issues took on more domestic implications. Between 1966 and 1975, the gap in presidential success narrowed to 55 percent support for foreign policy proposals and 46 percent for domestic policy proposals.[27]

A recent study finds that the "two presidencies" phenomenon occurs only for Republican presidents.[28] The difference stems from the tendency of congressional Democrats to support Republican presidents substantially more on foreign policy issues than on domestic votes. On the other hand, congressional Republicans are just as likely to oppose Democratic presidents on foreign policy as on domestic policy. Table 5.1 compares the differences in support since the Eisenhower administration. Support was significantly greater on foreign policy votes for Presidents Ford and Reagan (and somewhat less so for Eisenhower and Nixon), when compared to the records of Carter and Clinton. These two Democrats actually fared better in the domestic policy realm while Kennedy and Johnson had almost no differences in support. However, much of the difference simply reflects the lower levels of support that Republican presidents have on domestic issues. Fleisher and Bond conclude that "there may be two presidencies, but the phenomenon is limited and conditional."[29]

Table 5.1   Average Percent Agreement (Support) in the House (two presidencies; by presidential party and individual president), 1953–1996

PRESIDENT	OVERALL MEAN	FOREIGN	DOMESTIC	DIFFERENCE
Eisenhower	57.7	62.1	55.9	−6.2
Kennedy	66.3	70.5	64.3	−6.2
Johnson	69.2	68.1	69.8	+1.7
Nixon	61.1	61.6	61.1	− .5
Ford	56.9	57.9	47.0	−10.9
Carter	59.7	57.3	61.2	+3.9
Reagan	47.7	53.6	42.9	−10.7
Bush	48.7	51.8	46.3	−5.5
Clinton	57.0	55.3	59.8	+4.5
Republican	53.8	57.3	50.8	−6.5
Democrat	63.1	62.8	63.8	+1.0
Totals	58.5	60.1	57.3	−2.8

Source: Adapted from Steven A. Shull, *Presidential-Congressional Relations* (Ann Arbor: University of Michigan Press, 1997): Chapter 6; updated by Shull from CQs *Roll Call* (annual).

With the globalization of the economy, foreign policy issues are increasingly subject to the same political forces as domestic issues. On the other hand, as the response to the war on terrorism suggests, these trends can be reversed in crisis situations. Although the president retains some inherent advantages in making crisis decisions, these instances are only one part of the foreign policy agenda. Congress and the president will usually have more shared governance on issues such as trade and international competitiveness, immigration, base location, foreign and military aid, and international environmental issues. Regarding these issues, like domestic issues, the president must bargain and persuade to put his imprint on policy.

Taking a broader historical perspective, Figure 5.1 compares three types of presidential actions in foreign policy and national defense since 1957: taking a position on legislation before Congress, casting vetoes on foreign policy measures, and issuing executive orders. Of the three, legislative position taking shows an upward trend for both diplomatic and defense issues. Executive orders appear to be declining slightly (especially on diplomacy), while vetoes remain stable at a low level. This suggests the growing significance of Congress and the greater importance of legislation to the president's success and influence in foreign policy. No one can predict the possibility of future terrorism on America's shores. Certainly the United States is more vigilant and somewhat better prepared than before September 11, 2001. The desire of the country and the Congress for the president to lead the war on terrorism is a sobering reminder of how quickly trends can be reversed in the short run. But if a sustained fight against global terrorism is successful, it is likely that the balance between Congress and the president will tend to return to the familiar long-term patterns. The cases that follow provide some examples of the changing dynamic between Congress and the president regarding legislation, within the realm of foreign policy.

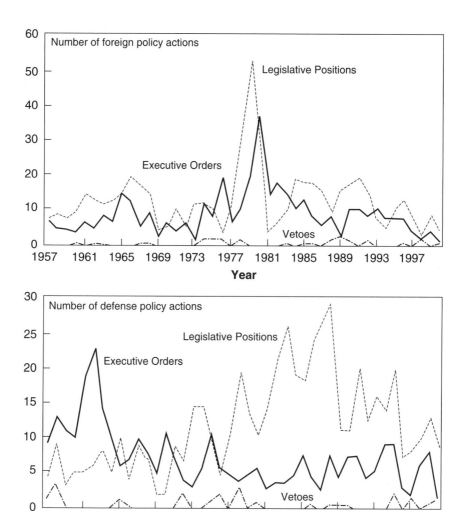

Figure 5.1   Presidential Behavior on Foreign and Defense Policy (1957–2000).

Note: Foreign includes aid and trade

Source: Early data from Lyn Ragsdale, *Vital Statistics on the Presidency,* revised edition. (Washington, D.C. Congressional Quarterly, Inc. 1998). Updated by authors. Figure prepared by Brandon Prins.

Presidential Leadership: The Persian Gulf War (1991)

On January 16, 1991, President George Bush's Press Secretary, Marlin Fitzwater, announced to the nation, "The liberation of Kuwait has begun." The president of the United States had succeeded in leading the country and the international community to act against the aggression of Iraq's Saddam Hussein. Bush dominated policymaking internationally by forging an unprecedented coalition of nations, composed of

Arab and Western countries. He dominated policy domestically by successfully urging Congress to give him the formal authorization to use force in the Persian Gulf. After weeks of a punishing air war, followed by a lightning ground war, the United States and its allies won. The jubilant nation gave President Bush the highest public approval ratings ever recorded.

The outcome of the war overshadowed a number of questions about earlier U.S. support for Iraq, which had allowed the invasion of Kuwait to occur in the first place. U.S. policymakers seemed to ignore ominous Iraqi troop movements until it was too late. By the last week in July 1990, American intelligence judged that Iraq was preparing to seize a small part of Kuwait. The Bush administration was unprepared when Iraq launched a massive invasion early in August, and its tanks rolled over Kuwait in a matter of hours. Saddam Hussein announced to the world that Kuwait had become Iraq's nineteenth province.

After joining the world in denouncing Iraq's aggression, the Bush administration's most immediate concern was the security of Saudi Arabia and its oil reserves. The large Iraqi army was in a position to continue its advance across the Saudi desert; if the Iraqis chose to do so, they could have controlled a huge proportion of the world's oil supplies. Unwilling to risk becoming an energy hostage to Iraq, Bush announced that U.S. troops and naval forces would be deployed immediately in Saudi Arabia and the Persian Gulf. The initiative, dubbed Operation Desert Shield, would attempt to deter further advances by Iraq. Many Arab nations, although they had historically been opposed to a U.S. military presence in the Middle East, supported the move.

The president initially received strong bipartisan support for the deployment of U.S. troops to the Gulf. Both houses of Congress passed a resolution in support of the president by nearly unanimous margins. The administration's other main strategy was diplomatic, urging the United Nations to impose economic sanctions on Iraq. Very quickly, the UN Security Council passed several resolutions condemning Iraq and implemented a virtual economic blockade around it. The Bush administration also worked to build a multinational force in Saudi Arabia, including troops from Egypt and other Arab states.

Within a matter of weeks, the Unites States had deployed over 200,000 troops and tons of equipment and materiel. Back home, the invasion had severe economic effects. Oil prices doubled at one point, to over $40 a barrel. Growing impatient with economic sanctions, the administration made a crucial policy change in November 1990, after Congress had recessed. The administration doubled the number of U.S. troops in the Gulf to over 400,000. This constituted a moved toward an offensive posture, since that number of troops could not be rotated out over a prolonged period of time. At the same time, the administration successfully pushed a UN resolution that authorized the use of force if Iraq did not withdraw from Kuwait by January 15, 1991. Dissent in Congress grew steadily, as the earlier bipartisan consensus eroded. Democrats and some Republicans warned the president that only Congress had the power to commit the nation to war. A confrontation was developing; the administration claimed that, as commander in chief, the president did not need congressional authorization.

Congress reconvened in January 1991, as the UN deadline approached. Although partisanship was restrained in public, support for the president had split Congress largely along party lines. On January 8, the administration switched gears. In a letter to congressional leaders, Bush requested that Congress adopt a resolution backing UN Security Council Resolution 678, which authorized the use of "all necessary means" to expel Iraq from Kuwait. Such a congressional resolution, the president wrote, "would help dispel any belief that may exist in the minds of Iraq's leaders that the United States lacks the necessary unity to act decisively."[30]

An emotional but solemn debate on the resolution began on Capitol Hill on January 10. Over the next three days, over 300 speeches were given on the House floor, and 94 of 100 senators rose to speak. The administration worked hard behind the scenes to ensure a majority in both houses. The biggest problem was in the Senate, where Majority Leader George Mitchell (D-Maine) and Senator Sam Nunn (D-Ga.), the influential chairman of the Armed Services Committee, led the opposition. Two Republican senators defected from the president's position, meaning that at least seven Democratic votes were needed for a majority.

Democrat Joseph Lieberman of Connecticut cosponsored the resolution in the Senate and helped Bush round up the needed Democratic votes. On January 12, the Senate passed the resolution by a vote of 52 to 47. Minutes later, the House of Representatives voted 250 to 183 for the same resolution. The administration's task was much easier in the House, where Armed Services chairman Les Aspin (D-Wis.) and Rep. Steven Solarz (D-N.Y.), an influential Northeastern liberal, worked hard for passage. House Republicans voted in favor 164 to 3, and 86 of 265 Democrats supported the resolution—a more comfortable margin than in the Senate. In the end, the debate was remembered as one of Congress's finest hours, and the vote represented a crucial political victory for the Bush administration.

On January 16, Desert Shield became Desert Storm as the air attack on Iraq began. Days later, both the House and Senate passed nearly unanimous resolutions supporting the president and U.S. troops. Within weeks, coalition forces had expelled Iraq from Kuwait, in the process destroying much of Iraq's vaunted military might. The U.S. stopped short of occupying Baghdad and forcing Saddam Hussein from office—a decision that would later be subjected to considerable second-guessing. Chaos gripped Iraq for weeks, with Kurds rebelling in the north and Shiite Moslems rebelling in the south. Saddam Hussein regrouped and reestablished control of the country. In the United States, the nation was euphoric. A jubilant George Bush said, "By God, we've kicked the Vietnam syndrome once and for all."[31]

How was President Bush able to dominate policymaking? Although the presidency has a number of political advantages in foreign and military affairs, congressional support in the crucial vote was far from guaranteed. The United States itself had not been attacked, and many people questioned how essential it was to restore Kuwait's ruling royal family to power. In addition, there was a clear alternative to military action. The economic sanctions initiated by the administration had not had time to work and there was strong sentiment among many members of Congress to give them more time.[32] Bush prevailed because he made his case and effectively sold it to Congress. The administration skillfully used the United Nations to its advantage, bringing international pressure on Congress. Although later evidence suggested that the administration was not as unified as it had appeared, it was clear and unwavering in defining its goals and ways to achieve them.[33]

The Gulf War had a number of constitutional, political, and policy impacts. With respect to the issue of war powers, some scholars consider that Bush's letter to Congress requesting authorization was important. Yale law professor Harold Koh noted that "the president blinked" in the "constitutional face-off."[34] Senate Majority leader Mitchell commented, "His request clearly acknowledged the need for congressional approval. The Constitution of the United States is not and cannot be subordinated to a United Nations resolution."[35] In terms of immediate political effects, the war was a bonanza for the administration. Immediately after the war, more Americans reported themselves as Republicans than Democrats for the first time ever.[36] The president's approval ratings approached 90 percent.

The war had several immediate policy consequences. It restored confidence in the American military and proved the capability of many of the advanced weapons that had been procured during the 1980s. The main objective of the policy—the expulsion of Iraq from Kuwait—was achieved. Much of Iraq's offensive military capacity seemingly was destroyed, including chemical and nuclear weapons. The process strengthened the United Nations and established important precedents for multilateral cooperation in the post-cold war world. Middle East peace talks between Arab nations and Israel began. The war also affected oil prices; a year after the war, gasoline prices in the United States were 20 percent lower.

Despite these achievements, questions about the impact of the war remain. Ten years later, Saddam Hussein still clings to power and is rebuilding the Iraqi military, which remains formidable. After the terrorist attacks in 2001, the George W. Bush administration seriously considered further action against Iraq as part of the larger war on terrorism. In the end, Bush Sr.'s political advantages proved fleeting, as public attention turned from the war to an economy mired in recession. A year later, Democrats once again had a 10 percent lead over Republicans in party identification, and Bush's approval ratings had plunged below 40 percent as he entered the election year.

Congressional Leadership:
Cuba Sanctions Legislation (1996)

On February 24, 1996, Cuban fighter pilots shot down an unarmed U.S. registered aircraft that had entered Cuban airspace, killing four American citizens. This confrontational act forced President Clinton and moderates in Congress to support pending legislation that greatly expanded economic sanctions against Cuba. Following Cuba's action, the options available to all parties were greatly constrained. Indeed, the White House and Congress reached agreement on the bill just four days after the incident. Castro had only himself to blame for making it politically impossible for the president and the Republican Congress to not take action on this issue.

The sanctions legislation culminated a long-festering disaffection with the single remaining communist dictatorship in the Western Hemisphere. In the United States, the Cuban vote was a powerful force in Florida, a state critical to winning the presidential election. In October 1995, conservative Republicans in the Senate, led by Jesse Helms (R-N.C.), Bob Dole (R-Kans.) and Phil Gramm (R-Tex.) opposed President Clinton's plans to increase cultural exchanges and travel to Cuba. They accused Clinton of seeking to limit a boycott of Cuba that had been in place for 35 years and pushed for a heavily modified sanctions bill that had passed the House overwhelmingly the previous month. The tactic these leaders used was to cut off debate by White House supporters by invoking cloture, which would have ended the filibuster against HR 924. They failed in this endeavor by a mere four votes on October 12, 1995. Clinton had threatened a veto and even some Republicans feared that the legislation "could strain relations with U.S. allies, spawn a flood of costly litigation, and trigger a backlash against U.S. companies abroad."[37] Although Clinton prevailed, he brought forth the wrath of conservatives who wanted even stronger sanctions.

This vote revealed the deep ideological divisions in the Senate, particularly among Democrats, over how best to deal with the Castro regime in Cuba. A short time later, the Senate passed more moderate sanctions legislation that contained fewer provisions to which the White House objected. Even this scaled-back version, which passed by a 50-vote margin on October 19, 1995, was opposed by many Democrats and two Republicans. But Clinton and his Democratic allies in Congress were undercut by the shoot-down of the plane. Four days later, February 28, 1996, the revised legislation passed both chambers by veto-proof margins after conferees agreed on a compromise version.

The Senate adopted the conference report to HB 927 on March 5, 1996, by a vote of 74 to 22; it had passed the House the previous day by an also-lopsided vote of 336 to 86. Highlights of the resulting Cuban Liberty and Democratic Solidarity Act (PL 104-116) include the following provisions:

1. It urged the president to seek an international embargo against Cuba through the United Nations.
2. It codified existing embargoes until Castro is replaced.
3. It prohibited the extension of loans and credits involving confiscated property until a democratically elected government appeared in Cuba.
4. It authorized the president to encourage democracy-building efforts in Cuba.

5. It withheld U.S. assistance to any nation supporting completion of nuclear facilities in Cuba.

In addition to condemning the attack of February 24, 1996, the most controversial provision sought to protect the property rights of U.S. nationals whose property had been confiscated by the Cuban regime by making the perpetrators liable for damages.

The Cuban Liberty and Democratic Solidarity (or LIBERTAD) Act, also known as Helms-Burton, was signed into law on March 12, 1996. Despite earlier presidential opposition, Clinton decided to go along with Congress. In signing the legislation, President Clinton made the following remarks:

> Today I sign with a certainty that it will send a powerful unified message from the United States to Havana, that the yearning of the Cuban people for freedom must not be denied. This bill continues our bipartisan effort to pursue an activist Cuba policy, an effort that began some four years ago with the Cuban Democracy Act.[38]

Rhetoric was hot in the Senate when Foreign Relations Committee Chairman Helms said, "There is no mistaking the bill's intent. 'Farewell Fidel,' that's the message of this bill."[39] Prior to the legislation, the president had been able to lift embargoes on his own but now that authority was transferred to Congress. The administration had obtained a provision that empowered the president to delay implementation of suits against foreign businesses. Still, the resulting law was stricter in other elements than that of the previous year and limited the president's discretion. Republicans did not want Clinton to do what he did on Vietnam, initiating diplomatic relations with the communist nation over congressional objections.

The case of sanctions legislation reveals the political intricacies and interrelationships among domestic, economic, and foreign policy in presidential-congressional relations. It also shows, in a dramatic fashion, how an international event can change the political environment and, as a result, negotiations between Congress and the president. Its elements of international intrigue and diplomacy might appear at first to be solely in the realm of foreign policy: After the attack on American citizens in the small airplane, Congress and President Clinton made retaliatory threats against Castro. However, the case also contains elements of trade and economic matters, since the law placed sanctions on any nation "trafficking" in Cuban money expropriated (confiscated) from U.S. citizens. Additionally, the Cuban sanctions law involved a heavy dose of domestic politics, pitting candidates for the presidency against one another in 1996. The legislation is an interesting example of shifting relationships, from initial congressional dominance to support for the presidential viewpoint, and back to Congress taking the predominant leadership position.

In addition to military implications, the legislation likely will inflict further economic hardship on the Cuban people, who remain among Latin America's most impoverished. Castro and his brother Raul blasted Helms-Burton as "a monstrous plan . . . to make Cubans surrender to hunger and need." During the annual celebration of the Cuban revolution, the Castro brothers claimed it would have little effect and that tourism would increase by nearly 20 percent during the year.[40] Clinton suspended all charter air travel from the United States to Cuba indefinitely. Helms-Burton raised potential complications with U.S. allies in the Americas and the European Union who resented having conditions placed on their trading relations. These nations threatened retaliation, stating that the lawsuits provision could "expose U.S. businesses to similar claims in foreign courts."[41] Private businesses were also subject to its provisions, wherein any economic involvement with Cuba that encompassed expropriated U.S. property was subject to legal action. In addition, foreign governments and companies involved in doing business with Cuba were barred from entering the U.S. except for medical conditions. Thus, the provisions were very wide-ranging and several foreign governments, Mexico and Canada among them, hinted at retaliation against U.S. companies in their countries.

The Helms-Burton Act generated much controversy not only among the international trade community, but also among scholars of international law.[42] Numerous lawsuits sought to clarify the vague or unresolved issues of the law, such as the liability of foreign citizens in U.S. courts or subjecting foreign countries to retroactive liability. Some provisions of the Act seemed inconsistent. Mexico announced that it would consider inducements to its companies to ignore the Act. Such actions and confusion over the law prompted President Clinton to name a special envoy to deal with criticisms and seek to promote Cuban democracy.

The legislation is a case of Congress making foreign policy. However, the president obtained the authority to suspend the rights of claimants to file lawsuits for six months if he asserted that delays would be in U.S. interests. Indeed, Clinton consistently suspended the law, thereby preventing U.S. citizens from suing foreign firms using confiscated property in Cuba. He stated that he would continue to do so as long as progress was being made in organizing other international actions against Castro's regime.[43] In the end, the president was able to blunt the impact of the policy during the implementation phase.

Consensus/Cooperation:
The Panama Canal Treaties (1978)

On April 18, 1978, with only one vote to spare, a two-thirds majority in the U.S. Senate ratified the treaty that would turn over operation of the Panama Canal to the nation of Panama in 2000. This followed an identical 68 to 32 vote in March over the neutrality treaty with Panama. Ratification of these two treaties was a victory not only for President Jimmy Carter, but also for Senate leaders who had navigated through a legislative minefield for two months. Immediately after the vote, Carter said, "These treaties can mark the beginning of a new era in our relations not only with Panama but with the rest of the world."[44]

There may be constitutional ambiguity about the war power, but responsibility for treaties with foreign nations is clear: The president negotiates treaties, and the Senate ratifies by a two-thirds vote. Since the days of George Washington, treaty negotiation has been an executive prerogative, with the Senate limited to approval or rejection of the final document. That approval has not always been easy to get. The defeat in the U.S. Senate of the Treaty of Versailles, negotiated by President Woodrow Wilson at the end of World War I, was a devastating blow to his presidency. As a result of difficulties with treaties, presidents in the modern era increasingly turned to executive agreements (which do not need Senate ratification), as shown in Table 5.2.

Renegotiating the control of the Panama Canal, however, could not be disposed of by executive agreement. A treaty with Panama had existed since 1903, and was revised in 1936 and 1955. By the 1960s, U.S. control of the canal was a sore point between the United States, Panama, and the nations of Latin America. Early in his first year in office, Jimmy Carter promised the Organization of American States that he was "firmly committed to negotiating. . . a new treaty which will take into account Panama's legitimate needs as a sovereign nation."[45] Over the course of the year, the administration finalized work on two separate treaties: one establishing the neutrality of the Canal Zone, and the second turning over control of the canal to

Table 5.2   Treaties and Executive Agreements, 1789–1998.

Years	Number Treaties	Number Executive Agreements	Executive Agreements as Percent of Total
1789–1839	60	27	34%
1839–1889	215	238	53
1889–1932	431	804	65
1933–1944 (Roosevelt)	131	369	74
1945–1952 (Truman)	132	1324	91
1953–1960 (Eisenhower)	89	1834	95
1961–1963 (Kennedy)	36	813	96
1964–1968 (Johnson)	67	1083	94
1969–1974 (Nixon)	93	1317	93
1975–1976 (Ford)	26	666	96
1977–1980 (Carter)	79	1476	96
1981–1988 (Reagan)	117	2837	96
1989–1992 (Bush)	67	1350	95
1993–1998 (Clinton)	168	1649	98

Source: Adapted from Harold W. Stanley and Richard G. Niemi, *Vital Statistics on American Politics* (Washington, D.C.: CQ Press, 2000): 329.

Panama on December 31, 1999. The treaties were signed on September 7, 1977. In October, the Panamanian people approved the treaties in a national plebiscite. Now the challenge for the president was to work with congressional leaders to secure the necessary votes for ratification. Given Carter's unspectacular legislative record in his first year, the prospects for getting a two-thirds majority seemed slim at best.

Lobbying was intense. Proponents and opponents battled both for Senate votes and public opinion. In late 1977, the Gallup poll revealed that a majority of Americans opposed the treaties. Conservative groups attacked what they called "giving away our canal." Senate Minority Leader Howard Baker (R-Tenn.) was lobbied at a University of Tennessee football game by a plane flying overhead with a banner that read, "Save Our Canal."[46] The American Conservative Union launched a massive grassroots campaign against ratification, spending hundreds of thousands of dollars. An impressive bipartisan group of former officials was brought in to support the treaties, including former President Gerald Ford, former Vice President Nelson Rockefeller, and former Secretaries of State Dean Rusk, Henry Kissinger, and William Rogers. Even conservative actor John Wayne was enlisted to publicize his support for the treaties.

Much of the work in building this support was done in the Senate itself. Minority Leader Baker and Majority Leader Robert Byrd (D-W.Va.) both announced their support in early 1978 and formed a bipartisan team to win ratification. The debate in the Senate began on February 8 and was carried nationwide on National Public Radio. As more and more senators announced their intentions, vote counters estimated that there were 62 senators in favor, 28 opposed, and 10 undecided.[47] Finally, opponents agreed to a vote on the neutrality treaty on March 16. Neither side knew whether it had the votes.

As the dramatic vote unfolded, all 100 senators sat at their desks. The administration had been busy in the hours leading up to the vote, sending 30 State Department officials to meet with senators and providing expensive maps and information packets. Vice President Walter Mondale, well known and respected in the Senate, worked the Hill hard. To secure the votes of those senators who still had major concerns, the administration and congressional sponsors agreed to accept several major "reservations" by the Senate. Unlike amendments, reservations do not change the text of the treaty but, according to international law scholars, carry the same weight.[48] In the end, Byrd and Baker got 68 votes for the treaty and claimed to have four in reserve (members who would have voted yes if they were needed to provide the decisive vote). This was a tremendous victory for proponents, but it did not guarantee victory on the more controversial treaty that would turn over the canal to Panama.

The debate on the second treaty resumed in April. One of the most compelling arguments concerned the effect that a defeat of the treaty would have on the nation's ability to conduct foreign policy. A reluctant supporter, Senator Herman Talmadge (D-Ga.) reasoned that "we do not want to destroy the bargaining power or diplomatic credibility of the United States."[49] Still, the treaties remained unpopular with

Americans. A Harris poll in April revealed that by 44 to 37 percent, a plurality of Americans believed the treaties were "not a good thing" for the United States.[50] Despite the polls, Senator Byrd appealed to the Senate to do what they knew was right rather than what was popular:

> There's no political mileage in voting for the treaties. I know what my constituents are saying. But I have a responsibility not only to follow them but to inform them and lead them. I'm not going to betray my responsibility to my constituents. I owe them not only my industry but my judgment.[51]

Opponents tried several last-ditch maneuvers to defeat the treaties. Senator Orrin Hatch (R-Utah) offered an amendment requiring the House to approve the transfer of U.S. property to Panama even if the treaties were ratified. The Senate rejected the amendment and the constitutional interpretation behind it. Dozens more amendments were tabled or defeated. As the final vote approached, the Senate adopted another sensitive reservation, giving the United States the right to keep the canal open. The vote was in doubt until the final hour, and this time the leadership had no votes in reserve. The result was the same, 68 to 32, with 52 out of 60 Democrats and 16 out of 38 Republicans voting for the treaty. Although a majority of Republicans opposed it, cross partisanship was key to success.

How were the legislative and executive branches able to cooperate effectively to gain ratification for such a controversial treaty? Clearly, the political environment was unfavorable for such an outcome, with opponents of the treaty fanning deep public fears. The president's congressional liaison efforts, much maligned in the previous year, were given high marks by senators. Individual leadership played a crucial role both in working the intricate rules of the Senate and in setting a high moral tone in the debate. Despite the interbranch conflict that characterized the 1970s, Congress evidenced a respect for the prerogatives of the executive branch in negotiating treaties. At the same time, the administration compromised by accepting a number of reservations to help alleviate congressional concerns. Cooperation emerged when both branches acted responsibly on a measure they believed was in the broad national interest.

What were the policy impacts of the Panama Canal treaties? Although it is impossible to say exactly what would have happened if the treaties had been defeated, Latin American experts agree that it would have been very damaging to U.S. relations with that region. In the years after ratification, the canal has remained open to shipping as responsibility was gradually shifted to Panamanians. Without the treaties, the canal might have been subject to sabotage, targeted for terrorist attacks, or shut down by local protests. Ratification also helped relations with Third World nations and was supported by U.S. allies. The treaties did not do anything to improve the government in Panama; the United States intervened there militarily in 1989. This was not primarily to safeguard the canal, however. Although the treaties did not solve all the conflicts between the United States and its Latin American neighbors, they represented a step toward that goal.

Deadlock/Extraordinary Resolution: Aid to the Nicaraguan Contras (1982–89)

In November of 1986, the American people first learned of a Reagan administration initiative to sell arms to Iran in hopes of winning the release of American hostages held in Lebanon. Soon thereafter, it was disclosed that some of the profits from those sales had been diverted to aid the Contra rebels in Nicaragua, in direct violation of a law passed by Congress. The Iran-Contra scandal became one of the top political events of 1987. Televised congressional hearings featured Lieutenant Colonel Oliver North, who, along with the late CIA Director William Casey, had masterminded the scheme. This episode, which tarnished the reputation of the Reagan administration, was the outgrowth of five years of bitter confrontation between Congress and the president over policy toward the Sandinista government in Nicaragua. It is an example of the inconsistent and disastrous policy results that can emerge from a pattern of institutional combat and deadlock.

For many years, Nicaragua had been ruled by the dictator Anastasio Somoza, who had the support of the United States. In 1979, a revolution toppled Somoza and brought to power Daniel Ortega and his cadre of Sandinista rebels. The Carter administration cut off assistance to the Sandinistas as the new Marxist government tilted toward the Soviet Union and Cuba. Anti-Sandinista rebels (the "Contras"), many of them loyal to the old dictatorship, still occupied some rural areas of Nicaragua. The United States offered the Contras humanitarian and military aid until Congress, citing the need for self-determination in Central America, cut off aid in 1980.

With the inauguration of Ronald Reagan in 1981, the White House gained a president firmly committed to checking the spread of communism in the Western Hemisphere. He was a strong advocate of military aid to the Contras. Over the next half-dozen years, Reagan would make scores of emotional speeches against the Sandinistas—scathing attacks on their human rights abuses, exporting of revolutionary violence throughout Central America, and ties to the Soviet Union. Reagan referred to the Contras as "freedom fighters" and patriots, deserving of significant aid from the United States in their struggle. Despite this rhetoric, Reagan did not convince even a plurality of the American people to support aid to the Contras.[52]

Public skepticism about the Contras reinforced congressional opposition to the policy, particularly in the Democratic House of Representatives. Opponents pointed to some of the problems associated with the Contras, particularly the lack of unity among rebel groups and the strong association some of the rebels had with the repressive Somoza regime. Military aid to the Contras began in 1982 through the CIA, which delivered arms, uniforms, and equipment to the rebels. The Reagan administration requested additional funds, but congressional opponents wanted to limit the use of this money to strictly nonmilitary purposes. One of the leading opponents to Contra aid was Rep. Edward Boland (D-Mass.), who chaired the subcommittee responsible for funding. He authored a number of amendments through the 1980s—the *Boland amendments*—to limit aid to the Contras.

The first Boland amendment was enacted on December 21, 1982, and extended through December of 1983 as part of the Defense Appropriation Act. It provided that no funds from the Defense Department or the CIA could be used to "furnish military equipment, military training or advice for the purpose of overthrowing the government of Nicaragua or provoking a military exchange between Nicaragua and Honduras."[53] The policy continued to seesaw back and forth, as the administration pushed for more aid, and congressional opponents sought the means to block it. In 1983, the second Boland amendment was adopted, giving the administration a partial victory. It provided $24 million (less than Reagan wanted) for direct and indirect support for paramilitary operations in Nicaragua.

The next year, conflict between the president and Congress continued to result in inconsistent policies. When it was revealed that the CIA had been involved in mining the harbor in Managua, Congress banned all military aid to the Contras. The third Boland amendment, which was in force from October of 1984 to September of 1985, prohibited spending any money that would "have the effect of supporting, directly or indirectly, military or paramilitary operations in Nicaragua by any nation, group, organization, movement, or individual."[54] The fourth Boland amendment brought another change: Congress authorized $27 million in humanitarian assistance to the Contras. In 1985 to 1986, the fifth Boland amendment represented yet another reversal, authorizing secret direct aid to the Contras.

During the 1980s, the issue of aid to the Contras consumed months and months of time in the White House and Congress. Congress debated and voted on the same basic issue over and over again. If one side lost a battle, its leaders knew that they would have another chance in a few months. The administration was frustrated because its foreign policy was undermined and because it was unable to deliver military aid with any consistency. Congressional opponents were frustrated that they could not stop the U.S. indirect intervention completely. This policy was a high priority to both branches, and emotions ran high. Toppling the Sandinistas, according to later testimony, was almost a daily preoccupation in the White House. This preoccupation and frustration with congressional opponents led to an attempt by key administration officials to develop an extraordinary resolution to the policy deadlock.

In 1984, National Security Advisor John Poindexter, his aide Oliver North, and CIA Director William Casey decided to divert to the Contras profits from the sale of arms to Iran, despite the Boland amendments. The president maintained "deniability"; testimony from his staff asserted that he was not informed of the illegal actions. When the scandal broke, it further inflamed the debate over aid to the Contras. Reagan's popularity plummeted, and the percentage of the public who supported military aid to the Contras diminished. President Reagan appointed former Senator

John Tower to head a commission to investigate the affair. The Tower Commission report in early 1987 was highly critical of the organization of the White House and the National Security Council. It concluded that President Reagan was not sufficiently in control of White House policy.

Congress used its investigatory powers to explore the case further. Americans around the country avidly watched the televised testimony of North and Poindexter. Congressional reactions ranged from comparing the administration's actions to a junta seizing power in the White House to justifying them as an appropriate response to congressional interference in foreign policy. North and Poindexter were later prosecuted, but their convictions were overturned because the appeals courts held that material revealed in their congressional testimony under a grant of immunity had influenced the verdicts in the trial courts. Reagan's popularity rebounded after a period of time, but it never reached the levels he had enjoyed previously.

The conflict between Congress and the president over aid to the Contras was not resolved until 1989. President Bush was committed to developing a compromise with Congress to prevent the disastrous process that had led to the scandal. In March of 1989, Secretary of State James Baker and congressional leaders agreed to approve a package of nonmilitary aid to the Contras through early 1990. In return, the president promised to request no further military aid and to make diplomatic overtures to the Sandinista government. The agreement allowed Congress to halt the aid within six months if any of four committees believed that the peace process was being undermined. In reaction to the deal, Bush noted that for the first time in years, both parties "were speaking with one voice."[55] Critics, however, argued that Bush had caved in to Congress, weakening the president's power in foreign affairs. Columnist David Broder wrote, "This evasion of the Constitution was so smelly it had to be accomplished through a side agreement, embodied in a letter from the Secretary of State."[56] The real resolution of the issue came soon after. In a democratic election, Violeta Chamorro defeated Sandinista Daniel Ortega for the presidency of Nicaragua. Within a matter of months, the Contras disbanded.

What explains the emergence of such a pattern of policy deadlock and attempts at extraordinary resolution? The divisions between branches arose from deep differences in ideology with regard to U.S. responsibilities for checking the spread of communism in Central America. The differences erupted into intense partisan conflict between the branches and grew worse as relations between Reagan and Congress deteriorated because of budget battles and other issues. Both sides were more concerned with winning the policy battle than protecting the integrity of the nation's foreign policymaking institutions and processes. In the political environment, there was no strong public support for aiding the Contras, but the public sentiment was ambivalent. Frustrated ideologues in the White House, disgusted with Congress, decided to take extraordinary measures to achieve their policy goals, regardless of the constitutional consequences. A severe failure of institutional performance and presidential leadership occurred.

What were the consequences of this conflict? Aiding the Nicaraguan Contras in the 1980s was a policy fiasco of the highest order. The policy was inconsistently applied because of the tug of war between branches. Neither side could win a complete victory, and the policy that emerged was the worst of both worlds. The aid did not succeed in overthrowing the Sandinistas. Although the flow of arms from Nicaragua to the communist rebels in El Salvador was reduced, it was not eliminated. People around the world—particularly in Latin America—criticized U.S. policy, even though there was little sympathy for the Sandinistas. Finally, the policy damaged the process of governing. The episode highlighted the worst consequences of divided government and interbranch combat.

Conclusion

The four cases in this chapter demonstrate a remarkable range in policymaking patterns in the realm of foreign affairs. In most of the cases, even when presidential leadership prevails, Congress shares in governing. Since the end of the cold war, presidential dominance appears diminished, especially on issues that are of great concern to members of Congress. On some foreign policy issues that have strong domestic consequences, such as the Cuban sanctions bill, Congress can play a leading role. That was true before the war on terrorism and will be true afterward. In general, however, a pattern of congressional dominance is unlikely to prevail in foreign policy. Protracted deadlock, to the extent seen in the case of aid to the Contras, is also not common. Despite the fact that the president can dominate government in time of a crisis, no single model is appropriate to characterize presidential-congressional relations in foreign affairs in the 2000s.

Several factors help explain the patterns of policymaking that emerged in the four cases. The political environment was instrumental in the Gulf War because of the strong domestic and international support Bush mustered for his policy. The environment was much more complex and probably less decisive in the other three cases, in which public opinion was either ambivalent or negative. Regarding the Panama Canal treaties, leaders made their case despite public doubts. In the case of Cuban sanctions, the Clinton administration position was hamstrung by an external event, the shooting down of American citizens by Cuban fighter planes. On the issue of aid to the Contras, the administration failed to make the case to the public. Public opinion since the late 1960s has generally judged foreign policy a less important problem than domestic policy. Except for the Gulf War (and the recent war against terrorism), public opinion was not instrumental in determining the outcome.

Individual leadership influenced the patterns that emerged. Bush provided clear and consistent direction to U.S. policy following Iraq's invasion of Kuwait. In winning ratification of the Panama Canal treaties, Carter and Congress showed leadership as well as a concern for the integrity of the policy process. Strong congressional leadership prevailed over more ambivalent presidential views on Cuban sanctions.

On the other hand, sharply differing policy preferences and the inability of leadership in either branch to constructively resolve differences led to a failed policy in Nicaragua. Particularly in foreign policy, strong and responsible leadership from both branches remains an essential component of successful public policy.

Notes

1. See Robert A. Dahl, *Congress and Foreign Policy* (New York: Harcourt, Brace, Javanovich, 1950); James A Robinson, *Congress and Foreign Policy Making* (Homewood IL.: Dorsey Press, 1967); Louis W. Koenig, *The Chief Executive* (New York: Harcourt, Brace, Javanovich 1975); John C. Donovan, *The Cold Warriors: A Policy Making Elite* (Lexington, MA.: D.C. Heath, 1974); I. M. Destler, *Presidents, Bureaucrats and Foreign Policy* (Princeton, NJ: Princeton University Press, 1974).
2. Aaron Wildavsky, "The Two Presidencies" *Transaction* 4 (December 1966): 7–14; reprinted in Steven A. Shull (ed.) *The Two Presidencies: A Quarter Century Assessment* (Chicago: Nelson Hall, 1991): 11–25.
3. Marcus Cunliffe, *American Presidents and the Presidency* (New York: McGraw Hill, 1972).
4. See Gary Orfield, *Congressional Power* (New York: Harcourt, Brace, Javanovich, 1975); Hugh G. Gallagher, "The President, Congress, and Legislation," in Thomas E. Cronin and Rexford G. Tugwell (eds.), *The Presidency Reappraised* (New York: Praeger, 1977); James L. Sundquist, *Politics and Policy* (Washington, D.C.: Brookings, 1968); John Johannes, *Political Innovation in Congress* (Morristown, NJ: General Learning Press, 1972); Randall B. Ripley and James M. Lindsay (eds.), *Congress Resurgent* (Ann Arbor: University of Michigan Press, 1993); Barbara Hinckley, *Less Than Meets the Eye* (Chicago: University of Chicago Press, 1994).
5. Cecil V. Crabb and Pat M. Holt, *Invitation to Struggle* (Washington, D.C.: CQ Press, 1989); Paul Peterson, (ed.), *President, Congress, and the Making of Foreign Policy* (Norman, OK.: University of Oklahoma Press, 1994); James A. Thurber (ed.), *Rivals for Power* (Washington, D.C.: CQ Press, 1996); Steven A. Shull, *Presidential-Congressional Relations* (Ann Arbor: University of Michigan Press, 1997).
6. *CQ Weekly* (December 22, 2001): 3062.
7. Quoted in William D. Rodgers, "Who's in Charge of Foreign Policy," *New York Times Magazine* (September 9, 1979): 49.
8. Samuel Huntington, *Common Defense* (New York: Columbia University Press, 1961): 124.
9. L Gordon Crovitz and Jeremy A. Rabkin (eds.), *The Fettered Presidency* (Washington, D.C.: American Enterprise Institute, 1989): 38–39
10. Stephen E. Ambrose, *American Rise to Globalism: American Foreign Policy, 1938–1980* (New York: Penguin, 1980): 13–14.
11. Harry S Truman, "Special Message to the Congress on Greece and Turkey," *Public Papers of the President* (Washington, D.C.: Government Printing Office, 1963).
12. George C. Marshall, "European Initiative Essential to Economic Recovery," *Department of State Bulletin* 16 (June 1947): 1160.
13. George F. Kennan, "The Sources of Soviet Conduct'" *Foreign Affairs* 25 (July 1947): 566–582.
14. Irving Janis, *Groupthink*, second edition, (Boston: Houghton Mifflin, 1982: Chapter 3.
15. Ibid., 14.
16. Graham Allison, "Conceptual Models and the Cuban Missile Crisis," *American Political Science Review* 63 (September 1969): 689.
17. Richard M. Nixon, *United States Foreign Policy for the 1970s: A New Strategy for Peace* (Washington, D.C.: Government Printing Office, 1970).
18. Jimmy Carter, *Department of State Bulletin* 76 (June 1977): 622.
19. Trade was an important issue, cutting across traditional foreign and domestic categories. See, for example, Bayless Manning, "Congress, the Executive, and Intermestic Affairs," *Foreign Affairs* 55 (1977): 306–324; Martha Gibson, "Issues, Coalitions, and Divided Government," *Congress and the*

President 22 (1995): 155–166; Brandon C. Prins and Steven A. Shull, "Enduring Rivals: Presidential Success and Support in the House of Representatives," unpublished manuscript.

20. *New Orleans Times-Picayune* (September 10, 1997): A-9.
21. Bill Keller, "The World According to Colin Powell," *New York Times Magazine*, November, 25, 2001): 30.
22. John Campbell, "The Disorganization of State," in Martin B. Hickman (ed.), *Problems of American Foreign Policy* (Beverly Hills: Glencoe Press, 1975): 168.
23. Steven A. Shull, *Presidential Policy Making: An Analysis* (Brunswick, OH: Kings Court Inc., 1979): Chapter 9.
24. Richard A. Watson and Norman C. Thomas, *The Politics of the Presidency* (New York: Wiley, 1983): 334.
25. Duane M. Oldfield and Aaron B. Wildavsky, "Reconsidering the Two Presidencies," *Society* 26 (July 1989): 54–59.
26. Wildavsky (1966): 10.
27. Lance T. LeLoup and Steven A. Shull, "Congress versus the Executive: The 'Two Presidencies' Reconsidered," *Social Science Quarterly* 59 (March, 1979): 704–719. As we noted in Chapter 3, Congressional Quarterly developed a new measure of "success" used by researchers (percentage of presidential vote positions upheld) as well as "support" (percentage of members in Congress voting to uphold the position taken by the president).
28. Richard Fleisher and Jon R. Bond, "Are There Two Presidencies? Yes, but Only for Republicans," *Journal of Politics* 50 (August 1988); 747–767.
29. *Ibid.*, 766.
30. *Congressional Quarterly Weekly Report* (January 12, 1991): 70.
31. *Newsweek* (March 11, 1991): 30.
32. *Washington Post National Weekly Edition* (March 18–24, 1991): 30.
33. Bob Woodward, *The Commanders* (New York: Simon and Schuster, 1991).
34. *Congressional Quarterly Weekly Report* (January 12, 1991): 70.
35. Ibid.
36. *Washington Post National Weekly Edition* (Feb. 18–24, 1991): 25.
37. *Congressional Quarterly Weekly Report* (October 14, 1995): 3156.
38. *Weekly Compilation of Presidential Documents*, Vol. 32 (March 18, 1996): 478.
39. *Congressional Quarterly Weekly Report* (March 2, 1996): 565.
40. *New Orleans Times-Picayune* (July 27, 1997): A-2.
41. *Congressional Quarterly Weekly Report* (March 2, 1996): 566
42. See, for example, *American Journal of International Law* 90 (1996): 419–434; 641–644.
43. WashingtonPost.com/WP-SER/WPlate (July 17, 1997): 2.
44. *Congressional Quarterly Weekly Report*, April 22, 1978: 917.
45. *Weekly Compilation of Presidential Documents* 13 (1977): 526.
46. *Congressional Quarterly Weekly Report* (January 21, 1978): 135.
47. *Congressional Quarterly Weekly Report* (February 4, 1978): 317.
48. *Congressional Quarterly Weekly Report* (March 18, 1978): 676.
49. Ibid.
50. Reported in *New Orleans Times-Picayune/ States-Item* (April 27, 1978). A-1.
51. Quoted in David Vogler, *The Politics of Congress* (Boston: Allyn and Bacon, 1980): 82.
52. *Congressional Quarterly Weekly Report* (March 15, 1986): 601.
53. *Congressional Quarterly Weekly Report* (November 26, 1983): 2487.
54. *Congressional Quarterly Weekly Report* (March 15, 1986): 602.
55. Ryan Barrileaux, "Presidential Conduct of Foreign Policy," *Congress and the Presidency* (Spring 1988): 1–23.
56. *Washington Post National Weekly Edition* 14 (May 15, 1989): 4.

CHAPTER 6

Civil Rights Policy

In order to win the war [against terrorism], we must make sure that the law enforcement men and women have got the tools necessary, within the Constitution, to defeat the enemy.

—PRESIDENT GEORGE W. BUSH (SEPTEMBER 2001)[1]

The United States is not so threatened that we have to throw away our rights with no consideration.

—CONGRESSMAN JOHN DINGELL (OCTOBER 2001)[2]

Civil rights—the ability of all citizens to share fully in the nation's political, economic, and social system—is a critical element of the policy agenda. Closely related are civil liberties—freedom from government infringement on rights of free speech, free press, and religion. The heritage of slavery and racial discrimination in the United States remains at the root of many current political disputes. Since the abolition of slavery in 1863, civil rights has followed an erratic policy course. Reconstruction Congresses in the 1870s and 1880s enacted legislation to protect civil rights of blacks, but they were swept aside by the courts and southern politicians. Not until the 1950s, after decades of struggle, did civil rights once again feature prominently on the nation's agenda. At that time, it was the Supreme Court, not Congress or the president, that took the lead.

When the legislative and executive branches became involved in the late 1950s and 1960s, more often than not they worked in tandem to enact legislation. Fervent opposition came from southern Democrats, who used every tactic available to block civil rights bills. The 1960 Civil Rights Act reflected this pattern of policymaking. Eighteen die-hard southern senators vowed to block the bill. Majority Leader Lyndon Johnson (D-Tex.) and Minority Leader Everett Dirksen (R-Ill.) assembled a bipartisan coalition of northern Democrats and moderate Republicans. They had the tacit if not active support of President Eisenhower. Faced with filibusters, quorum calls, and other delaying tactics, Johnson kept the Senate in session around the clock for months. Cots were set up for weary senators. Finally, Johnson and Dirksen wore down the opposition, and the bill passed.

Other major civil rights legislation in this era (notably the Civil Rights Act of 1964 and the Voting Rights Act of 1965) resulted from presidential leadership accompanied by legislative cooperation. In recent years, however, the environment for civil rights politics has changed, and so have the prevalent patterns of policymaking. Growing Republican strength in the South and sharp cleavages in the voting behavior of blacks and whites have increased partisanship and interbranch conflict. Both Presidents Reagan and Bush Sr. had confrontations with the Democratic Congress over civil rights legislation and the issue took on new political overtones. Democratic President Bill Clinton faced much the same challenge from a Republican Congress and a more conservative Supreme Court. President George W. Bush made more of an effort to reach across racial and ethnic lines and change the Republican reputation of not representing the interests of minority voters. Bush's main challenge in civil rights concerned the rights of Arab Americans and people of Middle Eastern decent following the September 11 terrorist attacks. The White House proposed much stronger powers for law enforcement in the war against terrorism, but civil libertarians feared that the administration was undermining many basic constitutional rights.

This chapter examines civil rights policy and patterns of presidential-congressional policymaking. We begin with a history of the evolution of civil rights policy, examine the current environment for civil rights, and then look at how Congress and the president make civil rights policy. We also look at the importance of leadership and agenda change. The four cases present examples of each of the four patterns of policymaking and their causes and consequences.

The Evolution of Civil Rights Policy

SLAVERY, THE CIVIL WAR, AND SEGREGATION

The economic system of the southern states, based on plantations and black slaves, became the dominant issue of the first half of the nineteenth century. Some early presidents actively opposed slavery: James Monroe proposed making the importation of slaves a capital offense; John Q. Adams challenged the institution of slavery as president and, later, in the House of Representatives.[3] Other presidents, however, avoided the increasingly controversial issue by suggesting that it was a problem that should be left to the states.[4]

A series of compromises kept the Union together through the 1850s, but the *Dred Scott* decision in 1857 helped push the country into civil war. In *Dred Scott*, the Supreme Court ruled that slaves were property and as such had no political rights, even in nonslave states. The high court also struck down the Missouri Compromise of 1820, since it had banned slavery in certain states. The justices were out of touch with a nation in which opposition to slavery was growing. Four years later the war started. The question of slavery would not be settled until hundreds of thousands of lives were lost. On January 1, 1863, the Emancipation Proclamation decreed that "all persons held as slaves within any State or designated part of a State the people whereof shall then be in rebellion against the United States shall be then, thenceforward, and forever free."[5]

To guarantee the civil rights of freed slaves, Congress proposed three amendments to the Constitution, which the states ratified. The Thirteenth Amendment banned slavery in the United States, but it was quickly circumvented. Southern states passed "black codes," restricting the rights of freed slaves. Congress responded by passing the Fourteenth Amendment, which was ratified in 1868. It contained seemingly clear language: "No state . . . shall deprive any person of life, liberty, or property without due process of law; nor deny . . . the equal protection of laws." The Fifteenth Amendment was intended to ensure the voting rights of blacks, stating that the right to vote could not be abridged because of a person's race, color, or condition of previous servitude. The women's suffrage movement argued that the amendments should apply to women as well, but in 1875 the Supreme Court ruled that the protections of the Fourteenth and Fifteenth Amendments did not extend to women.

Despite the constitutional guarantees in these three amendments, any semblance of equal rights for blacks was wiped out within 20 years. In the *Slaughterhouse* cases in 1873, the Supreme Court chose the narrowest possible interpretations of what it meant to abuse the "privileges and immunities" of blacks. Congress responded by passing a series of civil rights laws that forbade discrimination in public facilities and accommodations. In 1877, the last of the federal troops were removed from the South. The Reconstruction governments, dominated by Republicans and including a number of blacks, were swept out by conservative Democratic regimes. The Supreme Court helped these new governments undermine civil rights once more with the 1883 *Civil Rights* cases. The justices ruled that Congress could not ban discrimination in privately owned establishments. This opened the door to a series of "Jim Crow" laws (named for a slang expression for blacks), which systematically denied blacks equal access and opportunity.

The sanctioning of a separate, segregated society of blacks and whites in the deep South was completed in 1896 in the case of *Plessy v. Ferguson*. In this case, the Supreme Court upheld a Louisiana law that required those of "colored races" to ride in separate Pullman cars on the train. The Court ruled that such a law was constitutional as long as "separate but equal" facilities were provided. This now allowed the segregation of public as well as private facilities. The rollback of civil rights for blacks was not limited to Pullman cars and schools; the right to vote guaranteed by the Fifteenth Amendment was taken away as well. Between 1880 and 1900, most black voters in the states of the old Confederacy had been taken off the rolls of eligible voters.[6] Two generations after the Civil War, virtually all facilities were segregated—from bathrooms to drinking fountains to the court Bibles used to swear in witnesses.[7] Segregation and racism also existed in the North, but not to the same extent as in the dual society of the South.

THE CIVIL RIGHTS MOVEMENT

The movement to provide civil rights for blacks began quietly at the beginning of the twentieth century. In 1909, a group of black and white activists formed the National Association for the Advancement of Colored People (NAACP). Two years later, the Urban League was formed to improve the lives of blacks living in big cities. In contrast, voting rights for women were long in coming, perhaps because paternalism and protection were more characteristic of discrimination against women than discrimination against blacks. The national movement to give women the right to vote had gathered momentum after the turn of the century and would achieve its goal in 1920 with the ratification of the Nineteenth Amendment.

Most of the activity in the civil rights movement in the first half of the century took place in the courts rather than in the White House or Congress. Presidents, including Franklin D. Roosevelt, were unwilling to push civil rights legislation, and the power of the southern bloc in the Senate stymied Congress.[8] The House of Representatives passed an antilynching bill in the late 1930s and several bills banning the poll tax in the 1940s, but all of these died in the Senate. Meanwhile, lawsuits brought by the NAACP were chipping away at the legal basis of segregation. Harry S Truman was the first president to push for civil rights legislation to promote equality.[9] He issued an executive order integrating the nation's armed forces and urged the 1948 Democratic convention to adopt a civil rights plank in its platform.[10] This drove a number of southern Democrats out of the party.

On May 17, 1954, the U.S. Supreme Court struck a landmark blow for civil rights in overturning the "separate but equal" doctrine. The case of *Brown v. Board of Education* was a combination of cases from seven cities brought on behalf of black students by the NAACP. In the unanimous decision, Chief Justice Earl Warren's opinion attacked the basic nature of segregation in public education: "Separate is inherently unequal," the Court declared. School districts were ordered to desegregate "with all deliberate speed." Reaction to the *Brown* decision was predictable: Civil rights advocates were elated, while southern politicians denounced the decision and pledged to disobey it. The implementation proved difficult and often ugly. President Eisenhower was forced to order federal troops into Little Rock, Arkansas, when the state's governor refused to integrate the schools.

The civil rights movement did not stop with school integration; the system of segregation still prevailed throughout the South. In Montgomery, Alabama, a black seamstress named Rosa Parks was arrested when she refused to move to the colored section in the back of a public bus. In protest, the Reverend Martin Luther King Jr., organized a boycott of the Montgomery bus system.[11] A year later, the Court ruled that segregation on public transportation systems was illegal. Economic sanctions such as the bus boycott became increasingly important to the civil rights movement. In 1960, at a restaurant in Greensboro, North Carolina, a group of black and white college students refused to leave the lunch counter seats until all of them were served. Local sheriffs arrested them, but soon hundreds of other protesters took their place. Within a year, over 70,000 people had participated in sit-ins, and hundreds of facilities previously closed to blacks were opened to them.[12]

THE CIVIL RIGHTS AND VOTING RIGHTS ACTS

Because of actions by the courts and the growing protest movement in the South, civil rights gained more importance as a component of the policy agenda of Congress and the president. President Eisenhower requested an extension of the Civil Rights Commission and the abolition of literacy tests and the poll tax, but remained extremely cautious on civil rights.[13] In 1957, he signed a civil rights bill initiated by Congress. Although the bill was weak, it was an important milestone for the bipartisan pro-civil rights coalition in Congress in overcoming the opposition of the southern bloc. After the monumental battle over the 1960 civil rights bill, Eisenhower signed it into law. However, neither bill went very far in eliminating discrimination in public accommodations, voting, housing, and other areas.

During the 1960 campaign, John F. Kennedy voiced strong support for civil rights. After the election, however, he faced a Congress that had a slim Democratic majority and a powerful southern contingent. Fearing for the rest of his legislative agenda, Kennedy held back on civil rights legislation.[14] By 1963, President Kennedy was convinced he had to take strong action, regardless of the political consequences. Ugly racial incidents such as the murder of Medgar Evers and three civil rights workers in Mississippi strengthened his resolve. In June, he sent Congress the most sweeping civil rights bill ever. In August of 1963, Reverend Martin Luther King Jr., led a march on Washington; many people in the country were growing impatient for meaningful change. The bill had emerged from committee in November of 1963, the month Kennedy was assassinated.

Despite being a southerner and former civil rights opponent, Kennedy's successor, Lyndon Johnson, became a fervent civil rights supporter.[15] As president, he used his legislative skills and the lingering sympathy for Kennedy to push through the Civil Rights Act of 1964. For the first time, Congress enacted strong provisions promoting open accommodations, and protecting the rights of blacks and women in employment and other areas. The passage of the 1964 Civil Rights Act had an important effect on the nation's political alignment. Johnson's landslide victory in the 1964 presidential election reflected a significant partisan realignment among the nation's voters, black and white.[16] Richard Nixon attracted over 30 percent of the black vote in the 1960 presidential election, but in 1964 and subsequent elections, Republican candidates have garnered less than 10 percent of the black vote. At the same time, 1964 marked the first time in generations that the South—once solidly Democratic—voted for a Republican presidential candidate.

In 1965, enjoying large Democratic majorities in both the House and the Senate, Johnson helped usher through the Voting Rights Act of 1965. Despite the elimination of many of the old exclusionary devices, southern blacks still had difficulty registering and voting. In Mississippi, for example, less than 7 percent of eligible black voters were registered. This would jump to 60 percent a few years after the implementation of the Voting Rights Act.[17] The act made it possible to take legal action against an entire county or state, rather than acting on each occurrence of discrimination on a case-by-case basis.[18] In addition, it removed all remaining tests and devices used to prevent blacks from voting. The results were dramatic; in just a few years, there was a significant increase in the number of blacks—and whites—registered and voting in the South.

The 1964 Civil Rights Act also granted protections to women. The women's movement sought greater employment opportunities, demanded equal pay for equal work, and campaigned for the elimination of protective, gender-based distinctions in state and federal law. Dissatisfied with the pace of change, blacks in many American cities erupted in violence in the late 1960s. Militant groups opposed the nonviolent approach of Martin Luther King. The political victories felt hollow to African Americans who were unemployed and trapped in poverty. When King was assassinated and further violence erupted in 1968, the civil rights movement entered a new phase.

The Environment for Civil Rights Policy

The political environment in which Congress and the president make civil rights policy began to change around 1970. More groups were seeking protection for their civil rights. In the 1950s and 1960s, the focus was clearly upon the plight of blacks, who were the victims of vicious racism and discrimination. In the years since then, civil rights and liberties have encompassed new groups: women, Hispanics, Native Americans, the disabled, and homosexuals. On certain issues, these different groups come together with a common interest, but in many cases, the expansion of the civil rights agenda created competition among them.

In the early 1970s, the Equal Rights Amendment (ERA) became the highest priority for the women's movement. Passed by Congress in 1972, the amendment read: "Equality of rights under the law shall not be denied or abridged by the United States or by any state on account of sex." Its primary objective was to remove the presumption that women should be treated differently under the law. The amendment would have affected thousands of state and federal laws that make gender-based distinctions, such as those dealing with property and inheritance, child custody and support, and equal pay. The ERA gained an initial surge of support that brought it within a few states of the number needed for ratification. As the 1970s progressed, however, the political environment changed, and conservative attacks on the ERA began to take their toll. Charges that it would lead to unisex bathrooms, homosexual marriages, and women in combat concerned state legislators. Several states that had ratified the amendment earlier tried to rescind their approval. The ERA died in 1982.

Republicans and Democrats began to move in different directions on civil rights. Democrats, with their nearly unanimous black support, continued to press for more aggressive enforcement of existing laws and remedies needed to desegregate schools. Republicans, on the other hand, while emphasizing that they still supported civil rights, resisted many new changes. The Nixon administration criticized the Supreme Court and announced its opposition to busing.[19] Nixon's 1972 reelection campaign incorporated a "southern strategy" to capitalize on southerners, growing discontent with the Democratic party. Increasingly, the two parties disagreed on what measures to apply in overcoming the effects of past discrimination against women and blacks. Some Democrats argued that it was not enough simply to provide equal opportunities for minorities; more positive actions were necessary.[20] Affirmative action—giving preference to target groups—became increasingly controversial. The public supported affirmative action when defined as ensuring a broad pool of applicants, but large majorities opposed affirmative action when defined as preferential treatment or quotas.

The differences between Republicans and Democrats on civil rights, which were striking during the Nixon and Ford administrations, drew less attention during the Carter administration, when Democrats controlled both legislative and executive branches. Carter was a civil rights advocate; he took unprecedented steps to appoint blacks and women to positions in the executive and judicial branches (see Table 6.1). He also urged the bureaucracy to enforce existing laws aggressively. He was not particularly active in the legislative arena, however.[21] As affirmative action grew more controversial, the courts became increasingly involved in defining acceptable standards. In the *Bakke* decision in 1979, the Supreme Court allowed race to be considered as a factor in admission to medical school, but ruled against setting up quotas for minorities.

The shift in the environment for civil rights policy was reflected in different policymaking patterns after Ronald Reagan was inaugurated in 1981. In the 1980 election, he had received the lowest proportion of the black vote of any Republican candidate in history. Public opinion polls revealed that popular support for civil rights among whites, which had increased until the early 1980s, began to decline.[22] Reagan was opposed to busing, affirmative action, and aggressive enforcement of civil rights laws. He eased the enforcement of existing laws through the appointment of conservatives, executive orders, budget cuts, program changes, and reorganizations.[23] When called on to defend his civil rights record, Reagan simply noted that his actions in civil rights were consistent with his general objective of reducing the scope and intrusiveness of government in all policy areas. Reagan appointed conservatives to the Supreme Court and the federal bench (see Table 6.1). Within a few years, court decisions became more conservative with regard to affirmative action standards.

The conflict over civil rights grew increasingly bitter and partisan in the late 1980s and 1990s, pitting the Democratic Congress against Reagan and Bush Sr., and increasingly, the courts. The racial element in voting became more pronounced as well. In 1984, 2 of 3 whites voted Republican in the presidential election, while 9 of

Table 6.1   Characteristics of Federal District and Appellate Court Judges, 1963–2000.

CHARACTERISTICS	Johnson		Nixon		Ford		Carter		Reagan		Bush		Clinton	
	D	A	D	A	D	A	D	A	D	A	D	A	D	A
Political/ government experience	21	10	11	4	21	8	4	5	13	6	11	11	12	7
Judicial experience	34	65	35	58	42	75	54	54	47	60	50	62	52	59
Public law school	40	40	42	38	44	50	51	39	42	40	48	41	39	40
Same party	84	95	93	93	79	92	93	82	97	94	95	95	87	85
Past party activism	49	58	49	60	50	58	61	73	59	55	63	70	49	6
White	95	95	97	98	90	100	79	79	92	97	93	89	75	73
Male	98	98	99	100	98	100	86	80	92	95	81	81	71	68
Millionaires	–	–	–	–	–	–	5	10	22	18	35	43	39	50
Exceptionally or well qualified	7	28	5	15	–	17	4	16	55	59	59	65	59	80

Legend: D = district court appointments; A = appellate court appointments; – means information unavailable
Source: Adapted from Sheldon Goldman, "The Clinton Imprint on the Judiciary," *Judicature* 78 (September–October 1994): 72; *Judicature* 78 (May–June 1995): 287; *Judicature* 84 (2001): 242, 247. Values for presidents prior to Carter appear in earlier editions of this journal.

10 blacks voted Democratic.[24] Congress sought to reverse the 1984 Supreme Court decision of *Grove City College v. Bell,* in which the justices ruled that the college did not have to provide equal athletic opportunities for men and women based on Title IX of the 1964 Civil Rights Act. In this case, discussed later in the chapter, Congress amended the act in order to reverse the *Grove City* decision, finally succeeding in doing so over Reagan's veto.

The partisan pattern was repeated in the Bush Sr. administration as well, beginning during the 1988 presidential campaign. The Bush campaign ran the infamous Willie Horton commercials, which accused Democratic candidate Michael Dukakis of allowing dangerous criminals out on the street. They specifically mentioned Willie Horton, a black man who had raped a white woman while out on furlough from a Massachusetts jail. (At the time the incident occurred, Dukakis was governor of Massachusetts.) These ads infuriated many civil rights leaders and Democrats. Congress and President Bush clashed over the issue of "quotas" in the 1990s, as Congress attempted to overturn Supreme Court decisions that limited protection from job discrimination. In one of the cases treated later in this chapter, the administration and Congress were deadlocked for two years until the quota issue was finally resolved. One study finds Bush Sr. even more assertive and conservative on civil rights than Reagan.[25]

When Bill Clinton was elected president in 1992, he promised a government that looked like the American people, and made even greater efforts than Carter in appointing women and minorities to the executive branch and federal judiciary (see Table 6.1).[26] Clinton claimed to be a "new Democrat" and persuaded voters that he was genuinely moderate on most domestic issues. Regarding civil rights, however, Clinton expressed liberal views on affirmative action programs, although opposing quotas. In a major speech in San Diego in June 1997, Clinton stated: "I want to lead the American people in a great and unprecedented conversation about race." It seemed he to wanted to be remembered for fundamentally altering black-white relations by persuading Americans to change the way they view one another. Clinton began a yearlong series of town meetings to soothe racial tensions and appointed a presidential advisory board headed by historian John Hope Franklin.

In promising to "amend it, don't end it," President Clinton was bucking growing opposition to affirmation action programs. Critics, such as Governor Pete Wilson (R-Cal.), criticized the president as being out of touch, since public opinion polls showed growing opposition to affirmative action. Conservatives in Congress pushed legislation that would prohibit the use of "preferential treatment" in the awarding of federal contracts. However, moderates such as Representative Tony Hall (D-Ohio) and a dozen other white cosponsors in both parties, introduced legislation that would issue a formal apology for slavery, much as the United States had done for mistreatment of Japanese Americans interred during World War II. Clinton not only defended affirmative action and stepped up fair housing laws, but he became the first president to back measures to end bias against homosexuals (but see case later in this chapter). Thus, the climate was ripe for hostile relations with Congress on several fronts.

Despite his efforts in the campaign to reach out to minority voters, George W. Bush received only 8 percent of the black vote and 31 percent of the Hispanic vote in 2000.[27] In late January 2001, Bush took questions from the congressional black caucus for over 90 minutes. Although some members boycotted the meeting due to lingering suspicion over the controversial election outcome, the new president pushed his "compassionate conservatism." He expressed a commitment to electoral reform along with other issues of concern to black Americans, such as AIDs, health issues, and public education. Bush also mentioned his faith-based initiative, which he hoped would appeal to African-Americans. However, the president boycotted an international conference on civil rights because it advocated reparations for past slavery. In addition, Bush was particularly concerned about the plight of Hispanics, which was the largest minority group in his native Texas as well as in Florida, where his brother Jeb Bush was governor.

Bush's faith-based initiative intended to give religious groups greater access to federal funding to deliver services to the poor without losing their religious orientation. However, the proposal came under early criticism from both liberals and conservatives over concerns that it would blur the lines between church and state and permit religious groups to discriminate with federal money in hiring. The Urban League and other groups were concerned that politically connected organizations that discriminate would receive the bulk of the federal funds available. Undeterred, Bush named John Dilulio, a Democratic policy analyst from the University of Pennsylvania, to head the White House Office on Faith-Based and Community Initiatives. Although the plan narrowly passed the Republican-controlled House in July 2001, because of differences with the administration, Dilulio left the position after only seven months, making him the first high-ranking official to leave the Bush administration. This caused problems in the Democratic-controlled Senate, where passage was expected to be much more difficult without Dilulio's leadership.

Clearly, the environment for civil rights has turned significantly more politicized and partisan since the 1970s. A large gap between black and white support for the president developed in the 1980s. Figure 6.1 shows the trends since 1953. The

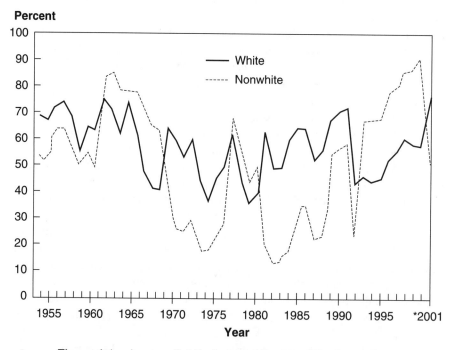

Figure 6.1   Average Public Approval Rating of the President, by Race, (1953–2001).

* *Note:* This value represents the average approval rating before and after September 11, 2001.
Source: Gallup Organization; early values from George C. Edwards III, *Presidential Approval: A Sourcebook* (Baltimore: Johns Hopkins University Press, 1990). Updated by authors. Figure prepared by Brandon Prins.

greatest gap appeared during the Reagan administration, when white support for the president was sometimes as much as 30 percentage points higher than black support. Although Bush Sr. initially received higher black support than Reagan, the gap in support remained. As might be expected, blacks and whites expressed very different views of Presidents Clinton and Bush Sr. Thus, the gap in how the races view the president remains large.

Making Civil Rights Policy

Congress has taken more of a leadership role in civil rights since 1970, particularly when a Democratic Congress was matched with a Republican president. As has occurred in recent years, Congress can reverse Supreme Court decisions if those decisions are based on interpretations of statutes enacted by Congress rather than on the Constitution itself. The Supreme Court in *Adarand Contractors Inc. v. Pena* (1995), restricted the use of race as a consideration in awarding federal contracts. This 5 to 4 decision was more in line with the views of Republicans, who gained control of Congress in 1995 and who were less likely to challenge conservative Court decisions than their Democratic predecessors. Congress can also use its power of the purse to thwart proposed cuts in civil rights agencies and their budgets. In 1986, Congress threatened to cut off all funds to the Civil Rights Commission because Reagan had weakened it dramatically. House and Senate Judiciary Committees often use hearings and testimony from prominent civil rights advocates to influence public opinion.

The president has a variety of means for shaping civil rights policy: appointments to the courts and the bureaucracy, executive orders, budget, administrative changes, and using the presidency to influence public opinion. Over the years, legislation has been an important vehicle for policymaking, although the number of bills has varied much more than for other policy areas. This is a function of the presidential and congressional policy agendas and the political environment of the time. Table 6.2 compares civil rights legislation on which the president took a position, listing the percentage of times that the vote in Congress was in support of the president's position. Positiontaking and executive order issuance illustrate presidential assertiveness while percent success reveals legislative independence.

These data suggest differences in presidential support in Congress as well as in the number of vote positions. The political alignments through 1963 restricted the legislation before Congress. The surge of activity during the Johnson administration stands alone in the postwar period. Not only was the volume of legislation greater, but working with both northern Democrats and Republicans, the administration received record levels of support. Legislative activity remained higher than average during the Nixon administration before declining through the rest of the 1970s. As the environment for civil rights changed in the 1980s, the amount of positiontaking on roll calls increased under Reagan and Bush Sr. Reagan's support on these votes was lower than the other presidents, with the exception of Eisenhower. Bush took

Table 6.2 Presidential-Congressional Actions in Civil Rights, 1953–1999

PRESIDENT	NO. OF POSITIONS TAKEN ON ROLL CALL VOTES	AVERAGE NO. OF VOTE POSITIONS TAKEN PER YEAR	PERCENT SUCCESS ON PRES. POSITIONS	EXECUTIVE ORDERS/YEAR
Eisenhower	6	1.5	50%	.3
Kennedy	3	1	67%	1.0
Johnson	101	20.2	98%	.6
Nixon	38	6.9	66%	.4
Ford	0	0	—	0
Carter	7	1.8	71%	2.5
Reagan	23	2.9	52%	2.1
Bush	19	4.8	65%	1.0
Clinton	4	1.3	56%	2.9
Average		5.1	66%	1.2

Source: These data are taken annually from *Congressional Quarterly Almanac* and from *Public Papers of the Presidents* and were collected by the authors.

more positions on civil rights votes than did Reagan and also received higher levels of support. Very few roll call votes occurred during the Clinton years. His level of support on the few votes on which he took positions was lowest among Democratic presidents.

Presidents average about 57 executive orders per year but just over 1 per year on civil rights matters. There is no clear trend in order issuance evident from Table 6.2, but it does reveal that Ford was just as nonassertive administratively as he was legislatively. The higher than average order issuance for Reagan and Clinton is consistent with earlier judgments about their relatively strong views on civil rights.[28] Clinton issued *far* more orders per year than any president, including orders regarding historically black colleges, education for Hispanics, and environmental justice.

Although these comparisons are interesting, they provide only part of the picture. The civil rights agenda, political leadership, and the environment are highly changeable and important. Policy initiation today comes as much from Capitol Hill as from the White House. While civil rights is a highly discretionary policy area, neither branch can lead on its own. The cases that follow show various patterns in different eras and some of their results.

Presidential Leadership:
The Antiterrorism (Patriot) Act (2001)

On October 26, 2001, less than six weeks after the terrorist attacks on the World Trade Center and the Pentagon, President George W. Bush signed the Patriot Act of 2001.[29] This antiterrorism law gave the Justice Department and law enforcement officials around the country sweeping new powers to wiretap, intercept emails, and detain aliens for up to seven days without charging them. A clear case of presidential leadership in response to a rapid and dramatic change in the political environment, the antiterrorism legislation is important in several respects. It is an example of significant congressional participation in shaping policy even when the executive branch is driving the process. Second, it shows how the legislative process can be adapted in order to streamline policymaking. Conversely, it is a case that suggests potential problems when Congress takes insufficient time to consider important legislation and fails to establish a clear legislative record for the courts to consider if the constitutionality of the legislation is questioned.

The terrorist attacks of September 11, 2001, profoundly changed America's political environment. Issues that seemed important just days earlier were swept off the political agenda in favor of mounting a war against terrorism on several fronts. The country rallied around the president as it had in past times of crisis. In the first few days after the crisis, Congress rubber-stamped presidential proposals for spending billions on the reconstruction of New York and on bailing out the airlines. This was definitely not politics as usual in terms of the president and Congress. But with the antiterrorism legislation that came to be known as the Patriot Act, Congress was more than a rubber stamp. They accommodated the president, but made some important changes in the law.

On September 19, 2001, only eight days after the attacks, Attorney General John Ashcroft sent Congress a set of proposals to expand law enforcement powers to fight terrorism. These proposals were crafted in the Justice Department in consultation with the White House staff and President Bush. Some of these issues were not new; Congress had rejected many of them in the years after the Oklahoma bombing in 1995, but now viewed them in a different light. Ashcroft's proposals included the following:[30]

- Greater powers for searches and surveillance including "roving" wiretaps, access to email and voice mail, and the ability to keep searches secret.
- Stricter immigration controls, broadening the definition of "terrorist" and the power to detain any noncitizen without charge indefinitely if considered a national security risk.
- Easier disclosure of information obtained from wiretaps, Internet information, student records, proceedings of grand juries, and tax information.
- Removal of the statute of limitations for prosecuting terrorists and increase penalties.

Ashcroft, with the support of the president, told Congress he wanted these new powers enacted within a week. Despite the unifying effect of the attacks and the desire to put partisanship aside and work closely with the president, Congress was not going to pass these dramatic changes to fundamental civil liberties without first examining them. The administration's antiterrorism proposals engendered an unusual coalition that, if not directly opposed, had grave concerns about the consequences for civil liberties. This coalition was made up of members of Congress from the right and left of their respective parties.[31] On the right, conservatives such as Georgia's Representative Robert Barr (R-Ga.), who had led the impeachment of President Clinton, objected to this expansion of government power into people's private lives. On the left, supporters of the American Civil Liberties Union (ACLU), such as Representative John Conyers (D-Mich.), considered a number of the provisions an unacceptable abridgement of civil rights and liberties.

House-Senate differences were an important element in the legislative dynamics of enacting the antiterrorism legislation. Initially, the House was much less receptive to the administration proposals while the Senate was more in favor. This impacted the pattern of negotiations. Although Senate Judiciary Committee Chair Patrick Leahy (D-Vt.) had a reputation as a civil libertarian, the Senate, working with the White House, crafted a bill that encompassed most of the Ashcroft proposals. Leahy got the administration to back off on provisions such as the unlimited detention of aliens and settle for the power to hold them without charge for up to seven days. Although Leahy and the ranking minority member, Orrin Hatch (R-Utah) were the key Senate negotiators, the antiterrorism bill never went to the Judiciary committee. It was formulated by the leadership and sent directly to the Senate floor. Anxious to move the legislation ahead, Senate Majority Leader Tom Daschle asked Democrats not to offer any amendments to the bill. Most went along but this infuriated Russ Feingold (D-Wis.), who insisted in offering three floor amendments, complaining bitterly about the process. All were easily defeated and after only three hours of debate, the Senate passed the bill by a vote of 96 to 1. Only Feingold voted against the bill.

Ironically, the administration found the most opposition in the Republican House. The House Judiciary Committee, acting in a bipartisan fashion, began to dismantle much of the administration's proposals. They reported a severely scaled down antiterrorism bill by an unusual unanimous vote in committee.[32] Despite this committee unanimity, under intense pressure from the White House, House Speaker Dennis Hastert moved to circumvent the Judiciary Committee entirely. On October 12, the Speaker brought an entirely different bill to the House floor, one much more like the Senate version. This infuriated Representative John Dingell (D-Mich.) who complained about throwing out the work of the committee: "I believe it was done in a sneaky, dishonest fashion that reflects very poorly on this body."[33] The House passed its version of the bill by a vote of 337 to 79. Three Republicans and 76 Democrats voted against the bill.[34] The Speaker acted to eliminate the need for a protracted House-Senate conference committee that would have to resolve serious differences between the two bills. However, some differences remained, such as the money-laundering provisions included in the Senate bill that were not in the House bill.

The political environment again changed the week of October 15 with the warning from the Federal Bureau of Investigation (FBI) of new terrorist threats and the anthrax scare. Members were under even more pressure to enact an antiterrorism bill and give law enforcement as many tools as possible in the war. Members of the House Judiciary committee, whose work was thrown out, changed their minds and supported the substitute bill.[35] House-Senate conferees, in consultation with the White House, worked quickly to make necessary compromises to get a bill out. The House decided to accept the Senate provisions for money laundering that Majority Leader Daschle said were essential. The Senate and the Bush administration, on the other hand, accepted the House provisions to *sunset* the search and surveillance provisions in 2005 (that is, that they would automatically expire unless Congress reauthorized them, or the "sun" would "set" on them).

Congressional leaders opted to move quickly to expedite passage of the bill; some members complained that they had not even had time to read it.[36] Much of the negotiation was held in secret. The House and Senate Judiciary Committees each held only one hearing on Ashcroft's proposals and in neither case did any opponents testify. Civil liberty groups were allowed to "brief" members but their comments never went into the record. The only committee report associated with the bill was that accompanying H.R. 2975, the bill dumped by Speaker Hastert. In working out the final conference agreement, negotiators opted to put the package in a House bill (H.R. 3162) that would then be passed in exactly the same form in both houses. The result of this tactic, however, was that there was no conference or committee report accompanying the final bill to explain congressional thinking. Nonetheless, after the final deal was struck and drafted into legislation, both houses enacted the Patriot Act. On October 24, the House passed the bill by a vote of 357 to 66. The next day, the Senate passed the same bill by a vote of 98 to 1.

As enacted by Congress and signed by President Bush, the Patriot Act of 2001 encompasses much of what Bush and Ashcroft had requested.[37] Law enforcement can conduct secret searches in certain circumstances and has expanded authority to search Internet and computer files. In addition, the act permits officials to get only one warrant to conduct many searches. The act also allows investigators to share grand jury information and strengthens laws against money laundering. The main concessions made by the administration concerned how long officials can detain noncitizens without formally charging them and the sunset provisions.

This is a clear case of presidential leadership, even though it might seem that President Bush did not have much of a personal impact. In this case, Attorney General Ashcroft represented the president and the administration in the policy process in terms of drafting the proposals and testifying before Congress. The president closely followed the process and his staff people were directly involved in the final negotiations and compromises. The administration received most of what they had asked for in an expedited fashion. Nonetheless, Congress looked at the proposals seriously and won some important concessions from the administration in protecting civil liberties. This legislative process was highly unusual. Committees and rank-and-file members do not usually stand for having their prerogatives overridden and procedures circumvented. But this was a function of the atmosphere in the country—a response to the public expectations of fast, decisive action against terrorism and support for the president.

What are the likely consequences of the Patriot Act? It is far too soon to tell at this writing. The legislation does seem to have aided law enforcement officials to act more aggressively against domestic terrorists, although the evidence is limited as yet. Some have expressed concern that in the rush to fight terrorism, important constitutional safeguards were forgotten. Senator Arlen Specter (R-Pa.) as well as several legal experts felt that the failure of Congress to provide any kind of a legislative history or record to accompany the legislation made it more likely that the courts may overturn key provisions.[38]

This case is potentially a good demonstration of the strengths and weaknesses of presidential leadership as a pattern of policymaking. On one hand, the president and Congress responded quickly and effectively and had tremendous public support. In addition to being timely and responsive, however, the policy consequences of presidential leadership can be hasty action and ill-conceived results. Civil liberties groups have already promised to challenge the constitutionality of the new antiterrorism law. The judicial branch will be one judge of the work of the legislative and executive branches. In addition, though, the Patriot Act should also be judged by the effectiveness of the war against terrorism, congressional willingness to extend the provisions after 2005, and whether in its implementation, a balance is struck between civil rights and domestic security.

Congressional Leadership: The Civil Rights Restoration Act (1988)

A bipartisan coalition in the House and Senate won a decisive political battle on March 22, 1988, overriding President Ronald Reagan's veto of the Civil Rights Restoration Act. The House voted 292 to 133 to override, while the Senate voted 73 to 24 (eight votes more than the two-thirds needed). Reagan had vetoed the bill only a week earlier, claiming that it would "vastly and unjustifiably expand the power of the federal government."[39] Despite a desperate, last-minute lobbying effort, members voted for the bill to become law over the president's objections.

The genesis of this legislative battle occurred four years earlier when the Supreme Court limited the application of four federal civil rights laws in the case of *Grove City College v. Bell* (1984). Grove City College was a four-year private institution that did not receive any direct federal assistance, although a number of students individually received Pell Grants or other federal assistance. One of the laws in question was the 1972 Education Act amendments, whose Title IX banned sex discrimination. Prior to the 1984 decision, the law was interpreted to mean that all programs and activities at a college or other institution must comply with sex discrimination prohibitions if any programs received federal aid. Grove City College, a small school, did not provide the same athletic teams for women as they did for men. College officials did not believe that they had to assure compliance with Title IX in their athletic programs or in any other activities that did not receive direct federal aid. They took their case to court, and it ended up in the U.S. Supreme Court.

In their 6 to 3 ruling, the Court agreed with Grove City College that only its financial aid programs had to comply with Title IX.[40] The effect of the decision was to restrict three other civil rights laws that dealt with discrimination on the basis of race, age, and disability. The decision was extremely unpopular with women's groups and members of Congress, who blasted the Court for undermining civil rights. A group of legislators immediately moved to introduce legislation that would reinstate the old interpretation, so that failure to comply in any program or activity would lead to elimination of all federal aid.

Enacting the Civil Rights Restoration Act proved difficult. President Reagan praised the Court decision and promised to veto any attempt by Congress to circumvent it. Proponents failed in 1985 and 1986 to get legislation through. More than 40 separate hearings were held on various versions of the bill. A number of unrelated issues became entwined with the civil rights debate, including the divisive issue of abortion. Catholic hospitals feared they might be required to permit abortions under the new law, which added to the conservative opposition. Reagan succeeded in blocking the legislation, primarily because of Republican control of the Senate. Although a number of Senate Republicans supported the Restoration Act, there were enough votes to support the president.

The 1986 midterm elections produced an important change in the Senate: The Democrats captured a majority of seats for the first time in six years. Many of the elections, particularly in the South, had been close; strong support from black voters had made the difference. These new Democratic senators were ardent supporters of the Civil Rights Restoration Act. In addition, following the Iran-Contra revelations, President Reagan's standing dropped in the opinion polls. He did not appear to be as formidable an opponent as he neared the last year of his presidency. Sensing victory, congressional leaders, such as Senator Edward Kennedy (D-Mass.), showed greater willingness to compromise so as to enlarge the base of support. Partial exemption of religious organizations, farmers, and food stamp recipients helped diffuse some of the opposition inside Congress.

The debate between the president and the Congress extended into 1988. Proponents continued to argue that the bill did nothing more than restore the interpretation of the statutes that had applied before 1984: It would eradicate discrimination subsidized by federal money. Some attacked the administration's anti-civil rights stance, noting Reagan's opposition to the landmark Civil Rights Act of 1964 at that time.[41] As the congressional vote neared, Reagan continued to threaten a veto. He charged that the bill

> . . . dramatically expands the scope of federal jurisdiction over state and local governments and the private sector. . . . It diminishes the freedom of the private citizen to order his or her life and unnecessarily imposes the heavy burden of compliance with extensive federal regulations and paperwork on

many elements of American society. The bill poses a particular threat to religious liberty.[42]

The stage was set for a showdown. There was never much doubt that the bill would pass; the question was whether the margin would be large enough to override the promised veto. The Senate passed the bill on January 28 by a vote of 75 to 14, with seven cosponsors missing the vote. In the House, Speaker Jim Wright helped speed passage of the bill by restricting all amendments. The House passed the bill on March 2 by a vote of 315 to 98. Both the House and Senate margins were more than enough to override the veto, but victory was by no means assured. In many previous cases, the president had successfully pressured enough Republicans to switch their votes and uphold his veto. Reagan vetoed the bill on March 16.

In a last-ditch effort to sustain the veto, the Reverend Jerry Falwell and the Moral Majority made the extreme claim that the bill "could force churches to hire a practising [*sic*] homosexual drug addict with AIDS to be a teacher or youth pastor."[43] Even congressional conservatives who opposed the bill felt Falwell went too far and was hurting rather than helping their cause. Finally, on March 22, the override vote was taken. In the Senate, all 51 Democrats voted to override, while Republicans split 21 to 24. Eight Republicans who had originally voted for the bill switched, voting to sustain the veto in the second vote. Although they wound up eight votes short, opponents of the bill claimed that they had actually been only two votes short of sustaining the veto. The margin was close in the House as well—292 to 133, only eight votes more than needed. Democrats voted 240 to 10 to override, while Republicans voted 52 to 123 against the override. Six Democrats and 29 Republicans switched their original vote to support the president. Nonetheless, congressional sponsors had dealt the administration a blow and successfully orchestrated the enactment of the Civil Rights Restoration Act.

How was Congress able to dominate the policymaking process? The political environment was generally supportive, since voting for a civil rights bill is usually considered positive, especially in an election year. The administration failed to mobilize opinion against the bill. Congressional sponsors were determined, working four years before finally succeeding. The 1986 elections were crucial, changing the composition of the Senate, so that a veto-proof majority for the bill became possible. Streamlined floor consideration in the House helped ease passage. In addition, President Reagan's diminished popularity, and his status as a lame duck in 1988, reduced the negative consequences for Republicans who voted to override the president's veto. Even though the vote had a strong partisan element, Congress could not have succeeded without bipartisan support—half the Senate Republicans, led by Minority Leader Robert Dole, voted to override.

What were the consequences and results of the Civil Rights Restoration Act? Congress clearly achieved its goal of reversing the *Grove City* decision. Colleges that received any federal aid once again had to prove compliance with antidiscrimination statutes dealing with blacks, women, older Americans, and the disabled. The federal courts subsequently have upheld the need for more equal athletic facilities for college women. The act had political consequences as well, setting the tone for a Congress anxious to assert its leadership against the lame-duck president. It also raised support for the civil rights bill as a possible campaign issue in 1988. George Bush, who as vice president supported the president, would have his own battles with Congress over civil rights.

Cooperation and Consensus: Same Sex Marriage Law (1996)

During the 1992 election campaign, Bill Clinton emerged as the first presidential candidate that openly sought the political support of gays and lesbians. In one of his first acts as president, Clinton directed the Secretary of Defense to review the existing policy of barring homosexuals from the military. He supported the resulting recommendation of "don't ask, don't tell," wherein homosexuals could stay in the service if they did not announce or practice their sexual preference. Clinton took considerable political heat from conservatives in Congress and elsewhere for this decision, but supporters called it courageous. With this background, many expected Clinton to oppose legislation restricting homosexual activities. However, the White House announced early in May 1996 that Clinton would sign the same-sex marriage ban proposed by Congress. Presidential spokesman Mike McCurry stated: "The president has very strong . . . personal views on the subject." However, McCurry stated that the president also "believed the measure was politically motivated . . . it is gay-baiting, pure and simple."[44]

The 104th Congress became much more conservative on social issues after the Republican takeover following the 1994 midterm election. Strong public opinion against gay marriages dominated the political environment. As a result, Clinton joined the consensus with Congress and supported the legislation. The political dynamic surrounding this case was also influenced by the upcoming 1996 presidential campaign, since Clinton was not anxious to hand this issue to challenger Bob Dole (R-Kan.), an early cosponsor of the same-sex marriage ban.

The issue became part of the policy agenda following a Hawaii Supreme Court ruling in May 1993 challenging a same-sex marriage ban as discriminatory. Three gay couples sued the state for the right to marry and the legislature was considering legalizing such marriage when Congress acted. Then, on May 21, 1996, the U.S. Supreme Court in *Romer, Governor of Colorado, et al. v. Evans et al.,* struck down a Colorado amendment banning laws that protect gays and lesbians from discrimination. (Eight states and over 100 municipalities ban such discrimination and such issues have appeared in many forums around the country.) Homosexual organizations around the country held rallies while opponents vowed to keep fighting. Another argument voiced is that allowing such unions would "cause a run on the federal treasury by gay couples seeking federal benefits."[45] Thus, conservatives found an economic reason to support the legislation as well as what they considered a moral one.

Both the House and the Senate introduced identical bills banning same-sex marriage in May 1996—representing federal intervention in an area of public policy normally left to the states. The rhetoric was heated on both sides of the issue, in what proponents called the Defense of Marriage Act. In the House, supporters argued that legalizing gay marriages might encourage children to become homosexuals and was contrary to what marriage had always meant in the United States. Opponents, including openly gay Representative Barney Frank (D-Mass.), stated: "How can you argue that a man and woman in love . . . are somehow threatened because two women down the street are also in love."[46] After defeating several amendments by Frank and others, the House Judiciary Committee approved the bill (H.R. 3396), voting along party lines.

Opponents of the legislation included the American Civil Liberties Union (ACLU), and the Gay and Lesbian Rights Project, both of whom testified before the Senate Judiciary Committee. The former called the bill unconstitutional and bad public policy. "For 200 years, Congress has left it to the states to decide who they will marry and to the courts to make sure they respect each other's decision on that. That is a fine tradition, which ought to be respected."[47] Representative John Lewis (D-Ga.) said that "you cannot tell people they cannot fall in love."[48] Senator Edward Kennedy stated, "America will only be America when we free ourselves of discrimination."[49]

Senate debate focused on the definition of marriage, the rights of states to make that definition for themselves, and whether federal benefits would apply to gay spouses. Edward Kennedy (D-Mass.) led the opponents and sought separate votes on the marriage bill and other legislation to prohibit job discrimination against homosexuals (S 1056). Kennedy prevailed in this effort when a bipartisan agreement allowed separate votes on these two measures. The compromise "allowed senators to take an election-year stand against gay marriages but show their tolerance directly thereafter with a vote to outlaw workplace discrimination."[50] This position seemed identical to President Clinton's, who expressed opposition to the former but support for the latter. The votes in the Senate were 85 to 14 in passing the same-sex marriage prohibition but a much narrower defeat (49 to 50) for the job rights bill. Prospects for the latter during the upcoming 105th Congress looked bright since one supporting senator was absent during the voting and Vice President Gore would be available to break a tie vote if that occurred in the Senate. The immediate result, however, was that congressional Republicans gained back-to-back victories on a sensitive social issue dear to the conservative agenda.

All the "no" votes for the same-sex marriage ban in the Senate on September 10, 1996, were cast by Democrats and included only one southerner (Charles Robb, D-Va.). The legislation became PL 104-99 upon signing by President Clinton on

September 21, 1996. The new law barred federal recognition of gay marriages and specified that states need not recognize same-sex marriages even if legal in other states.

Democrats claimed that Republicans were trying to cause a rift in the Democratic party ranks in both chambers and also to embarrass President Clinton. Senator Kennedy stated: "We all know what is going on here. I regard this bill as a mean-spirited form of Republican legislative gay-bashing cynically calculated to try to inflame the public eight weeks before the November 5 election."[51] At the signing, President Clinton stated, "I have long opposed government recognition of same-gender marriages and this legislation is consistent with that position." He also stated in the same message that "I want to make clear that the enactment of this legislation should not, despite the fierce and at times divisive rhetoric surrounding it, be understood to provide an excuse for discrimination, violence, and intimidation against any person on the basis of sexual orientation."[52]

Although disappointed with Clinton's stand on the same-sex marriage ban, gay rights groups had no alternative but to support his reelection effort. David Smith of the Human Rights Campaign stated: "This is a wedge issue, but we're too smart to fall for that."[53] Patricia Ireland, president of the National Organization for Women (NOW), concurred: "The president is first and foremost a politician and his duty is to get reelected. A lot of people are willing to give him a pass."[54] Proponents like Dole said that "this is a huge string of victories for the pro-family movement," while Ralph Reed, then executive director of the Christian Coalition, stated: "These are the bricks in the wall that allow you to build a turnout of religious conservatives."[55]

This case represents consensus and cooperation on a prominent social issue, even if in reality there was less consensus between Congress and the president than appeared. The political environment and impending election had much to do with the timing and the outcome of the legislation. However it was motivated, Democrats, including President Clinton, were able to benefit from working with Congress by supporting the marriage ban, but also making a public record by pushing to end employment discrimination against homosexuals. The Clinton administration would have preferred to not have this legislation at all, but once it was on the agenda, his administration worked constructively with Congress to get the most acceptable legislation possible.

Deadlock/Extraordinary Resolution: The Civil Rights Act (1991)

On November 21, 1991, President George Bush signed the Civil Rights Act of 1991, reversing the effects of Supreme Court decisions that had made it harder for workers to bring job discrimination suits. This followed a bitter, partisan two-year deadlock with Congress, during which political symbols and strategies for the 1992 elections were as important as civil rights policy. A year before, Bush had vetoed a similar bill, insisting that it would have forced companies to use hiring quotas. In a show-down before the 1990 elections, Congress failed by a narrow margin to override Bush's veto. In the end, extraordinary means were necessary to break the deadlock, centering on closed-door negotiations between moderate Republicans and Bush, who were faced with sudden changes in the political environment.

Like the Civil Rights Restoration Act of 1988, this case had its impetus in over-turning an unpopular Supreme Court decision. In this case, however, neither branch could dominate, and they remained deadlocked until a means for resolution could be found. Legislation was introduced in response to a series of decisions that limited employee recourse in the case of discrimination on the job. One of the court deci-sions the proponents found most objectionable was the 1989 case of *Wards Cove Packing v. Antonio*. This decision reversed a 1971 ruling that required employers to justify employment practices that were detrimental to the employment opportunities of women and minorities; employers had to prove that there was a "business neces-sity" to justify practices that resulted in the exclusion of target groups.

The *Wards Cove* decision reversed the presumption: The Court ruled that the burden of proof now fell to the employee to prove that the company had no legiti-mate reason for its hiring criteria. Several other adverse decisions were targeted by the 1990 civil rights bill. One provision of the act would overrule a decision that made it harder to punish racial harassment on the job. The bill also would permit women and religious minorities to be awarded monetary damages in the case of dis-crimination. Under the old law, they were entitled only to back pay.

Senator Edward Kennedy (D-Mass.) and Representative Augustus Hawkins (D-Calif.) introduced legislation on February 7, 1990. The White House indicated its opposition and was represented in the Senate by Orrin Hatch (R-Utah), a staunch opponent of Kennedy on civil rights. The bill caused much consternation in the Senate, particularly among Republicans, who were split on the issue. The bill was reported by the Senate Labor and Human Resources Committee on April 4 and moved to the Senate floor for debate. In the tradition of civil rights legislation, oppo-nents filibustered. Minority Leader Robert Dole (R-Kan.) originally a supporter of the bill, split with the Democratic leadership over the timing of a cloture vote. "If we're going to be treated like a bunch of bums on this side of the aisle," Dole com-plained, "there won't be any agreements on anything."[56] On July 17, cloture was adopted, and the debate ended. The next day, the Senate approved the bill by a vote of 65 to 34, just short of the two-thirds needed to override. Divisiveness was present on the House side as well; Republicans walked out of several committee meetings to protest the tactics of the Democrats. The bill was marked up by both the Education and Labor Committee and the Judiciary Committee, and it was passed on August 3 by a vote of 272 to 154—also just short of a two-thirds majority.

The White House remained opposed to the bills, despite the support for the leg-islation from influential Republicans such as Senator John Danforth (R-Mo.) and members of the president's own cabinet, such as Health and Human Services

Secretary Louis Sullivan. With elections approaching, the civil rights bill became a political football. Democrats accused the president of trying to use the quota issue to drive white voters further into the Republican camp. The president accused the Democrats of favoring racial quotas. The confrontation would come to a head in October, after the House-Senate conference report passed both houses and was sent to the president's desk. On October 22, Bush vetoed the bill, saying, "I deeply regret having to take this action with respect to a bill bearing such a title."[57] Two days later, the Senate voted to override. Both sides knew it would be close. By a single vote, 66 to 34, the president's veto was sustained, and the deadlock continued.

When the 102nd Congress opened in 1991, proponents made the Civil Rights Act the first bill introduced. It looked as if 1991 would be a replay of 1990: The House passed the bill in June by a vote of 273 to 156. Meanwhile, President Bush continued to rebuff efforts by Danforth to negotiate a compromise, insisting the bill would still result in quotas. Democrats continued to promote the president's opposition as a campaign issue, while many Republican supporters of the legislation felt caught in the middle. After passing the bill, House leaders left it to Senate Republicans to try to make a deal with the president. The deadlock continued through the summer, until several changes in the political climate helped facilitate a resolution.

First, the confirmation hearings over Clarence Thomas's nomination to the U.S. Supreme Court exploded into controversy when a former subordinate charged him with sexual harassment. Suddenly the issue of sexual harassment and discrimination against women in the workplace was foremost in voters' minds. Bush was leery of a backlash from the hearings. In addition, he owed a political debt to Danforth, who was instrumental in orchestrating the narrow confirmation victory for Thomas. Second, former Ku Klux Klan leader David Duke, campaigning for governor of Louisiana as a Republican, raised many of the same issues as Bush in opposition to quotas. Now, mainstream Republicans, including the president, wanted to distance themselves from Duke. Many Republicans feared that a nay vote on the civil rights bill would be more damaging than before.

In this context, several moderate Republican senators who had previously supported the president on the civil rights votes, including Virginia's John Warner, notified Bush that they now felt compelled to vote for the bill and override a veto. Based on the one-vote margin in the Senate the year before, this switch appeared to foreshadow what would have been the first override of Bush's presidency. Instead, the president decided to cut a deal. A week of backroom meetings between the administration, Danforth, and several other Republican senators finally produced a compromise. They agreed to leave one of the most divisive issues for the courts to decide, thus allowing both sides to claim victory. Although Bush made concessions, he argued that "We didn't cave. . . . I can say to the American people that this is not a quota bill."[58] Some Democrats scoffed at this. Senate Majority Leader George Mitchell said that Bush had "found a fig leaf to cover a hasty retreat." In any event, the deadlock was finally broken. On October 30, the Senate passed the bill by a vote of 93 to 5. The House passed the bill in November by a 381 to 38 margin, and President Bush signed it on November 21.

What caused this pattern of deadlock to emerge, and why was it finally resolved? The key elements behind this case are divided government and the more partisan environment for civil rights that developed since the Reagan era. Congress was able to dominate in 1988, overriding Reagan's veto of an earlier bill, but lacked the votes to override Bush. Clearly, political calculations were all-important, causing a division within the Republican ranks. The Thomas hearings and the Duke candidacy helped tip the balance among Republicans toward resolution. The leadership of Senator Danforth and several of his colleagues was instrumental in resolving the deadlock, which was accomplished in private meetings rather than the open atmosphere of congressional hearing rooms.

What were the results and consequences of the Civil Rights Act of 1991? Several changes were clear—particularly the ability of women and religious minorities to collect punitive damages in cases of discrimination. On perhaps the most important issue surrounding the *Wards Cove* decision—quotas—both branches agreed to disagree and let the courts decide. A more conservative judiciary, due in large measure to Reagan and Bush Sr. appointees, did begin to chip away at some previous employment discrimination decisions. This compromise by Congress may not have been decisive or effective policymaking, but it did allow a resolution of many other issues.

Conclusion

Patterns of presidential-congressional policymaking have evolved through several distinct stages since the *Brown* decision in 1954. Neither branch took a leadership role in civil rights at first, leaving it to the courts to change public policy. When Congress and the president became more involved, the Democratic party found itself deeply divided between its powerful southern wing and the rest of its members. A substantial moderate wing of the Republican party also strongly supported civil rights and became the ally of northern Democrats in their civil rights battles. Congressional dominance of policymaking characterized the 1957 and 1960 Civil Rights Acts. By the mid-1960s, the most dominant patterns were presidential leadership and cooperation, as displayed in the 1964 Civil Rights Act and the 1965 Voting Rights Act.

Those patterns changed in the 1970s. On one hand, civil rights policy receded somewhat from the legislative arena to the bureaucracy and the courts. At the same time, the political alignment over civil rights began to change during the Nixon administration. Unified party control of government during the Carter administration left both branches largely in agreement, although very little legislation was enacted during Carter's four years. He used administrative reforms and executive orders to restructure the civil rights bureaucracy. Nonlegislative tactics reemerged somewhat under President Clinton, who was the only Democratic president since Truman to face a Republican Congress. Clinton's willingness to compromise, even on his deeply held views on civil rights, allowed the same-sex marriage law to become a case of cooperation rather than congressional leadership.

The most prevalent pattern in the 1980s and 1990s was interbranch conflict, as reflected in the cases of the 1988 and 1991 Civil Rights Acts. In the former case, congressional dominance emerged when unified Democrats were able to attract enough Republican votes to override Reagan's veto. In the latter case, deadlock emerged when Bush Sr. was strong enough to have his veto sustained in his confrontation with Congress.

Civil rights differs from other policy areas in several notable respects. The importance of civil rights groups, instrumental in prompting government action 30 years ago, have weakened considerably. The federal courts play a more important role in defining the civil rights agenda than they do in foreign policy, economic policy, or social welfare policy. The courts' importance helps shape the agenda and relationship between Congress and the president. Given the transformation of the Supreme Court by the Reagan and Bush Sr. appointments, the direction in civil rights decisions is clear: restricting applications of affirmative action, limiting minority preferences, and narrowly interpretating civil rights laws.

The focus of civil rights shifted during the administration of George W. Bush because of the war on terrorism. The pattern of presidential leadership in enacting the Patriot Act of 2001 stands in stark contrast to the other three cases. Not since LBJ in 1964–65 has a president been able to lead so effectively in this policy area. Whether civil rights policy again becomes partisan or divides the branches may depend on the war on terrorism and how the civil rights policy agenda changes in the 2000s.

Notes

1. Quoted in Elizabeth A. Palmer, "Committees Taking a Critical Look at Ashcroft's Request for Broad New Powers," *CQ Weekly* (September 29, 2001): 2263.
2. Quoted in Elizabeth A. Palmer, "House Passes Anti-Terrorism bill that Tracks White House's Wishes," *CQ Weekly* (October 13, 2001): 2400.
3. See James D. Richardson, *A Compilation of the Messages and Papers of the Presidents 1789–1897*, (Washington, D.C.: U.S. Congress), 10 volumes.
4. See R. Bardolpf (ed.), *Civil Rights Record* (New York: Thomas Crowell, 1970): 20.
5. Charles E. Silberman, *Crisis in Black and White* (New York: Vintage, 1964): 23.
6. U.S. Commission of Civil Rights, *Voting 1961* (Washington, D.C.: Government Printing Office, 1961): 91–97.
7. Harrell R. Rodgers Jr. and Charles S. Bullock, *Law and Social Change* (New York: McGraw Hill, 1972): 17.
8. Barbara Sinclair, "Agenda, Policy, and Alignment Change from Coolidge to Reagan," in Lawrence C. Dodd and Bruce I. Oppenheimer (eds.), *Congress Reconsidered*, third edition (Washington, D.C.: CQ Press, 1985): 291–314.
9. P. H. Vaughn, "The Truman Administration's Fair Deal for Black America," *Missouri Historical Review* 70 (March 1976): 291–305.
10. *Congress and the Nation* I: 1945–1964 (Washington, DC: Congressional Quarterly, Inc. 1965): 1597.

11. Martin Luther King Jr., *Stride Toward Freedom* (New York: Harper, 1958).

12. Joel B. Grossman, "A Model for Judicial Policy Analysis: The Supreme Court and Sit-in Cases," in Joel B. Grossman and Joseph Tanenhaus (eds.), *Frontiers of Judicial Research* (New York: Wiley, 1969): 247.

13. Stephen E. Ambrose, *Eisenhower* (New York: Simon and Schuster, 1984).

14. Theodore C. Sorensen, *Kennedy* (New York: Harper & Row, 1965): 535.

15. Eric F. Goldman, *The Tragedy of Lyndon Johnson* (New York: Knopf, 1969): 515.

16. Edward G. Carmines and James A. Stimson, *Issue Evolution* (Princeton, NJ: Princeton Univeristy Press, 1989): 56–58

17. Rodgers and Bullock (1972): 271.

18. Ibid., 62.

19. Jonathan Schell, *The Time of Illusion* (New York: Vintage, 1975): 40–44.

20. Paul M. Sniderman and Michael G. Hagen, *Race and Inequality: Study in American Values* (Chatham, NJ: Chatham House, 1985).

21. J. H. Shattuck, "You Can't Depend on It: The Carter Administration and Civil Liberties," *Civil Liberties Review* 4 (5) (1978): 10–27.

22. Steven A. Shull, *American Civil Rights Policy from Truman to Clinton: The Role of Presidential Leadership* (Armonk, NY: M. E. Sharpe, 1999).

23. Steven A Shull, "Presidential Influence versus Bureaucratic Discretion," *American Review of Public Administration* 19 (September 1989): 197–215.

24. *National Journal* (November 12, 1988).

25. Shull (1999): 87–88.

26. *New York Times* (November 13, 1996: 1) reported that since entering office, Clinton had appointed more women and minorities to the Cabinet and federal courts than any prior president.

27. Gerald Pomper, "The Presidential Election," in Gerald M. Pomper (ed.), *The Election of 2000* (New York: Chatham House, 2001): 138.

28. Shull (1989).

29. Elizabeth A. Palmer, "Terrorism Bill's Sparse Paper Trail May Cause Legal Vulnerabilities," *CQ Weekly* (October 27, 2001): 2533–2535.

30. Palmer (September 29, 2001): 2264.

31. Ibid., 2263–2265.

32. Palmer (October 13, 2001): 2399.

33. Ibid., 2400.

34. *CQ Weekly* (October 13, 2001): 2425 *(vote #302)*.

35. Jennifer A. Dlouhy and Keith Perine, "Deal Clears Way for Final Passage of Antiterrorism Legislation," *CQ Weekly* (October 20, 2001): 2475–2476.

36. Palmer, (October 27, 2001): 2534.

37. Ibid.

38. Ibid., 2535.

39. *Congressional Quarterly Weekly Report* (March 19, 1988): 709.

40. *Grove City College v. Bell,* 465 US 555 (1984).

41. *National Journal* (March 19, 1988): 757.

42. *Public Papers of the President* (March 1, 1988): 287.

43. *Congressional Quarterly Weekly Report* (March 19, 1988): 709

44. cnn.com.conUS/9605/21/gay.reax/indx (July 12, 1996): 1.

45. *Congressional Quarterly Weekly Report* (July 13, 1996): 1976.

46. *Congressional Quarterly Almanac* (1996): B-27.

47. Ibid., B-28

48. Ibid.

49. Ibid.

50. Ibid., B-29.

51. *Congressional Quarterly Almanac* (1996): 5–29.
52. *Weekly Compilation of Presidential Documents*, Vol. 32, 1996: 1829.
53. *Congressional Quarterly Almanac* (1996): B-29.
54. Ibid.
55. Ibid., B-30.
56. *New Orleans Times-Picayune*, July 18, 1990: A-3.
57. *New York Times*, October 23, 1990: A1.
58. *Congressional Quarterly Weekly Report*, October 26, 1991: 3124

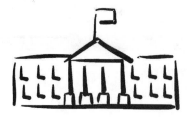

CHAPTER 7

Economic and Budget Policy

Year after year in Washington, budget debates seem to come down to an old tired argument: on one side, those who want more government, regardless of the cost; on the other, those who want less government, regardless of the cost.

—GEORGE W. BUSH, 2001

Careful stewardship of the economy was one of the lessons George W. Bush learned from his father's one-term presidency. Even as he focused his attention on the war against terrorism in 2001 and 2002, he and his advisors were mindful that voters thought George Bush Sr. had been too concerned about foreign policy and not concerned enough about the economic problems of the average American. He and his advisors were determined not to repeat this mistake.

Economic and budget issues are difficult for presidents, however. Congress has just as great a stake in prosperity and reelection as the president. The chief executive's economic tools are blunt, slow, and sometimes ineffective. Congress constitutionally has the power of the purse and shares policymaking with the president. More than any other set of issues on the policy agenda, economic and budget issues divide the two parties. Since the mid-1970s, budget votes in Congress have been party-line votes on nearly every occasion.[1] Policy positions on taxes and spending help define the two parties as much as any issue. This means that divided government has a greater impact on economic and budget policies and that interbranch conflict is almost guaranteed on these issues when party control is divided.

Confronting a difficult decision to raise taxes in 1967, President Lyndon Johnson, the former Senate majority leader, believed that he understood some of the fundamental differences between Congress and the president in making tough economic choices:

The president is concerned with the economic well-being of the entire nation. Congress, by contrast, is the product of 50 states and 435 local constituencies, each representing only one piece of the national jigsaw puzzle.[2]

LBJ's characterization—the presidency unified and coordinated, and Congress torn between protecting local benefits and acting in the national interest—is still commonly accepted, but is less true than 35 years ago. Because of the congressional budget process, Congress can take a national perspective as well as the president. Granted, legislators struggle with the budget because of the difficulty of making the many desirable parts fit into a responsible whole.[3] They like to promote spending to benefit local constituents. However, both branches face difficult choices. A president's political goals and campaign promises may clash with economic reality. Before looking at the four different patterns of presidential-congressional policy-making in economic and budget policy, we examine the historical evolution of policy, the economic and political environment, and the specialized institutions that each branch relies on in making economic choices.

The Evolution of U.S. Economic and Budget Policy

EARLY GOVERNMENT POLICIES

U.S. policy is based on principles of market capitalism, just as it was at the time of the founding. As society and the economy changed over 200 years, however, public policy evolved to include an expanded role for government in the economy. The nation's first economic policies concerned trade and tariffs to protect developing industries, the establishment of a national bank, and the assumption of debts of the states by the federal government.[4] In its first century, the nation and the economy grew rapidly. The country was transformed from an agrarian nation to an industrial one. Millions moved from farms to work in factories in the cities. Revolutions occurred in transportation, communication, energy, and production. With these fundamental changes in the economy came new problems: monopolies and trusts, growing disparities between rich and poor, harsh working conditions, slums, and crime. The social consequences of unregulated market capitalism proved to be unacceptable, and government intervention into the economy became more widespread.[5] Congress created the Interstate Commerce Commission (ICC) in 1887, when it became apparent that it was necessary to regulate the chaotic railroad network spreading across the country. In 1890, Congress enacted the Sherman Antitrust Act and "trust-busting" presidents Teddy Roosevelt and Woodrow Wilson continued the fight against monopolies.

As the economy modernized and the demands on government grew, the policy agenda broadened. New institutions and processes were needed to deal with the increasingly complex problems. In the case of monetary policy, Congress and the president created the Federal Reserve System in 1913, which was more removed from the political fray, and empowered to regulate credit, interest rates, and the money supply.[6] Originally intended to consist of only 12 regional banks, the Federal Reserve Board (the Fed) evolved into the equivalent of a national bank.

Despite the changes in the late nineteenth and early twentieth centuries, U.S. economic policy remained restrained. Reliance on private business, not government, to spur the economy inspired the 1920s view that "what's good for General Motors is good for America." That view changed after the stock market crash in 1929 and Great Depression that followed.

ACCEPTANCE OF AN ENHANCED GOVERNMENT ROLE IN MANAGING THE ECONOMY

The Depression had a devastating effect on the U.S. economy.[7] One of four Americans were unemployed, and wages for those who were working fell to as little as five cents an hour. Grassroots pressure began to build for the federal government to take positive action to deal with the economic crisis. Inaction by President Herbert Hoover helped Franklin D. Roosevelt win the 1932 presidential election in a landslide. Roosevelt moved quickly to restore confidence and to change the role of government in managing the economy. The most important change was discretionary fiscal policy: using taxing and spending to stimulate economic activity and growth in accordance with the theories of British economist John Maynard Keynes. Preventing depressions through the management of surpluses or deficits in the budget would become a critical part of the policy responsibility of Congress and the president.[8] The use of budget deficits to help stimulate the economy would also become the most controversial part of Keynesian economics.

The revolution in the institutions and responsibilities of American government during the remarkable 12-year presidency of Franklin D. Roosevelt was closely connected to economic policy. The Bureau of the Budget (BOB), created in 1921, was originally located in the Treasury Department.[9] As part of the creation of a presidential bureaucracy, BOB became part of the Executive Office of the President in 1939. This move implicitly recognized the central role of taxing and spending in managing the economy and the president's increased responsibility for promoting the nation's prosperity. During World War II, the economy was largely run by the executive branch in Washington. Scarce resources were rationed, and government officials coordinated production of war materiel. The president's role in a more centralized system of economic planning also helped change public perceptions and expectations.

The Employment Act of 1946 translated the theories of Keynes and the policies of Roosevelt into law. Congress and the president were mandated to "use all practicable means" to promote "maximum employment, production, and purchasing power."[10] Although Congress intended to play a major role in economic policymaking, the legislation made more important changes in the power of the presidency. Under the Employment Act, the president was responsible for submitting not only the annual budget to Congress, but also an annual Economic Report of the President.

To formulate this annual report, the Employment Act created the Council of Economic Advisors (CEA). The president's chief economist became a key advisor and represented the president before Congress. To review the president's policies, the Employment Act created a new Joint Economic Committee in Congress.[11]

MANAGING THE POST-WORLD WAR II ECONOMY

The politics of guiding the nation's economy continued to evolve under the presidencies of Harry S Truman and Dwight Eisenhower. Republicans captured Congress in 1946, leading to divided government and partisan battles over taxes and spending; the postwar economic consensus evaporated. Keynesian economics reached its zenith under Presidents Kennedy and Johnson in the 1960s. The dominant approach was on the demand side: policies oriented to increasing consumer demand through greater government spending. The Kennedy-Johnson tax cut, adopted in 1964, was successful in stimulating economic growth while keeping inflation at relatively low levels, but the nation's economic waters were about to become choppy. As mentioned in the introduction to this chapter, rapidly growing expenditures for social programs and the war in Vietnam had an inflationary impact on the economy. The Johnson surtax, finally adopted in 1968, did little to stem the tide of rising prices. In 1971, Republican Richard Nixon surprised many observers by imposing mandatory wage and price controls. This move, which was controversial within conservative ranks, did not prove effective. When controls were removed, prices quickly jumped, making up for lost time.

Presidents Ford and Carter faced difficult economic problems and a growingly assertive Congress that was anxious to take a lead in economic and budget policy. The passage of the Congressional Budget Act of 1974 (see Chapter 4) was a crucial turning point in the balance between the president and Congress in terms of budget policy. Presidents Ford and Carter also served in a time of *stagflation:* double-digit inflation and unemployment.[12] Fiscal policy seemed to be less effective and a marked shift in emphasis to monetary policy occurred when President Carter selected Paul Volcker as chairman of the Federal Reserve Board in 1979.

Despite the predominance of Keynesian theory in guiding economic policy in the 1950s and 1960s, conservative critics such as Milton Friedman advocated a different approach.[13] Friedman argued that only monetary policy—not fiscal policy—could ultimately control inflation. By the late 1970s, monetarism was gaining adherents around the world. Newly appointed Federal Reserve Chairman Volcker embarked on a restrictive monetary policy, carefully managing the growth of the nation's money supply. Other critics of Keynesian economics favored government economic policies that focused on the *supply side* of the economy: helping entrepreneurs, investors, and businesses who produce economic growth. Supply-side economist Arthur Laffer argued that high taxes in the United States were discouraging investment and causing the economy to stagnate.[14] Widespread public unhappiness with inflation and astronomical interest rates set the stage for Ronald Reagan's victory over Carter in the 1980 presidential election. The influence of both monetarism and supply-side economics would be felt strongly in the 1980s.

Supply-side economics became the nation's economic policy with the election of Ronald Reagan in 1980. His 1981 economic and budget plan included deep across-the-board cuts in income taxes, major reductions in domestic spending, and a huge defense buildup. The 1981 plan, masterminded by Budget Director David Stockman, ushered in a decade of economic growth—but with it came unprecedented budget deficits as well as growing animosity between Congress and the president.

After his landslide reelection in 1984, Ronald Reagan announced that comprehensive tax reform would be the highest economic priority of his second term. A bipartisan coalition took almost two years to enact the most thorough revision of the nation's income tax system in history. However, confrontation with Congress over the budget remained the rule. A frustrated Congress enacted a plan for mandatory deficit reduction in 1985 and 1987. The stock market crash in October 1987 led to a budget summit and a two-year agreement with Congress

MANAGING THE POST-COLD WAR ECONOMY

Budget deficits continued to dominate the economic and political debate after the fall of the Berlin Wall in 1989 and the disintegration of the Soviet Union. Many believed that after defeating communism, the United States could significantly cut defense spending. But the "peace dividend" proved much smaller than expected and President George Bush was forced to deal with serious budget deficits. He initially adopted a less confrontational approach to Congress in 1989, reaching a budget summit agreement only months into his administration.[15] But the consensus collapsed when the deficit situation took a critical turn for the worse. Bush faced one of the most unfavorable budgetary situations in history, as the size of the projected deficits exploded. The deficit situation was so serious that President Bush felt compelled to renege on his famous "read my lips; no new taxes" pledge made during the 1988 campaign. The result was a deficit-reduction package cutting nearly $500 billion over five years with about a third coming from new taxes, a third from defense cuts, and a third from domestic cuts. The tax increase alienated many Republicans, who believed Bush had sold out on their party's best national issue.

The U.S. economy fell into recession in the early 1990s, exacerbating budget-deficit problems. Deficits continued at stubbornly high levels despite the 1990 deficit-reduction package, even though they would have been much worse without the legislation. Focusing on Bush's sinking popularity after the end of the Gulf War, Bill Clinton won the presidency in 1992 with his campaign mantra, "It's the economy, stupid." He, too, faced an immediate deficit crisis and had to trade his planned tax cuts for a deficit-reduction package in 1993. The plan cut the deficit by $430 billion over five years, with about half coming from new taxes and half from spending cuts. A bitter political battle ensued, with the president expending much political capital. Clinton's package passed by one vote in the Senate, and not a single Republican voted in favor. A year later, Congress blocked his healthcare reform proposal, and the Democrats lost control of Congress in 1994.

Combined with an improving economy, the 1990 and 1993 deficit-reduction packages set the deficit on a downward course over the next five years. In Clinton's first year, the gap between revenues and spending was $290 billion. In 1995 and 1996, up against Speaker Newt Gingrich and the Republican Congress, Clinton faced a bitter 18-month stalemate over balancing the budget. It was marked by two controversial shutdowns of the government, near-default on U.S. debt obligations, and 16 stop-gap budgets (see case that follows). In 1997, Congress and the president finally agreed on a bipartisan plan to balance the budget. By his sixth year in office, the budget was balanced for the first time in 30 years. After 16 years of conflict over the deficit, both parties were helped by stronger-than-expected economic growth, using the nation's prosperity to deliver promised tax breaks and new spending programs to constituents.

George W. Bush was chosen in a close and controversial election. By the time he was inaugurated, the U.S. budget had shifted from years of red ink to projected surpluses. But those surpluses did not last long, as Figure 7.1 shows. Bush's top campaign promise had been for a massive tax cut, comparable to Reagan's 20 years earlier. Given a Republican Congress, he pushed for the tax cut from the minute he

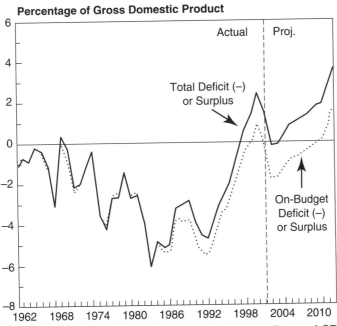

Figure 7.1 Total Deficits and Surpluses as a Share of GDP, 1962–2012

Source: Congressional Budget Office, 2002.

took office. It was one of his most important legislative accomplishments even though it was scaled down by Congress (see case that follows). But the economic environment shifted quickly with a recession made worse by the terrorist attacks of September 11. Suddenly, unemployment jumped from 4 percent to nearly 6 percent, 2 million people were laid off, and the stock market dropped despite 11 interest rate cuts by the Fed.

U.S. economic policy has evolved dramatically since Franklin D. Roosevelt. Fiscal policy has become less effective, and monetary policy is more important. Federal outlays are more inflexible because of entitlements (discussed in the next chapter) and other mandatory spending. The globalization of the economy has made the United States less autonomous in establishing economic policy: Congress and the president are subject to decisions made by governments and traders in Europe and Asia more than ever before. The budget is now one of the central instruments of domestic policymaking, encompassing not only economic consequences but a host of policy goals. All of these trends make economic policy and budget setting more complicated *and* more important to the president and Congress.

The Economic and Budgetary Environment

Economic conditions are a crucial aspect of the environment in which Congress and the president operate, affecting public support and policy options in a host of areas. By the late 1990s, the U.S. economy was performing better than it had in three decades. Unemployment dropped below 4 percent, inflation to 2 percent, and the stock market soared, increasing personal wealth. Figure 7.2 shows four major economic indicators between 1980 and 2000, projected through 2010: growth in gross domestic product (GDP), inflation, unemployment, and interest rates. Until the recession of 2001, the economic news was markedly improved over that of a decade earlier, when the economy grew but U.S. productivity lagged behind. Inflation, which plagued the 1970s, was brought under control.

In the 2000s, globalization and free trade issues are increasingly important to the public as demonstrated by the violent protests during the World Trade Organization's meetings in Seattle in late 1999. Many environmentalists and labor unions oppose the expansion of free trade because it shifts jobs to countries with lower labor standards, including child labor, and lower environmental standards.

The performance of the economy directly affects the budget and the deficit and an economic slowdown can quickly undo attempts at deficit reduction. An increase of 1 percent in unemployment increases the deficit by $33 billion in the first year alone, because tax collections fall by $28 billion, and outlays such as unemployment compensation increase by $5 billion. Similarly, an increase in interest rates expands the deficit because the government must pay more to finance its debt. Economic slumps increased the deficit in 1982, 1991, and 2002. This had political consequences for the presidents as well. Reagan's lowest public standing occurred in

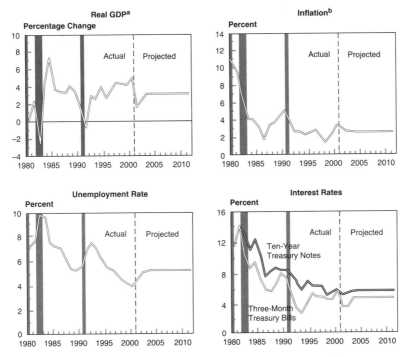

Figure 7.2   Economic Trends and Projections

Sources: Congressional Budget Office, December 2001.

1982, when unemployment hit 10 percent. Although the recession was not as severe in 1991 to 1992, the weak economy contributed to George Bush's defeat in the presidential election. Just as poor economic trends can hurt the electoral hopes of politicians, positive economic trends can make it easier to reach policy solutions, such as the 1997 balanced-budget agreement; they also help with reelection.

BUDGET TRENDS

Trends in government taxing and spending also affect the policymaking environment for Congress and the president. One of the most important changes since the 1960s is the growth of mandatory entitlements such as Social Security, Medicare, and Medicaid. This growing budgetary commitment has increased conflict and made choices all the more difficult. Figure 7.3 looks at the main categories of federal outlays in the 2002 budget, which totaled $2 trillion. Social Security is the largest outlay, taking up nearly one-fourth of all spending, followed by defense (16 percent) and Medicare (12 percent)—the three largest categories of programs. Nondefense discretionary programs (19 percent of all spending) include virtually all domestic agencies and departments and the bulk of other government programs. This part of

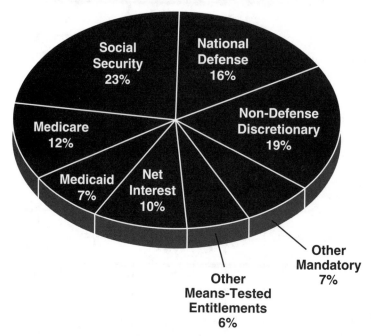

Figure 7.3   Major U.S. Budget Outlays (as a percent of total outlays)

Source: Office of Management and Budget, 2001.

the budget has shrunk significantly over the past decades, putting a squeeze on many government activities and programs. Major budgetary issues at the beginning of the twenty-first century surround Medicare and Social Security, which are discussed in detail in the next chapter.

Tax laws and the government's revenue sources are also an important part of the picture. Federal revenues come from four main sources: personal income taxes, Social Security and Medicare payroll taxes, corporate income taxes, and excise taxes. Table 7.1 looks at the source of federal revenues in 2000 projected to 2006. Half of revenues come from personal income taxes. Payroll taxes, the second largest source of tax revenue, have increased steadily, from only 10 percent of all revenues in 1960 to 30 percent today. Corporate income taxes and excise taxes have declined as a source of revenue over the past 30 years. Cutting taxes is a major priority of Republicans. Democrats are not always against tax cuts, but they focus more on the issue of who bears the tax burden. This was a major source of contention in budget debates throughout the period and in the case of Bush's tax cut in 2001.

Economic and budget trends play a critical role in setting the context for presidential-congressional policymaking. The four years of budget surpluses moderated but did not eliminate partisanship between parties and branches over economic and

Table 7.1 Sources of Federal Revenues (FY 2000–2006). ($ in billions)

SOURCE	2000 ACTUAL	ESTIMATE 2001	2002	2003	2004	2005	2006
Individual income taxes	$1,004	$1,073	$1,079	$1,092	$1,118	$1,157	$1,197
Corporate income taxes	207	213	219	227	235	244	252
Payroll taxes	653	690	726	766	806	856	896
Excise taxes	69	71	74	76	78	81	82
Estate and gift taxes	29	31	29	27	28	25	22
Customs duties	20	21	23	24	25	26	28
Miscellaneous revenues	43	38	43	45	48	49	51
Total revenues	$2,025	$2,137	$2,192	$2,258	$2,339	$2,438	$2,529

Source: Office of Management and Budget, 2001

budget issues. The recession made worse by the terrorist attacks once again increased conflict.

Making Economic and Budget Policy

PRESIDENTIAL ECONOMIC INSTITUTIONS

How does the presidency make economic and budget policy? The Treasury Department, the Office of Management and Budget (OMB),[16] and the CEA are key organizations for managing the economy. However, these institutions often had different interests and priorities, so presidents needed to develop some means for coordinating economic and budget decisions. In the 1960s, Presidents Kennedy and Johnson attempted to coordinate economic policymaking in the presidency by forming the economic "troika": budget director, CEA chair, and Treasury secretary. Along with the chair of the Federal Reserve Board, who remained largely independent of the president, this group formed an essential part of what has been called the "economic subpresidency."[17] Broadly speaking, the Treasury Department provides revenue estimates, the OMB supplies expenditure projections, and the CEA establishes the economic forecast.

Before he was forced from office by the Watergate scandal, President Nixon had initially attempted to institute a more formal economic policymaking process in the presidency, creating a Cabinet committee. Dissatisfied with this system, he then designated Treasury Secretary John Connally as the administration's "economic czar," in charge of all administration economic policy. Ford established an Economic Policy Board within his administration in an attempt to better coordinate policy. Carter also attempted to shuffle responsibilities to improve his control

Ronald Reagan created a Cabinet Council on Economic Affairs (CCEA) to coordinate policy by bringing together members of the Executive Office of the

President, the Cabinet, the bureaucracy, and the White House staff. Their mission was less one of policymaking than implementing a fixed agenda.[18] The budget process became the force driving domestic policy. The deficits created by the 1981 tax cut and defense buildup became the brakes that the administration used to curtail the size and scope of government. The Bush Sr. administration inherited the big deficits of the 1980s and sought some resolution with Congress through summits. Budget Director Richard Darman, Chief of Staff John Sununu, and CEA Chairman Michael Boskin dominated policymaking.[19] The Clinton administration had a fluid economic policy group, with the president participating actively. Clinton's appointment of Wall Street financier Robert Rubin as secretary of the Treasury was an attempt to demonstrate his "pro-business" policies. Perhaps adhering to his own campaign advice about the economy, the Clinton administration presided over the best economic performance in 30 years. George W. Bush had an even more pro-business makeup than his predecessor. He actively used both Secretary of Treasury Paul O'Neill and his White House staff to lobby Congress on behalf of his economic proposals. In general, recent presidents have used their entire White House and Cabinets to help work on economic and budget issues.

Congressional Institutions

When Congress finds a way to overcome decentralization, it increases its influence over the budget and economic policy. When the national budget was created in 1921, Congress attempted unsuccessfully to centralize its fragmented appropriations and revenue processes and consider the budget as a whole.[20] In 1946, at the time of the enactment of the Employment Act, Congress once again attempted to centralize economic decisionmaking by creating a legislative budget.[21] Congress was not able to influence monetary policy much either at this time. Even though Congress had oversight responsibility, the Federal Reserve remained substantially independent.[22]

As we saw in Chapter 4, the most important change in congressional institutions came with the passage of the Budget and Impoundment Control Act in July of 1974. In the ensuing decades, the Budget Act shored up the capacity of Congress to make economic and budget policy and strengthened its hand in negotiating with the president. The Budget Act made it possible for Congress to deal with macro-level economic decisions: the overall budget totals.[23] It required the adoption of a budget resolution to set the parameters of the budget and created House and Senate Budget Committees to draft the congressional budget. The act specified a timetable for congressional action and changed the fiscal year of the federal government. To improve congressional information, the Congressional Budget Office (CBO) was created. One of the most potent elements of the budget process was *reconciliation,* which allowed major taxing and spending changes to be enacted in a single bill.

In response to the deficit crisis and the growing deterioration of its own decisionmaking processes, Congress took a dramatic step in 1985 by adopting a mandatory deficit reduction law.[24] Their plan was to establish fixed deficit targets for the next five years, as well as a procedure for mandatory across-the-board cuts if Congress could not reach the target. This process was eventually abandoned in 1990, and Congress turned to expenditure control through appropriations caps and other devices to reduce the deficit. Congressional budgeting was unstable during the 1980s and 1990s, leading to a great deal of criticism. But despite the improvisational nature of congressional budgeting, it worked. Through the use of reconciliation, restrictive rules, and enhanced enforcement procedures, Congress emerged in a stronger position to challenge the presidency than at any time in recent history. The cases that follow show the dramatic range of patterns that take place in making critical choices on economic and budget policy.

Presidential Leadership: The Tax Cut (2001)

On May 26, 2001, President George W. Bush celebrated the most important legislative victory in his first six months in office. The U.S. Senate gave final passage to a bill that would reduce taxes on the American people by $1.35 trillion over 10 years, the largest tax cut in 20 years. Despite his narrow and controversial election to the presidency, Bush was able to enact the cornerstone of his domestic agenda. Senate Majority Leader Trent Lott (R-Miss.), called the vote an "exceptionally sweet victory."[25] Sweet, yes, but by no means an easy victory. It was achieved only after months of negotiation with Congress—both Republican and Democratic members—and major compromises by the president. Yet at the end of the day, it was a case of presidential leadership, because the Bush administration set the agenda and played the more dominant role in shaping the policy.

The tax cut package had its birth long before Bush's inauguration as the forty-third president of the United States. Along with education reform, tax cuts were at the center of the Bush campaign and a favorite theme among Republicans and conservatives. Bush faced a very different economic environment than what Bill Clinton confronted eight years earlier when he proposed *raising* taxes to reduce the deficits. Instead, Bush received news that surpluses were projected as far as the eye could see and would be even bigger than expected in 2001. This gave Bush the luxury of pushing for a politically popular tax cut rather than an unpopular tax increase. The president was anxious to move quickly because of the mounting concern that the U.S. economy was slowing down or even heading for recession. Even Democrats acknowledged that some tax cuts were appropriate, but they wanted much smaller cuts targeted toward lower income groups.

The political environment was unusual in 2001 because of how extraordinarily close the electorate was divided between Republicans and Democrats. The weakness of Bush's electoral mandate was balanced by the fact that Republicans controlled the presidency, House, and Senate for the first time in 48 years. However, the margin in the House was tiny and the Senate was tied 50 to 50 for the first time in history (Republican Vice President Cheney supplied the tiebreaking fifty-first vote). Some

Democrats were still bitter about the election and they were determined to oppose the president. Other Democrats felt the tax cuts would result in a return to budget deficits and would only help big business and the wealthy. Bush pledged to work for bipartisan support for this proposal. In the end, he gained only a handful of Democratic votes but they proved to be the margin of difference.

The administration started its lobbying campaign only days after Bush took office.[26] The first week of February, Treasury Secretary Paul O'Neill came to Capitol Hill to outline the administration's proposal while the president mixed public events with private meetings to promote his proposals. "I want the members of Congress and the American people to hear loud and clear," the president said. "This is the right-size plan, it is the right approach, and I'm going to defend it mightily."[27] The president's proposals would reduce taxes in several important ways:[28]

- *Reduce income tax rates:* Create a new 10 percent bracket, and lower the rates on all other brackets, including from a maximum of 39 percent to a maximum of 33 percent. Cost = $724 billion.
- *Phase out estate taxes:* Eliminate what the Republicans call "death taxes" and gift taxes. Cost = $236 billion
- *Child credit:* Increase the tax credits for taxpayers with children. Cost = $162 billion
- *Eliminate the "marriage penalty"*: Provide tax relief to two-income married couples who pay more tax than one-income couples at the same income level. Cost = $88 billion
- *Charitable contributions:* Increase the number of taxpayers who are allowed to deduct contributions to charities. Cost = $80 billion
- *Research and development tax credit:* Give large corporations a benefit for spending on R&D. Cost = $24 billion.
- *ESTIMATED TOTAL COST (including other provisions not listed here) =* **$1.62 trillion** over 10 years.

Within weeks of the introduction of Bush's proposals, alternative plans began surfacing in Congress. White House Chief of Staff Andrew Card came to lobby a group of Senate moderates who would be crucial in determining the eventual outcome. "We don't want to watch you guys make sausage," Card was reported to say.[29] Their reply: "Cover your eyes!" The House, with its stricter rules and stronger party leadership, was firmly under control of the Republicans despite the narrow 11-vote margin. They wanted to move quickly and not bother with bipartisanship. House Republicans rammed a bill through the House on March 8 without accommodating any Democratic concerns. This infuriated southern conservative "Blue Dog" Democrats in the House as well as the Senate, who promised they would remember how they were treated. Two moderate Republican senators, James Jeffords (R-Vt.) and Lincoln Chaffee (R-R.I.) indicated they would oppose a tax cut as large as $1.6 billion. This spelled trouble in the 50-50 Senate unless the administration could sway moderate Democrats to his side. It soon became clear that a handful of senators in the middle of the ideological spectrum would have a great deal of influence over Congress's final version of the tax cut.

Congressional rules and institutions, particularly the budget process, proved extremely important in determining the fate of the Bush tax cut. Under congressional rules, before Congress can enact individual tax and spending measures, it must pass a budget resolution that specifies the overall totals of the budget. The budget resolution determines how much "room" is in the budget for tax reductions. Then, House and Senate tax-writing committees determine the specifics.

A critical element for the tax cut battle was the reconciliation process. Originally designed to foster deficit reduction, Republicans now wanted to encompass the tax cuts in a reconciliation bill to give it "procedural protection" during consideration. That is, under the rules of the budget process, if the tax cuts were part of a reconciliation bill, it would take a supermajority to change the bill on the floor and would protect it from a Senate filibuster because of time limits on debate.[30]

The House passed its budget resolution on March 28 by a near party-line vote of 222 to 205, with only three Democrats voting for it and two Republicans voting against it.[31] The House resolution allowed $1.64 trillion for tax cuts over 10 years, about what the president asked. Things did not go as well in the Senate. Responding to concerns by Democrats and several Republicans that the tax cuts were too big, senators passed a budget resolution on April 6 that limited tax cuts to $1.27 trillion, significantly below what the president had requested. The key vote was taken two days earlier when three Republicans joined with the Democrats to reduce the tax-cut ceiling.[32] Over the next month, House, Senate, and White House negotiators tried to hammer out a compromise budget resolution. The negotiations involved primarily Republicans but also several key moderate Democrats. They finally agreed on a $1.35 trillion target for the tax cuts and that it would be implemented as a reconciliation bill. Although some 20 percent less than Bush had wanted, the agreement on the budget resolution meant that the likelihood of getting a major tax cut was high.

Attention now turned to the House Ways and Means Committee and the Senate Finance Committee that had the responsibility to write the specific tax-cut bills. Predictably, the House markup would make some minor changes but encompass the bulk of the president's requests. The House passed its version of the tax cut by a vote of 230 to 197 on May 16, having picked up a handful more Democratic votes. On the Senate side, things were more complicated. The team of Charles Grassley (R-Iowa), the Finance Committee chair, and Max Baucus (D-Mont.), the ranking minority member, agreed to work toward a bipartisan compromise that could pass the Senate. That put them partially at odds with Majority Leader Lott who threatened to overrule the committee and take legislation directly to the floor. The administration was still lobbying hard and negotiating to get as many of its desired provisions included in the $1.35 trillion total.[33]

Two unexpected factors helped spur a quick resolution to the tax-cut package. First, new projections were beginning to suggest the economy was slowing and that there might not be as large a budget surplus to give back in the form of tax cuts. Second, as the tax-cut package was reaching its final conclusion, Senator Jeffords announced he was becoming an Independent and that the Democrats would take over the Senate. Shock waves ran from Capitol Hill to the White House. The administration abandoned its reluctance to compromise and urged their Republican allies in Congress to make the best deal they could as quickly as possible. They made concessions on lowering rates and in targeting the cuts more toward low-income families. President Bush urged the Congress to finish its business immediately, noting "our economy cannot afford any further delays."[34] House-Senate conferees quickly tied up loose ends and sent the compromise package back to their respective houses.

The House passed the final bill 240 to 154. Twenty-eight Democrats voted for the bill, and 29 abstained. In the Senate, 12 Democrats supported the compromise and 7 abstained. Two Republican senators, Lincoln Chaffee and John McCain (R-Ariz.) voted no. In a hurry to recess for Memorial Day weekend and with one of the senators needing to go to the hospital immediately for back pain, the Senate even attenuated its final debate. The bill signed into law by President Bush was promoted as a great victory for the administration, but the White House promised to submit further legislation to get additional cuts that Congress had deleted. The final bill did much of what the president had proposed. Top rates were lowered but not to the 33 percent Bush wanted. Rate cuts reduced taxes by $875 billion over 10 years. Estate and gift taxes were reduced by $138 billion, the "marriage penalty" by $63 billion, child tax credits reduced taxes by $172 billion, and retirement provisions reduced taxes by $29 billion.[35]

What determined the pattern of presidential leadership and why is it not a case of cooperation given the extensive input of Congress? The political environment was conducive to presidential leadership. Bush was in his honeymoon period and the tax cut was one of his top priorities. The economy still looked good and there was surplus money to pay for tax cuts. Congress did have extensive input but that is normal today in economic and budget policy, even when the executive branch leads policy. Bush, in the end, did set the agenda and get 70 to 80 percent of what he wanted. Compare this case to the 1986 Tax Reform Act that follows, where the two branches were much more equal in shaping policy.

What about the impact? With so little time since its enactment, it is not yet possible to tell. On one hand, by 2002, Democrats were blaming the Bush tax cuts for the budget deficits that had reappeared. On the other hand, the economic argument for major tax cuts to stimulate the economy became even stronger as the recession and the events of September 11 unfolded. The consequences of the largest tax cut in 20 years might take a decade or longer to assess.

Congressional Leadership:
The Shareholder Lawsuits Bill (1995)

The United States has become a litigious society, with lawsuits continuing to proliferate over everything from McDonald's coffee that was too hot to Johnny Carson suing a neighbor for a dog fouling his yard. As the prevalence of coffee-room lawyer jokes suggests, the attorneys that bring these suits on behalf of plaintiffs have been subject to growing criticism. One of the less publicized provisions of the Republicans' Contract with America was legislation to reduce frivolous lawsuits that threatened emerging, high-tech industries. In 1995, guided by the new Republican majority but with bipartisan support, Congress led the policy process by passing legislation limiting lawsuits by shareholders against companies. In doing so, Congress ran into the opposition of President Clinton, who vetoed the bill. Undeterred, both the House and Senate mustered two-thirds majorities to override the veto and pass the shareholder lawsuits bill into law.

Some of the most egregious examples of unnecessary lawsuits in recent years have come in the area of shareholders' suits against companies for securities fraud. A small group of attorneys have made a fortune by watching for companies whose stock price has dropped, reviewing the records for previous optimistic performance projections, then suing on the grounds that the company had defrauded stockholders.[36] Particularly hard hit were high-tech companies, whose stock prices tend to be extremely volatile. Certain attorneys even *paid* stockholders to join class-action suits. Some investors bought small stakes in companies simply to look for opportunities to sue. Companies usually settle these suits out of court rather than spend the time and money to defend themselves. The CEO of America Online said that "frivolous lawsuits are such a problem that high-tech firms can now be lumped into two groups: those that have been sued and those that will be sued."[37]

On the other side of the issue were several groups, including trial lawyers and consumer rights organizations. A number of state attorneys general and securities regulators also opposed the bill. They argued that reformers wanted to go too far to curb the rights of stockowners to protect themselves against fraud and abuse by unscrupulous companies. They noted that there were only about 250 class-action securities suits filed per year and that not all were frivolous. The division of interest groups caused potential problems for President Clinton because it pitted Democratic-leaning trial lawyers and consumer groups against the high-tech industries in California that he was so carefully wooing with the 1996 presidential election coming up.

House Republicans moved quickly on the bill during the ambitious first 100 days of the 104th Congress, their first taste of having a majority in Congress in 40 years. Representative Christopher Cox (R-Calif.) was the prime author of the bill, H.R.1058. The Telecommunications and Finance Subcommittee of the House

Commerce Committee drafted the shareholder lawsuit bill in February and passed it by a voice vote. The full committee passed it on February 16, 1995, by a vote of 33 to 10. It garnered significant Democratic support. The bill prohibited lawyers from paying shareholders for joining a suit and required that the losing party in the suit pay all costs. It placed other restrictions on plaintiffs in terms of how many suits they could be party to and exempted from liability companies that were sued on the basis of projections. Opponents claimed that the bill went too far and was "the stripping of citizens of a mechanism by which they can defend themselves against malefactors of great wealth."[38] Nonetheless, the bill passed the House easily by a vote of 325 to 99 on March 8 with bipartisan support.

The Senate took up the bill in May and scaled back several provisions. To prevent small investors from buying stocks just to sue, the Senate required that the largest investor in a stock be the lead plaintiff in any suit. The bill also included safe harbor provisions to protect companies that wanted to make growth and earnings projections, as long as there was no intent to deceive. During the Senate debate, the lead sponsor, Senator Peter Domenici (R-N.M.), pointed out that most of the damages in these lawsuits went to the lawyers, with stockholders getting only 14 cents of every dollar.[39] He was assisted in getting the bill through the Senate by Christopher Dodd (D-Conn.), who was also general chairman of the Democratic National Committee. Despite his partisan job, Dodd worked with Domenici and other Republicans to get the bill passed. It did so on June 28 by a vote of 70 to 29.

Over the summer and fall, Congress and the president, Republicans and Democrats, were sharply divided on many issues, particularly budget issues. During this time, however, informal negotiations between the House and Senate resolved most of the differences in the two versions of the shareholder lawsuits bills. The conference committee finished work on the bill on November 28 and sent the compromise version to the House and Senate for final approval. It passed the Senate on December 5 and the House on December 6 by comfortable margins and was sent to the president for his signature.

President Clinton and his congressional liaison office had maintained a low profile on the issue during the year as the administration concentrated on other matters. It was clearly a congressional policy initiative with widespread support. But the president was heavily lobbied by interest groups after the bill was passed and sent to him for his signature. The trial lawyers—big Democratic contributors—were strongly against the bill and pressed for a veto. Conversely, high-tech industry lobbyists warned that the bill was so important to California that Clinton might lose that state in 1996 if he vetoed the bill.[40]

Clinton waited until the last possible minute to decide what to do with the bill. It would become law without his signature on December 19 at midnight. After meeting with advisors late into the evening, Clinton vetoed the bill. It was a difficult decision. Clinton claimed that he opposed frivolous lawsuits but felt that the bill had gone too far, particularly with the safe harbor provisions. A White House statement read: "The president supports the goals of this legislation, but he is unwilling to close the courthouse doors on the investors who have legitimate claims."[41] Many on Capitol Hill were stunned at the veto and promised to override it immediately. Even Democrats were surprised given the prominent role played by Dodd, one of the president's most loyal soldiers in Congress. It did not take long for Congress to respond. Only 13 hours after the veto, the House voted 319 to 100 to override, far more than the two-thirds needed. Two days later, the Senate voted to override by a closer margin of 68 to 30, still enough to enact the bill into law (PL 104–67).

Why did this case evolve the way it did? What does this case tell us about presidential-congressional policymaking, particularly when Congress takes the lead? The political environment in 1995 was exceptional, with the new Republican Congress virtually setting the agenda of the nation for much of the year. As part of the Contract with America, the shareholder lawsuits bill was part of this agenda. Unlike many other provisions, this attracted significant support from the Democratic minority on the other side of the aisle. This case was more typical of inside-the-Beltway politics, rather than the highly publicized economic issues such as the budget or proposed Medicare cutbacks. It was fought out by organized interests—high-tech companies, trial lawyers, and consumer advocates—in the halls and cloakrooms of Congress. This was also Congress leading, with relatively little input from the administration.

Nonetheless, the administration had stakes in the bill. It was torn, however, between political and policy objectives and divisions between groups that supported it. His hesitation cost Clinton the first veto override of his administration, an event with political consequences and a sign of weakness. Although the veto may have shored up the political support among the trial lawyers, high-tech companies were furious with his veto. During the 1996 campaign, some of the CEOs who had supported him in 1992 withheld support. The Republican Congress, however, not only had enacted another provision of the Contract but had won a political victory over the president as well.

Consensus/Cooperation: The Tax Reform Act (1986)

The conventional wisdom held that tax reform—especially comprehensive tax reform—was impossible in the American political system. Despite many obstacles, on October 22, 1986, President Ronald Reagan signed into law the most sweeping overhaul of federal income taxes in history. How did Congress and the president work together to make the impossible possible? Jimmy Carter had called the nation's tax system a disgrace during the 1976 campaign, but he never even submitted a comprehensive reform package during his presidency. Tax reform seemed particularly improbable in the partisan, politicized Washington environment after the 1984 election campaign, in which President Reagan had hammered Democratic presidential candidate Walter Mondale on the tax issue. With budget deficits at record levels,

Reagan's pledge not to raise taxes had driven legislative and executive branches farther apart.

Tax reform was also seen as highly unlikely because, with fiscal constraints on the spending side in the Reagan years, it had become increasingly popular to deliver benefits through tax preferences or loopholes. Granting special exclusions, exemptions, deductions, deferrals, and lower rates had become an ingenious if costly method for legislators to deliver benefits to constituents. By 1985, these special "tax expenditures" cost the Treasury over $400 billion per year.[42] The decline in fiscal responsibility of the House Ways and Means and Senate Finance Committees—Congress's tax-writing panels—further dimmed prospects for reform. Four years earlier, the Economic Recovery Tax Act (ERTA) looked like a bidding war. David Stockman characterized the process as "pigs feeding at the trough." Legislators were unable to resist the temptation to buy support by creating tax preferences.[43]

Tax reform was also considered impossible because of the array of powerful interest groups lined up against it. Any given group may have benefited from only one or two of the thousands of special provisions, but they would go to any lengths to protect their special loopholes. Interests ranging from investment bankers to timber companies to university presidents had something to protect in the old tax system. When Congress debated comprehensive reform, hundreds of highly paid lobbyists milled around outside of the hearing rooms. Authors Jeffrey Birnbaum and Alan Murray described the scene:

> In the hallway outside the committee room, more lobbyists stand nervously, like so many expectant fathers crowded into the waiting room of a maternity ward. These hallway loiterers include the top ranks of Washington's tax lobbying world—men and women who are paid $200, $300, and even $400 an hour to influence legislators and preserve tax benefits worth millions of dollars to their anxious clients. . . . A few of the lobbyists huddle around the back door of the committee room, hoping to catch a senator coming in or going out, hoping for one last chance to make a pitch before the vote. The desperation in their voices makes it clear that big money is at stake. Their expensive suits and shiny Italian shoes give this hallway its nickname: Gucci Gulch.[44]

Tax reform came into being through a carefully orchestrated collaboration between executive and legislative branches. The tax reform movement in Congress allied two diverse groups. Liberal reformers, such as Representative Richard Gephardt (D-Mo.) and Senator Bill Bradley (D-N.J.), who wanted to eliminate special preferences for the rich, joined with conservative supply-siders, such as Representative Jack Kemp (R-N.Y.) and Senator Robert Kasten (R-Wis.), who wanted lower rates. Both sides agreed that the tax base had to be broadened, which meant eliminating many special tax preferences. The Bradley-Gephardt and Kemp-Kasten bills had received a great deal of attention before 1985 but had never been seriously considered by either house of Congress.

The equilibrium changed when Ronald Reagan announced that comprehensive tax reform was the number one domestic priority of his second term. While the building blocks were in place, the political obstacles remained. In 1984, the president had instructed the Treasury Department to prepare a comprehensive tax reform plan. The details of the plan were carefully guarded until after the election. In December 1984, the Treasury Department unveiled a bold plan. It called for the elimination of many sacred cows in the tax code, so it immediately generated controversy. The Reagan administration was cautious, however, and did not endorse the plan as its own. The White House wanted time to review some of the more controversial provisions before actually submitting a plan to Congress.

The Reagan administration did not submit a plan until June 1985, six months into the second term. Remembering the budget blitz of 1981, many observers felt that the president had failed to capture the momentum of his landslide reelection. The revised plan, dubbed "Treasury II," retained many of the comprehensive features of "Treasury I." House Ways and Means Chairman Dan Rostenkowski (D-Ill.) quickly pledged Democratic support for the approach of the president's plan, if not all the specifics.

Legislative and executive branch leaders agreed on several ground rules to minimize conflict and make cooperation possible. First, all reform proposals had to be "revenue neutral"—neither raising nor losing revenue—to keep tax reform from being dragged into the bitter deficit dispute. Second, reformers agreed that for strategic purposes, approximately two-thirds of all taxpayers had to pay the same or less in taxes under the new system as compared with the existing system. Third, reformers determined that the number of tax brackets (15 at the time) would be sharply reduced, to as few as 2 or 3. Fourth, all sides decided that the effort would be bipartisan, avoiding as much as possible the divisions that characterized most budget and economic issues. These strategic premises did not assure victory, but did mean that tax reform would get farther than it had in decades.

The House took up the president's proposal first, reflecting its constitutional primacy in dealing with revenue measures. Rostenkowski confronted the legions of lobbyists in "Gucci Gulch" and watched in frustration as his committee voted to allow a number of the special preferences back into the bill. In October 1985, it appeared that a tax reform was doomed when the Ways and Means Committee voted to reinstate a $7 billion tax break for banks.[45] However, Rostenkowski worked out a deal with members who wanted to retain the deduction for state and local taxes, and the bank loophole was reconsidered and defeated. When the bill finally cleared committee and went to the full House in December 1985, a number of Republicans had grown disenchanted. Feeling left out of the negotiations among the White House, Republican Senate leaders, and Democratic House leaders, they staged a revolt. President Reagan promised to deal with the concerns of the House Republicans when the bill reached the Senate and urged them to support the committee version. However, on December 11, these Republicans joined with several dozen Democrats and defeated the rule under which tax reform was to be debated. It was a major crack in the bipartisanship that had characterized the process, which threatened to kill tax reform. Five days later, the president rescued the process by personally coming to Capitol Hill to convince House Republicans to support the bill. Although not all of them were convinced, the bill passed the House the next day.

The Senate Finance Committee, chaired by Republican Robert Packwood of Oregon, began drafting its version of tax reform in the spring of 1986. The markup seemed to confirm the worst fears and predictions of defeat. One by one, committee members chipped away, voting to restore provisions favoring special interests. After weeks of battering, Packwood withdrew his plan and contemplated giving up, but a key breakthrough occurred. Packwood took his committee members behind closed doors, away from the lobbyists, the reporters, and the glare of television lights of the hearing room. He asked members how low rates would have to drop before they would be willing to give up the special preferences they had already adopted in open sessions. Most members responded that the top rates would have to come down to 30 percent or below. Packwood showed them how it could be done.

Throwing out the decisions made over the previous month, the Senate Finance Committee reported a radical tax reform bill, with two brackets and a top rate of only 27 percent. By turning the decisionmaking process around in private, Packwood succeeded in getting his committee to report the bill to the Senate by a remarkable vote of 20 to 0. This may have been the single most important event in making tax reform a reality. The lobbyists were stunned to see their special tax provisions thrown out. The strong committee vote made tax reform irresistible on the Senate floor, where it passed by a vote of 97 to 3 on June 24, 1986.

The conference committee considering the two versions of the bills ran into its share of problems, but eventually it adopted a plan closer to the more daring Senate bill. The final version contained two brackets, with rates of 14 and 28 percent. The bill was approved by both the House and Senate in September and signed into law by the president in October. The impossible had been accomplished.

Several factors explain the emergence of a pattern of cooperation leading to the successful enactment of tax reform. Both branches worked actively on specific details of the legislation and demonstrated a willingness to negotiate and compromise. Bipartisanship was critical. With the exception of the House Republicans, all participants avoided the temptation to make political hay out of their differences. Tax reform was originally a congressional initiative, but it could not have been enacted without active, aggressive support from President Reagan, whose popularity and landslide election victory helped him to move the legislative process, particularly in the House, when it became stalled. Decisionmaking processes and individual leadership were exceptionally important in this case. The leadership of Senator Packwood was particularly noteworthy. Private negotiations, in which bargaining and trading could be done honestly, were instrumental in the crafting of the Tax Reform Act of 1986.

What were the results of the Tax Reform Act? One immediate result was that the top rate of personal income taxes fell to its lowest level since the 1920s. Although the revenue code remained complex, the reduction in the number of brackets was a significant improvement. For many supporters, the greatest benefit of tax reform was to restore some of the integrity to the tax system by eliminating hundreds of loopholes. However, the tax code would be changed again in ensuing years, with top rates being raised as part of the deficit reduction packages in 1990 and 1993. Whatever simplification was enacted was gradually eroded over the next decade. In particular, many new complex tax breaks were added back into the tax code as part of the balanced budget agreement in 1997.

Deadlock/Extraordinary Resolution: The Balanced Budget Standoff (1995–1996)

Perhaps no issue was more important to the new Republican Congress in 1995 than balancing the federal budget. They approached the issue aggressively, seeking total victory over the repudiated congressional Democrats and a weakened President Clinton. House Republicans concocted a plan with nearly a trillion dollars in spending cuts over seven years, including sharp reductions in Medicare, enough cuts to allow them to incorporate $350 billion in tax cuts during the same period. They tried to force the president to go along by threatening to shut down the government and default on federal debt if necessary. Although he gradually moved toward their position and agreed to seek a balanced budget, throughout 1995, Clinton stood up to Speaker Gingrich and the Republicans. Clinton's approval ratings soared while the Republicans' tumbled. Eighteen months after the battle over the fiscal 1996 budget started, a truce was called without an agreement on a plan to balance the budget. Both sides decided that the deadlock would best be resolved by the 1996 elections.

As the hectic first 100 days of the 104th Congress drew to a close, committees in both the House and Senate were getting down to the business of crafting a comprehensive plan to balance the budget. The House Budget Committee, headed by Representative John Kasich (R-Ohio) and the Senate Budget Committee, chaired by Senator Peter Domenici (R-N.M.), began hearings on the budget resolution for FY96. On February 6, 1995, President Clinton, chastened by the 1994 election results, had submitted a cautious budget that included no major initiatives or deficit reduction. Republicans lambasted the president for abdicating leadership, claiming he "took a walk" and "put up the white flag."[46] Not content just to shape the FY96 budget for the fiscal year that would begin on October 1, 1995, the Republicans proposed a package of rescissions (canceling spending already approved) for the current year (FY95) budget. In May, Clinton vetoed the rescissions bill and the

Republicans lacked the votes to override, a pattern that would be repeated over the next year. A compromise rescissions bill was finally approved in July.

The House balanced budget plan went to the floor in May. It was an ambitious attempt to make major reductions in government, including the elimination of 14 federal agencies. The House plan would cut spending by $1.04 trillion, including $288 billion in Medicare reductions, and cut taxes by $353 billion.[47] The Senate plan was somewhat more modest, making tax cuts contingent on a plan that would actually balance the budget. Democrats attacked the bills, claiming the Republicans wanted to balance the budget on the backs of the young, the poor, and the elderly. Still on the defensive, however, Clinton on June 13 put out his own plan for a balanced budget over 10 years. Some Democrats attacked the president for capitulating to the Republicans, but he argued that his plan would not harm society's most vulnerable. Republicans ignored the president's plan. After House and Senate versions passed by nearly party-line votes, the budget resolution went to conference. The conference committee worked out the differences between the two versions, and on June 29, the budget resolution laying out the Republicans' balanced budget plan passed. The budget resolution is binding only on subsequent congressional actions and does not have to be signed by the president to take effect.

Implementing the blueprint contained in the budget resolution would take place on two fronts. First, the 13 individual appropriations bills containing discretionary spending that must be passed by October 1 would provide Republicans an opportunity to make sharp cuts in existing programs. Second, the bulk of the balanced budget package would be contained in a massive reconciliation bill, encompassing multiyear cuts in entitlements and other spending, along with tax reductions. With partisan conflict at every stage, the pace was slow, and the administration's resolve was growing. By October 1, only two spending bills had passed, and Clinton had vetoed one of them. Congress passed a six-week stop-gap spending bill as a big battle was shaping up over the reconciliation bill.

The Republican strategy was to try to force Clinton to approve their balanced budget plan by threatening to shut down the government and default on the debt if he did not sign their bill. The statutory debt ceiling, which gives the government the authority to borrow, was set to expire in mid-November 1995.[48] The Republicans bet that, rather than allow a first-ever default on federal debt, Clinton would accept their budget plan. They were wrong. As the November 13 date for the expiration of the temporary spending bill approached, Clinton stepped up his counterattacks on Congress for trying to blackmail him into signing the bill. The Republicans passed another temporary spending bill and a debt extension with provisions that Clinton had promised not to accept. He vetoed both and on November 14, "nonessential" federal employees were sent home as the government closed down for six days. The Treasury was able to manipulate funds to avoid a default on government bonds.

Republicans did win one important concession from the president. As they were negotiating over another temporary funding bill, Clinton agreed with the seven-year timetable to balance the budget as long as it included his priorities for healthcare, education, and the environment. Now, both sides wanted a balanced budget—the only question was how to do it. That concession by Clinton would not make compromise any easier. The Republican version of the reconciliation bill passed Congress; the president vetoed it on December 6. Clinton released a new budget plan of his own on December 7. As the stalemate continued, the government shut down again on December 16 as federal workers were sent home right before the holidays. Voters were getting fed up with the antics in Washington.

It was the Republican Congress rather than the president that paid the political price for the budget deadlock. Clinton's approval rating shot up over 50 percent, the highest rate in two years, as support for Newt Gingrich and the Republicans tumbled.[49] The public saw Clinton sticking to principles and standing up for the little guy. News stories featured unhappy tourists locked out of national parks and monuments and disgruntled government workers not allowed to go to the office. To make matters worse, the stock market dropped over concerns with the budget deadlock. After the holidays, members of Congress returned to Washington and, spurred by rank-and-file discontent over the political consequences of their strategy, the Republicans backed away from their hardball tactics. Robert Dole, worrying about the negative consequences to his presidential bid, said, "Enough is enough. I do not see any sense in what we have been doing, frankly. Maybe I missed the point. . . . If there is any point to be made, I think that point should have been made by now."[50]

Ironically, with concessions by the Clinton administration, the two sides were not as far apart as they had been earlier, and agreement seemed to be within reach. In November, the White House and Congress were as much as $350 billion apart. By January, this had closed to $66 billion.[51] But as yet another temporary spending bill expired, Republicans were desperate to avoid another shutdown. In essence, the Republicans gave up on getting a budget agreement. Newt Gingrich said, "I don't expect us to get a seven-year balanced budget with President Clinton in office."[52] Meanwhile, no budget had passed, leaving many agencies and departments in financial chaos. In the spring of 1996, halfway into the fiscal year, fewer than half of the appropriations bill had been enacted, and the fourteenth temporary spending bill had to be passed to avoid another shutdown. An increasingly confident White House lambasted the Congress for not completing its work on the budget. Meanwhile, the cycle for the FY97 budget was already starting, although Clinton delayed submission of the plan by over a month and submitted only the rudiments of a regular budget.

The deadlock over the balanced budget plan was not so much resolved as it was postponed. In late April, both sides agreed to a bill that would fund agencies through the end of the fiscal year. Both sides still had their own versions of a balanced budget plan, and both sides planned to use the failure to reach a compromise in the 1996 presidential and congressional elections. There was no extraordinary resolution of the 1995–96 budget deadlock. Instead, it was resolved in part by the mixed message of the election. With the reelection of Bill Clinton by a substantial margin and the trimming of Republican majorities in Congress, the 1996 elections set the stage for eventual agreement on a balanced budget plan in 1997.

This case is an interesting example of how divided government and party differences over economic and budget policy can result in partisan bickering, deadlock, and potentially harmful results. Nothing positive was accomplished by the government shutdowns or threats to default on the federal debt. The case certainly reveals enhanced congressional capacity to lead government in terms of defining issues and formulating solutions. However, it also shows the limits of congressional leadership when there is substantial opposition from the White House. The Republicans were unable to pressure Clinton into accepting their plan, and their tactics backfired politically. In retrospect, many Republicans believe it was a mistake to force the government shutdowns to pressure the president.

The pattern of deadlock that emerged was a result of the unique political environment of 1995, the dramatic election results of 1994, and the strength and unity of the Republican majority in the House. It was possible for Congress to push as hard as it did because of the institutions linked with the congressional budget process that had developed over the past two decades. Personal leadership was also important. Speaker Newt Gingrich and Majority Leader Dick Armey were perhaps too swept up in their own successes and miscalculated the president's resolve and the public reaction. President Clinton, who had been reduced to holding a press conference to deny he was "irrelevant" right after the Republicans captured Congress, boosted his leadership ratings by standing up to Congress. In terms of policy, despite losing the political battle, Republicans may have won the policy battle by getting the president to commit to a balanced budget by 2002 and bringing him closer to their position in many areas. Undoubtedly, lessons were learned on both sides. In 1996, Clinton was reelected easily and the Republicans held Congress, but narrowly. This created a very different context in 1997, when President Clinton and many of the same Republican leaders were able to negotiate in good faith for the most part, and helped by a booming economy, achieved a plan to balance the budget after all.

Conclusion

Both branches know the high stakes involved in economic and budget issues. Accordingly, dominance by either branch is relatively rare. Congressional leadership may be rarer, because the political stakes are so great for the president. In the case of the shareholder lawsuits bill, the president identified his position in the bill too late, and Congress was not willing to let him obstruct their work at the last minute. Congress is more likely to lead on less-publicized economic issues, like the shareholder lawsuits bill, or public works and other pork-barrel legislation that distributes local benefits. It is much more exceptional for the legislative branch to try to lead the president on comprehensive national economic and budget legislation, as the 104th Congress did in 1995. This case may be unprecedented in modern times in terms of congressional attempts to dominate policymaking. But despite all their initial political advantages, the result was still deadlock. The case remains instructive, however, in defining both the potential and the limits of congressional power in economic policymaking.

In this era of greater coequality of the branches, strong presidential leadership of Congress may be getting equally rare, occurring only in an unusual political environment. The classic case is Franklin Roosevelt's "Hundred Days" during the depths of the Depression in 1933, when Congress was willing to enact virtually anything the president proposed. This may not occur again absent a comparable economic calamity. In this perspective, George W. Bush's success with his tax cut in 2001 demonstrates a more collaborative form of presidential leadership. While we argue that it still constitutes presidential leadership because the president did dominate in shaping the outcome, Congress forced major changes and a 20 percent reduction in the size of the tax cut. Comparable recent cases are Clinton's 1993 deficit-reduction package and Ronald Reagan's 1981 budget and economic plan, which also included a large tax cut. Significantly, all three of these cases of reshaping budget priorities took place in the president's first year in office.

If the two branches disagree significantly, and neither can dominate, the alternative is either cooperation or deadlock. Bipartisan cooperation seemed missing on economic and budget policy in the 1980s, making the interbranch cooperation exhibited in the Tax Reform Act of 1986 all the more exceptional. Furthermore, there was no imminent crisis looming to force legislative and executive negotiators to the bargaining table as was the case in the 1983 Social Security bailout (a case described in the next chapter). Tax reform occurred because of an unusual ideological congruence between both branches and both parties, boosted by effective leadership that mustered the political will to stand up to the powerful interests opposing tax reform.

Economic and budget questions have been defining issues for America's two political parties. Because the presidency and Congress have been under divided party control for much of the last 30 years, the most prevalent pattern in budget and economic policymaking in recent years has been interbranch conflict that is predominantly partisan. This conflict has increased the use of extraordinary resolution. Some form of interbranch summit was employed to resolve the budget deadlocks nearly a dozen times since 1981. In 1993, a unified Democratic Congress and president barely prevailed in the most partisan of atmospheres. The 1995–1996 budget stalemate resulted in multiple government shutdowns and more than a dozen temporary budgets. The 2001 tax cut resulted in a presidential victory only after making whatever concessions were necessary at the end. The future of presidential-congressional policymaking will look much like the past. While the length of the 2001–02 recession and the seriousness of budget deficits through 2005 will matter, as long as the two parties define themselves largely by economic and budget issues, it will remain an area of continued conflict.

Notes

1. Lance T. LeLoup, *Budgetary Politics,* fourth edition (Brunswick, Ohio: King's Court, 1988): Chapter 5.
2. Lyndon B. Johnson, *The Vantage Point: Perspectives on the Presidency 1963–1969* (New York: Holt, Rinehart and Winston, 1971): 440.
3. Allen Schick (ed.), *Congress and the Making of Economic Policy* (Washington, D.C.: American Enterprise Institute, 1983).
4. Louis M. Hacker, *The Course of American Growth and Development* (New York: Wiley, 1970): 55.
5. Daniel R. Fusfield (ed.) *The Age of the Economist* (Glenview, IL: Scott Foresman, 1982).
6. John Wooley, *Monetary Politics* (New York: Cambridge University Press, 1984).
7. Robert Heilbroner, *The Making of Economic Society* (Englewood Cliffs, NJ: Prentice-Hall, 1962): 122–123.
8. Robert Lekachman, *The Age of Keynes* (New York: Random House, 1966).
9. Larry Berman, *The Office of Management and Budget and the Presidency 1921–79* (Princeton, NJ: Princeton University Press, 1979).
10. Steven K. Bailey, *Congress Makes a Law* (New York: Columbia University Press, 1950): 57–58.
11. The original name of the committee was the Joint Committee on the Economic Report of the President.
12. Congressional Budget Office, *The Fiscal Response to Inflation* (January 1979): 67.
13. Friedman's general political and economic ideas are discussed in Milton Friedman, *Capitalism and Freedom* (Chicago: University of Chicago Press, 1962).
14. D. I. Museman and A. B. Laffer, *The Phenomenon of Worldwide Inflation* (Washington, D.C.: American Enterprise Institute, 1975).
15. *Congressional Quarterly Weekly Report* (April 15, 1989): 804–805.
16. LeLoup (1988): 108.
17. James Anderson, "Managing the Economy: The Johnson Experience," paper presented at the American Political Science Association Annual Meeting, August 27–30, 1980: 6.
18. Chester Newland, "Executive Office Policy Apparatus: Enforcing the Reagan Agenda," in Lester M. Salamon and Michael S. Lund (eds.), *The Reagan Presidency and the Governing of America* (Washington, D.C.: Urban Institute Press, 1984): 135–168.
19. *Wall Street Journal* (August 3, 1989): A16.
20. Lance T. LeLoup, *The Fiscal Congress: Legislative Control of the Budget* (Westport, CT.: Greenwood Press, 1980): 6.
21. Jesse Burkhead, "Federal Budgetary Developments, 1947–48," *Public Administration Review* 8 (Autumn 1948): 267–274.
22. Woolley (1984): 154.
23. Allen Schick, *Congress and Money* (Washington, D.C.: Urban Institute Press, 1980).
24. Lance T. LeLoup et al., "Deficit Politics and Constitutional Government: The Impact of Gramm-Rudman-Hollings," *Public Budgeting and Finance* 7 (Spring 1987): 83–103.
25. Daniel J. Parks, "Tax Debate Assured a Long Life As Bush, GOP Press for New Cuts," *CQ Weekly* (June 2, 2001): 1308.
26. David Sanger, "Bush Tax Plan Sent to Congress, Starting the Jostling for Position, *New York Times* (February 9, 2001): A1.
27. Daniel J. Parks with Andrew Taylor, "The Republican Challenge: Roping the Fiscal Strays," *CQ Weekly* (February 10, 2001): 318.
28. Congressional Budget Office, *An Analysis of the President's Budget Proposals for Fiscal year 2002,* (April 2001).
29. Lori Nitschke, "Proposals to Alter Bush's Tax Plan Multiply Despite White House Appeals for Unity," *CQ Weekly* (February, 17, 2001): 377.
30. Andrew Taylor, "Law Designed for Curbing Deficits Becomes GOP Tool for Cutting Taxes," *CQ Weekly* (April 7, 2001): 770–771.
31. *CQ Weekly,* [vote 70] (March 31, 2001): 744.

32. Daniel J. Parks, "It's the Day of the Centrist As Bush Tax Cut Takes a Hit," *CQ Weekly,* April 7, 2001: 769.
33. Glenn Kessler, "Senate Clears Budget Plan," *Washington Post,* May 11, 2001, A1.
34. Lori Nitschke, "Tax Cut Deal Reached Quickly As Appetite for Battle Fades," *CQ Weekly* (May 26, 2001): 1251.
35. *CQ Weekly*, (June 2, 2001): 1305.
36. *Congressional Quarterly Almanac 1995* (Washington, D.C.: Congressional Quarterly Inc, 1996): 2–90.
37. Benjamin Weiser, "High-Tech Firms Decry Frivolous Suits," *Washington Post* (March 7, 1995): D3.
38. *Congressional Quarterly Almanac* (1995): 2–91.
39. Ibid., 2–92.
40. Jerry Knight, "A Measure of Security on Securities Suits," *Washington Post* (December 7, 1995): B11.
41. John F. Harris and Sharon Walsh, "Clinton Vetoes Measure to Limit Securities Suits," *Washington Post* (December 20, 1995): A8.
42. Ronald F. King, "Tax Expenditures and Systematic Public Policy," *Public Budgeting and Finance* 4 (Spring 1984): 21.
43. Catherine Rudder, "Fiscal Responsibility and the Revenue Committees," in Lawrence Dodd and Bruce Oppenheimer (eds.), *Congress Reconsidered,* third edition (Washington, D.C.: Congressional Quarterly Press, 1985): 221–224.
44. Jeffrey H. Birnbaum and Alan S. Murray, *Showdown at Gucci Gulch: Lawmakers, Lobbyists, and the Unlikely Triumph of Tax Reform* (New York: Random House, 1988): 4.
45. Ibid., 124–126.
46. "Clinton's Budget: No Cover for GOP," *Congressional Quarterly Almanac* 1995 (Washington, D.C.: Congressional Quarterly Inc., 1996): 2–5.
47. "GOP Throws Down Budget Gauntlet," Ibid., 2–30.
48. See Linda Kowalcky and Lance T. LeLoup, "Congress and the Politics of Statutory Debt Limitation," *Public Administration Review* 53:1 (January/February 1993): 14–27.
49. Richard L. Berke, "Clinton's Ratings over 50% in Poll as GOP Declines," *New York Times* (December 14, 1995): A1.
50. *Congressional Quarterly Weekly Report* (January 6, 1996): 53.
51. Ibid., 53–55.
52. *Congressional Quarterly Weekly Report* (January 27, 1996): 213

CHAPTER 8

Social Welfare Policy

We can never insure one hundred percent of the population against one hundred percent of the hazards and vicissitudes of life, but we have tried to frame a law which will give some measure of protection to the average citizen and to his family against the loss of a job and against poverty-ridden old age.

—President Franklin D. Roosevelt upon Signing
the Social Security Act of 1935[1]

From countries in which a small elite rules over impoverished masses, to the "cradle-to-grave" welfare states of Scandinavia, nations adopt certain policies that affect social welfare and economic equity among their citizens. In the United States, social welfare policies are influenced by values rooted deep in the nation's history and political culture. Although Americans have a more egalitarian tradition and a less rigid class structure than many other developed nations, questions of wealth and poverty and disputes about "fairness" and "social justice" cause intense political division and policy conflict. Those issues frequently divide Republicans and Democrats, the president and Congress.

Unlike a budget, which must be approved every year, social welfare policy is subject to long periods of relative dormancy. Only extraordinary circumstances, such as the impending bankruptcy of Social Security, can create inexorable pressure to act. When such forcing mechanisms are absent, social welfare policies require long-term political mobilization to create major changes, much like civil rights.

Despite comprehensive welfare reform in 1996, many social welfare issues remain unresolved. The failure of the Clinton administration's healthcare reform left 40 million Americans still without health insurance. The other major issue is the future of Medicare and Social Security in the twenty-first century. Despite numerous commissions and studies, the effect of the impending retirement of the baby boomers on Social Security and Medicare has not been fully addressed by Congress or the president. George W. Bush proposed the partial privatization of Social Security but that is very controversial, and the disappearance of budget surpluses after the September 11 attacks make it even more difficult.

The Evolution of Social Welfare Policy

Rugged individualism, materialism, the work ethic, and respect for private property rights were important values in early America.[2] Land was plentiful and cheap compared with Europe. Because there was no nobility in America, there was no sense of "noblesse oblige": the view that the wealthy and powerful had a duty to help the poor. Respect for these values, and ease of access to opportunity, created a general belief that people were largely responsible for their own condition.[3] Accordingly, economic inequality was accepted as part of the natural order. Economic historian Louis Hacker observed: "Easy access to property led to . . . acceptance of the uneven distribution of wealth and income and the private decisions made by entrepreneurs."[4]

The industrial revolution and the transformation of the American economy from agrarian to industrial widened the gap in wealth between rich and poor. Americans were not without sympathy for the elderly, the disabled, and the infirm, who were provided for through private charity. However, not until the Progressive era at the turn of the twentieth century was serious consideration given to the view that poverty may be the result of the social and economic system. Robert Hunter's *Poverty,* published in 1904 and based on his years in the backstreet tenements of New York, suggested that although there is a poverty that "some men deserve," there is also a poverty born of "unjust social conditions which punish the good and the pure."[5]

While Otto von Bismarck was establishing a social security system in Germany in the 1880s and other nations in Europe followed suit, the dominant view in the United States continued to be that poverty was a private problem, not a public one. It took the ravages of the Great Depression in the 1930s to make the federal government accept the responsibility of protecting the social welfare of its citizens. It was a difficult transition, which required a major political realignment and the emergence of the Democratic New Deal coalition under President Franklin D. Roosevelt.

THE SOCIAL SECURITY ACT OF 1935

When he took office, Roosevelt did not have a program or specific set of policies in mind. He was clear, however, in his commitment to use the resources of government aggressively to improve the welfare of the millions of Americans who were suffering from the Depression. Roosevelt assembled a group of international scholars and experts—the "brain trust"—to study the experience of European nations that had already adopted more extensive social welfare systems. The drafters settled on two kinds of programs, contributory and noncontributory. In the contributory programs, both employers and employees paid into a trust fund and received benefits when they retired or were laid off. Anyone who contributed—regardless of income— would be entitled to benefits. Noncontributory programs provided assistance for people with no means of support, such as the elderly, the disabled, and dependent children. These programs were means-tested: Eligibility depended on income levels. Some critics felt the new law would lead to socialism, but the bill was popular on Capitol Hill and sailed through Congress virtually intact. Roosevelt signed the Social Security Act into law in 1935.

The main feature of the law was the program called *Social Security: Old Age Survivors Disability Insurance (OASDI)*. A contributory program, Social Security provided monthly payments to retirees, disabled workers, and their dependents. Determined that the program would not be dismantled by a Republican president or Congress in future years, each contributor was assigned an account (Social Security number) in which their earning history was recorded to assure benefits when needed. Social Security became extremely popular with the American public and remains so, to the point that politicians have found it difficult to modify. A national program, it is administered by the Social Security Administration in Washington. Unlike an insurance program in which contributions are held and accrue earnings, Social Security runs on a "current financing" basis. Benefits are paid out of the trust fund from current contributions, with a reserve in the fund of around six to nine months. Social Security can run into financial trouble if the commitments to pay grow faster than the contributions from those working. It has no means test.

A second contributory program created by the 1935 Act was *unemployment compensation,* designed to provide income to those who lose their jobs. It is administered by the states, and benefits vary from one state to another. The program is funded by state and federal taxes on employers and no means test is required. Benefits usually last for 26 to 39 weeks. To qualify, recipients must prove that they are actively looking for a job.

The main noncontributory program created in 1935 was *Aid to Families with Dependent Children* (AFDC), commonly called *welfare.* The program was administered by states, which determined benefit levels and eligibility. Benefits varied greatly from state to state. In 1988, benefits were five times higher in Alaska than Mississippi, for example. Originally, eligibility also varied; some states paid benefits only to one-parent families. AFDC was funded jointly by states and the federal government and was means-tested. All of this changed in 1996 with the adoption of comprehensive welfare reform. Unlike Social Security, AFDC was never very popular. It embodied the notion of a "giveaway," and recipients were often called "welfare bums" or worse. Other noncontributory means-tested programs created by the Social Security Act included Old Age Assistance (OAA), Aid to the Blind (AB), and Aid to the Disabled (AD). These were designed to help the elderly and others who were not eligible for Social Security payments. In 1974, these programs were consolidated as *Supplementary Security Income* (SSI), financed and administered by the federal government.

Much of the social welfare system in the United States was established by the landmark Social Security Act of 1935. With a highly supportive political environment and a responsive Congress, it was a clear case of presidential leadership in policymaking. Today, Social Security constitutes the single largest expenditure in the federal budget.

THE 1960s WAR ON POVERTY

Extraordinary economic circumstances prompted the expansion of social welfare policies in the 1930s. New Deal policies and World War II finally brought the U.S. economy back to full employment, and the 1940s and 1950s were decades of relative prosperity. Poverty and social problems were removed from the public mind and the policy agenda. In the 1960s, however, misery and poverty in America were rediscovered. During the 1960 presidential campaign, John F. Kennedy, traveling though West Virginia while campaigning in that state's crucial Democratic primary, was shocked at the rural poverty he observed. If elected, he promised, something would be done about it.

Once again, presidential leadership was the catalyst. Assuming the presidency after the assassination of Kennedy, Lyndon Johnson declared war on poverty and proposed "Great Society" programs to eradicate it from the country. The case of presidential leadership in this chapter deals with the Economic Opportunity Act of 1964, an important initiative that created programs significantly different from the Social Security Act 30 years earlier. Instead of cash transfers through contributory and noncontributory programs, the act established new agencies and services to help the poor directly. Programs created by the Economic Opportunity Act included the Neighborhood Youth Corps, Head Start, the Job Corps, and work-study and literacy programs. The War on Poverty created great expectations, but many of its agencies and programs were under attack only a few years later.

The Great Society program with the most significant long-term financial implications for the nation was the Medicare Act of 1965. By this time, most Western industrialized nations had adopted some form of national healthcare or government insurance to help pay healthcare costs. Lyndon Johnson's landslide election in 1964 and enhanced Democratic majorities in Congress made it possible to enact a program to provide healthcare for the elderly. With growing support in Congress for Medicare, supporters expanded it to include Medicaid—assistance to the poor for paying their medical bills. Medicare, which is not means-tested, and Medicaid, which is, are the fastest-growing items in the federal budget.

The War on Poverty was short-lived, swept aside by the Vietnam War in the late 1960s. Many of the Great Society programs were controversial, and social welfare proposals increasingly divided government along partisan lines. Richard Nixon offered a Family Assistance plan to revamp the welfare system. Surprisingly liberal for a Republican president, this plan would have set a minimum level of income below which the government would pay families rather than tax them. But despite some bipartisan appeal, the program bogged down in Congress, where Nixon lacked the clout of Roosevelt or Johnson.

THE RAPID GROWTH OF ENTITLEMENTS

After the failure of the Family Assistance plan, initiatives to restructure healthcare, Social Security, or the welfare system proved impossible to pass. The most important development in the 1970s in social welfare was the rapid growth of entitlements, which programs like Social Security and Medicare came to be called. Entitlements—benefits guaranteed to recipients if they meet certain eligibility requirements—mushroomed from $65 billion in 1970 to $267 billion in 1980, an increase of over 400 percent.[6] As a share of the budget, social welfare entitlements increased from 33 percent of outlays in 1970 to 47 percent in 1980. Part of the increase was a result of high inflation in the 1970s, but much of the growth was attributable to the liberalization and expansion of programs. Social Security benefits were "indexed" in 1972: Benefits automatically increased as the consumer price index rose. The expansion of benefits put a financial strain on the Social Security trust fund, requiring a major increase in payroll taxes in 1977. Food stamps, an entitlement begun in the late 1960s, rose 1,000 percent in a decade. Conservatives became concerned about the exploding costs of social welfare programs.

Ronald Reagan's economic and budget proposals in 1981 included plans to curtail entitlement growth. Yet the president was careful to claim that the "social safety net" would be protected, particularly the popular Social Security program. The administration pledged to eliminate unintended benefits, reduce benefits for middle- and upper-income recipients, and consolidate and eliminate less-crucial programs. House Democrats blocked some of the cuts, but the administration succeeded in restricting eligibility for food stamps, tightening eligibility for AFDC, eliminating extended unemployment compensation benefits, increasing deductible copayments for Medicare recipients, cutting federal Medicaid reimbursements to the states, and eliminating Social Security benefits for college students. Nonetheless, the administration was disappointed in the reductions it had achieved.[7] Congress rejected most of the subsequent cuts proposed by the Reagan administration through the 1980s, and as deficits grew, budget issues became increasingly divisive.

Democrats accused the administration of trying to balance the budget on the backs of the poor. Despite a tax increase in 1977, the Social Security system was again threatened with bankruptcy in the early 1980s. Congressional Democrats used the Social Security issue in election campaigns, accusing Republicans of attempting to cut benefits to the elderly. A proposal floated by the administration in 1981 to make major cuts in Social Security resulted in an outcry from senior citizens and congressional Democrats. The issue was used against Republicans again in the 1982 midterm elections. The Social Security bailout case in this chapter explores in detail how it took extraordinary resolution, using a bipartisan commission, to break the deadlock and restore the financial solvency of the system.

Throughout the 1990s, entitlement spending, particularly for healthcare, increased far more rapidly than the rest of the budget. The election of Bill Clinton in 1992 put reforms much more ambitious than Medicare reform on the policy agenda.

HEALTHCARE REFORM

Despite the fact that the Democrats controlled both Congress and the presidency for the first time in 12 years, President Clinton and Congress could not agree on a system to guarantee healthcare to all Americans. Advances in medical technology have given the United States the most sophisticated healthcare system in the world, but also the most expensive. Healthcare spending, including both public and private, is some 13 percent of the gross domestic product (GDP) and rising. In addition to rising costs, 38 million people or 15 percent of the population, have no health insurance at all.

Clinton named his wife, Hillary Rodham Clinton, to head the administration task force to formulate healthcare reform. The process of sorting through all the expert recommendations took over nine months. The range of options ran from a single-payer system (such as in Canada) to more modest reforms, using existing private insurance and Medicare. The administration chose the middle ground and in late 1993 unveiled its 1,200-page plan. It would have done several things:

- Require all employers to provide healthcare insurance for their workers (75 percent already did).
- Create a series of purchasing alliances in the states that would operate like health maintenance organizations (HMOs) to provide competition and reduce costs.
- Create a National Health Board to monitor the system and impose cost controls if needed.
- Expand Medicare to cover the poor and unemployed and cover the cost of prescriptions for senior citizens.

In his 1994 State of the Union address, Clinton dramatically pulled out a pen and promised to veto any bill that would not provide universal healthcare coverage. Republicans accused Clinton of nothing less than a "government takeover of healthcare." A coalition of big insurance companies, hospitals, and doctors launched a massive national media campaign against the plan.[8] The blitz of negative spots featured "Harry and Louise," Mr. and Mrs. Average American, talking about rationing of services, losing choice, and government takeover. Support for the president's plan dwindled. Even Democrats largely ignored the administration's proposal and no bill ever even came up for a vote.

The failure of healthcare reform is important in the evolution of social welfare policy in the United States. The political environment was initially supportive of healthcare reform, with the public strongly supporting both universal coverage and mandatory employer participation. But opponents tapped into deep public cynicism and mistrust of government.[9] There were serious flaws in the policy design, a plan that was overly complex and bureaucratic. The process of presidential formulation had been closed, not allowing potential opponents to participate. Unsuccessful healthcare reform contributed to Clinton's falling public support and the Republican

sweep in the 1994 elections. Ironically, two years later, under the divided government that resulted from those elections, the most significant social welfare policy
change in 30 years emerged: comprehensive welfare reform

The Social Welfare Policy Environment

WEALTH AND POVERTY IN THE UNITED STATES

The context for presidential-congressional policymaking in social welfare begins
with deprivation in American society: poverty, hunger, homelessness, and inadequate healthcare. The gap between rich and poor—measured by the distribution of
wealth and income—is another potentially important environmental factor. The federal government has had an official definition of poverty since 1964, when the
Social Security Administration computed the "poverty line" at an income level three
times the cost of an economy food plan (assuming the poor spend one-third of their
income on food).[10] The figure was $3,000 for a family of four in 1964 compared
with $17,603 in 2000.[11] Under the official definition, the percentage of Americans
living below the poverty line between 1959 (measured retroactively) and 2000 is
shown in Figure 8.1. The figure shows that much progress in eliminating poverty has
taken place in the last 40 years, reducing rates from 22.4 percent in 1959 to 11.3 percent in 2000. This still leaves more than 30 million Americans living below the
poverty line today, however.

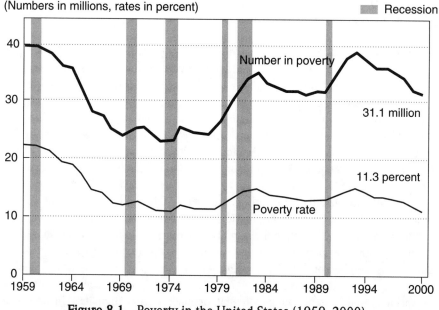

Figure 8.1   Poverty in the United States (1959–2000).

Source: U.S. Bureau of the Census, *Poverty in the United States 2000* (2001).

The incidence of poverty varies in accordance with demographic characteristics such as race, age, gender, and type of family unit.[12] Blacks are three times more likely than whites to live in poverty, and Hispanics twice as likely. Since the early 1970s, a feminization of poverty has occurred, measured by the number of single-parent households headed by a female. By the 1980s, almost half of these households were below the poverty line. More than half of the poor in the United States are children. Conversely, poverty rates for the elderly have dropped sharply since 1970. The elderly now constitute the most affluent age cohort in the country. With welfare reform and a robust economy, the number of welfare recipients has plummeted around the country from 12.8 million when welfare reform passed in 1996 to around half that by 2002. Welfare reform also reduced the number of Americans who received food stamps.[13]

At the same time that the incidence of poverty has fallen, the gap between rich and poor in the United States has widened.[14] Wealth (the amount of money and other assets owned) is less equitably distributed than income. The top 10 percent of the population owns one-third of the nation's private wealth and owns 62 percent of all corporate stock. In 1970, the richest 1 percent of families in the United States held 27 percent of the wealth. By 1995, the figure had grown to 36 percent, near the peak share attained in 1929. At the bottom of the economic ladder, the poorest 10 percent of the population owed more than they owned. The gap between rich and poor has steadily increased since 1970.

PUBLIC ATTITUDES AND PARTISAN DIVISIONS

Despite these inequities, the American public does *not* generally support welfare programs or policies to redistribute income from the rich to the poor. Compared to citizens of other nations, Americans do not believe it is the responsibility of the government to guarantee a minimum income or pursue policies that would significantly redistribute income.[15] Despite the underclass, the homeless, and families without health insurance, the vast majority of Americans supported the elimination of AFDC. Conversely, support for Social Security is nearly unanimous.

For decades, Republicans and Democrats have had sharply different social welfare agendas. Conservative opposition to the liberal "welfare state" took shape during the implementation of Roosevelt's New Deal. Since the 1930s, social welfare policies have also often reflected deep divisions between the parties. Studies of roll-call voting in Congress showed pronounced partisanship on social welfare policy issues.[16] After the 1972 campaign, when Nixon attacked Democratic nominee George McGovern's guaranteed income plan, partisan and ideological cleavages between branches widened.

The debate heated up in the 1980s, when the failures of the War on Poverty were attacked. Charles Murray created a stir with his book, *Losing Ground,* which argued that the condition of poor people—particularly blacks—had worsened during the 1960s and 1970s despite the rapid increase in federal spending.[17] Michael Harrington, who helped launch the War on Poverty, argued that Murray ignored the reduction in poverty among the elderly, improvements in healthcare, and gains in nutrition.[18] John Schwartz's study, *America's Hidden Success,* concluded that far from causing more poverty, the programs had led to dramatic improvements in a number of areas.[19]

The election of Democrat Bill Clinton in 1992 began to change the nature of partisan and ideological divisions on social welfare policy. As governor of Arkansas, Clinton had championed welfare reform, and pledged during his presidential campaign to "end welfare as we know it." As he had with the balanced budget and some other issues, Clinton moved to the center, partially co-opting a traditional Republican issue. As welfare reform was debated in the 1990s, this political shift caused divisions within the Democratic party. Although more moderate Democrats were glad to be on the right side of a popular issue, traditional liberals decried the president's abandonment of the poor.

The successful bipartisan collaboration on welfare reform did not depoliticize social welfare issues. Democrats had long played on public fears that Republicans would make cuts in the popular entitlements for the elderly—Social Security and Medicare. When the budget was balanced in 1998, more attention was paid to the financial viability of these two large programs. With the election of George W. Bush in 2000, both parties tried to inoculate themselves by promising not to touch the Social Security trust fund surplus. This continued through 2001 until the September 11 attacks and the recession made it less important to protect the surplus than to deal with the war against terrorism and economic recovery.

CONCERN FOR THE FUTURE OF MEDICARE AND SOCIAL SECURITY

The fact that Social Security and Medicare are such popular programs has often stifled debate and made it more difficult to develop responsible long-term solutions. In 2001, Social Security was the largest government expenditure, totaling $429 billion or 23 percent of federal spending. Adding Medicare and Medicaid, total expenditures were $798 billion or 48.3 percent of all outlays.[20] These figures are projected to increase rapidly as the baby boom generation prepares to retire. In 1996, spending for these two entitlements was equivalent to 7 percent of the nation's GDP. By the year 2030, Congressional Budget Office projections show that share of the economy doubling to 14 percent.[21] In 2000, 3.4 workers supported every Social Security recipient. In 2030 this will drop to 2.1 workers and in 2075 to only 1.9 workers for every recipient.[22] This means that the younger generations will be required to pay significantly more without much assurance that comparable benefit levels will be available when they retire. Figure 8.2 shows the projected increases in spending for Medicare, Medicaid, and Social Security between 2000 and 2030 as a proportion of GDP.

In May of 2001, George W. Bush established a 16-member commission "to study and report . . . specific recommendations to preserve Social Security for seniors while building wealth for younger Americans."[23] Bush urged the commission to come up with a financially viable means of allowing some portion of Social Security to be privatized, permitting younger workers to invest a portion of their contributions and

**Percent
of GDP**

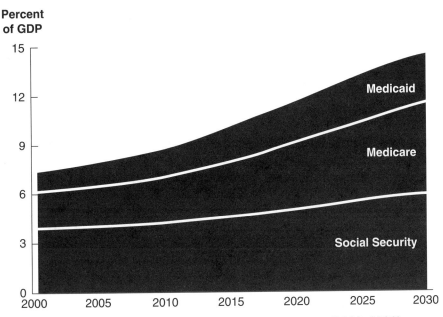

Figure 8.2 Projected Growth in Major Entitlements (2000–2030).

Source: Congressional Budget Office (October 2000 estimates).

receive higher returns. Knowing that this issue was potential dynamite, Bush hoped that the commission would provide some political cover for his administration to go forward. The commission was unable to agree on a single recommendation, and when they reported in late 2001, provided three possible plans. However, the environment for reform was considerably different than it had been a year before. First, the collapse of the stock markets in 2000 and 2001 had soured many investors on the lure of privatized Social Security accounts. Second, the war on terrorism and the recession eliminated the budget surplus that would have been needed to implement some of the reforms. Third, the terrorist attacks of September 11 had resulted in increased trust in government and somewhat blunted the impetus to take the most respected program of all—Social Security—from the hands of the government to the private sector. These issues and the future viability of Social Security and Medicare will continue to pose a challenge to the president and Congress throughout the 2000s.

Making Social Welfare Policy

Which branch shapes social welfare policy? Between 1933 and 1969, four of five presidents were Democrats. Leadership in social welfare emanated most frequently from the presidency, particularly Roosevelt, Truman, and Johnson. As in other policy areas, compared with earlier years, today there is more of an equal balance between congressional and presidential initiatives.

Presidents may create ad hoc organizations within the presidency to accomplish their goals as George W. Bush did. President Clinton engaged a massive task force to develop his plans for healthcare reform. President Johnson also assembled a high-powered team to develop the War on Poverty. Most frequently, policy initiatives are more modest and handled through a subset of domestic policy advisors.

Party leaders in Congress have assumed a critical role in formulating social welfare policy and responses to presidential initiatives. Key committees in Congress include the House Ways and Means Committee and the Senate Finance Committee, which have jurisdiction over Social Security, Medicare, Medicaid, and most entitlements. Banking committees in the House and Senate, the House Education and Labor Committee, and the Senate Labor and Human Resources Committee also play important roles in social welfare legislation. In the face of conflict and deadlock, smaller groups of party and committee leaders play an enhanced role in policymaking.

Other actors are important in the social welfare policy process. The growth of social welfare programs since the 1930s created a large bureaucracy in the federal executive branch. The Department of Health, Education, and Welfare (HEW) was created in 1953 to administer programs. It was divided into the Department of Education and the Department of Health and Human Services (HHS, eliminating the politically troublesome word *welfare* from the title) in 1979. The states have become key players in making national policy in the area of social welfare. States like Wisconsin were instrumental as policy laboratories in experimenting with various workfare programs and welfare reform. Operating through various organizations, such as the National Governors' Conference, states have had significant policy impact.

Social Security and Medicare programs are supported by influential clientele groups. The 30 million senior citizens are well organized and powerful, a potent voting bloc. Groups such as AARP (American Association of Retired Persons), the National Committee to Preserve Social Security and Medicare, and other seniors' groups flood the Hill with mail and lobbyists. Welfare mothers, in contrast, are fewer in numbers, unorganized, and relatively powerless. Their cause remains unpopular with the general public, which makes legislators skittish about any welfare issues. The four cases that follow show in more detail the changing role and responsibilities of various participants and the different patterns of legislative-executive policymaking in the social welfare arena.

Presidential Leadership:
The Economic Opportunity Act (1964)

Weeks after assuming the presidency following the assassination of John F. Kennedy, President Lyndon Johnson wanted to launch his presidency with a bold initiative—one that bore his imprimatur, not Kennedy's. Since Kennedy's domestic agenda was mostly stalled on Capitol Hill, there was a tendency to see Johnson's program as a compendium of unfinished business.[24] Despite facing the same congressional majorities, Johnson recognized that he benefited from a mood of national unity. In addition, he brought to the White House his record for effective legislative leadership from his tenure as Senate Majority Leader during the 1950s. With an election only 10 months away, members of Congress were mindful of their own electoral fortunes as they considered new social welfare legislation.

Johnson signaled his decision to launch a War on Poverty on January 5, 1964, only three days before his State of the Union address to a joint session of Congress. The White House released a three-page statement on a task force report entitled, "One-Third of a Nation," promising a "program to attack the roots of poverty."[25] The report was authored by Daniel P. Moynihan, an undersecretary of Labor appointed by Kennedy. Three days later, in his nationally televised address, Johnson declared his antipoverty goals to the nation.

Anxious to get his proposals to Congress, Johnson ordered his staff into high gear to produce a plan. Several Kennedy proposals were still pending in Congress, including the Youth Employment Act and a bill for a domestic Peace Corps. Johnson wanted a more comprehensive program to attack the roots of poverty and, for political reasons, one that was uniquely his. On January 31, the president named Sargent Shriver (Kennedy's brother-in-law) to serve as his special assistant to develop the War on Poverty proposals. Shriver, highly successful as head of the Peace Corps, had a "can-do" reputation of innovation and effective public relations. Shriver chose Moynihan, Adam Yarmolinsky from the Defense Department, and James Sundquist from the Department of Agriculture to join his task force in drafting the legislation.[26]

John Donovan, who chronicled the passage of the War on Poverty, noted the absence of any Texas influence in the key group, which was a "team of Eastern liberal intellectual-politicians under the leadership of a member of the Kennedy family."[27] Although other agencies and administration figures had input into the process, the Shriver task force took charge. Suspicious of old-line bureaucratic interests, the drafters sought a way to administer the program that would avoid agency turf battles. They suggested creating a new agency—staffed by younger, more aggressive personnel—rather than assigning new functions to an existing department.[28] This was a potential threat to the Department of Labor, HEW, and other agencies, but the task force had strong presidential backing. Eventually a new entity, the Office of Economic Opportunity (OEO), located in the Executive Office of the President and reporting directly to the president, would administer the poverty program.

The Economic Opportunity Act's approach to reducing poverty was fundamentally different from that of the Social Security Act of 30 years earlier. Rather than create entitlements, the act provided a number of services and programs to serve the poor directly.[29] Title I established three youth programs that were similar to the Kennedy programs already pending. A new addition was a work-study program to aid college students. Title II, urban and rural community action programs (CAPs), was an entirely new creation and a dramatic policy innovation. Title III of the act was a rural poverty program, authorizing the OEO to make grants to low-income rural families. Title IV allowed the OEO director to make loans to employers to create stable jobs for long-term unemployed and low-income families. Title V, "Family

Unity through Jobs," provided for grants to carry out pilot job training and work projects for AFDC recipients. Title VI created the Office of Economic Opportunity to administer and coordinate the programs.

Title II contained the most radical new element of the administration plan. CAPs were programs that:

1. Mobilized both public and private resources to attack poverty
2. Provided direct services and assistance to the poor
3. Would include "maximum feasible participation" of the poor
4. Would be administered by a nonprofit group rather than by existing agencies.[30]

The concept of a CAP was inherently "anti-establishment," creating competing centers of power in local government to obtain resources and develop new programs. Although easily approved by Congress, CAPs would prove to be the most controversial part of the new law.

The Economic Opportunity Act was conceived of and written in a matter of weeks, and sent to Capitol Hill on March 16, 1964. Congress responded quickly. An ad hoc subcommittee of the House Education and Labor Committee opened hearings on the bill the next day, with Adam Clayton Powell (D-N.Y.) as chair. The bill moved quickly through committee; Republican efforts to make changes in the legislation were turned aside. The committee had a tradition of division between majority and minority factions, but rarely were Republicans completely ignored as they were with this bill.[31] In three weeks of hearings, dozens of witnesses testified in favor of the bill, with only a handful of opponents appearing before the subcommittee. Donovan wrote, "Testimony was largely in terms of generalities; the questioning, by and large, was anything but probing."[32] The potentially divisive CAPs received scant attention.

Conservative Congressman Phil Landrum (D-Ga.) was chosen to manage the bill on the House floor. This decision troubled some civil rights and labor groups, but the administration, confident that northern liberals would support the president's program, sought to garner support from southern Democrats. With an election approaching, the Democratic administration was not bothered by Republican opposition to the bill. Congress made some changes in the bill, but in less important titles. Legislators added two new programs for adult literacy and assistance for migrant farm workers. The Senate made some changes to the provisions dealing with rural poverty programs.

Aided by aggressive lobbying, the Economic Opportunity Act sailed through the same Congress that bottled up less ambitious programs the year before under President Kennedy. The Senate adopted the bill on July 23 by a comfortable 61-to-34 margin,[33] and two weeks later, the House passed the bill by 226 to 185. Of the 100 southern Democrats, 60 supported the administration. Republicans opposed the bill 22 to 145. There was a price to be paid for the support of southern Democrats.

Adam Yarmolinsky, one of the key architects of the administration program, managed to antagonize several crucial Democrats. To assure southern votes, Shriver had to agree to exclude Yarmolinsky from the Office of Economic Opportunity once it was organized.[34]

What factors produced presidential leadership of policymaking in this case? The Economic Opportunity Act was reminiscent of Roosevelt's hundred days. It was drafted in the executive branch and enacted by Congress within months, with few revisions. Observers of the process concluded, "Congress was asked not to draft the War on Poverty, but rather, to ratify a fully prepared administration program, and invited, though hardly encouraged, to propose marginal changes."[35] Although the majorities in Congress were the same as they had been in 1963, the political environment and presidential leadership had changed.

What were the results of the Economic Opportunity Act? Clearly, the policy was both timely and decisive. Despite the fact that it was a dramatic new approach to poverty, the bill was written in a matter of weeks and passed with minimal changes in a matter of months. Yet only a few years later, the OEO was under attack and even its most ardent supporters were disappointed. The debate over its effectiveness continues today, including serious questions about the design of the policy.

Congressional Leadership: Catastrophic Healthcare Insurance (1988–1989)

"Older Americans worry about two things—their finances and their health," said HHS Secretary Otis Bowen in 1987, "and wonder which will run out first."[36] As healthcare costs spiraled in the 1980s, millions of citizens and their families faced financial ruin in case of catastrophic illness. Five percent of the population (disproportionately senior citizens) account for around 50 percent of all public and private healthcare costs in the United States. Under Medicare rules, as the costs of acute care for the elderly mounted, the proportion paid by the government fell. After 60 days in the hospital, in 1987, beneficiaries had to make a copayment of $130 a day.[37] The copayment rose to $260 after 90 days, and Medicare payments ceased altogether after 150 days. Many of the more affluent elderly supplemented their healthcare coverage with private "medigap" policies, but the majority were vulnerable to catastrophic illness.

Congress had long wanted to do something about the growing problem. The obstacles were the budget crisis of the 1980s and doubt that President Reagan would support the expansion of any social welfare programs. Legislators saw their opening in the president's 1986 State of the Union address. Reagan directed the secretary of Health and Human Services to develop recommendations "on how the private sector and government can work together to address the problems of affordable insurance for those whose life savings would otherwise be threatened when catastrophic illness strikes."[38] Secretary Bowen issued a report on November 20, 1986, recommending an expansion of Medicare coverage to cap at $2,000 per year the amount that any recipient would have to pay out of pocket for covered services.

Capitol Hill received the Bowen report more enthusiastically than the White House. The administration was deeply divided over the recommendations; conservatives were adamantly opposed to a government program that would supplant private insurance. Embroiled in the Iran–Contra affair and recovering from prostate surgery, Reagan did nothing to resolve the controversy within his own administration. In his 1987 State of the Union address, he promised only to send legislation to Congress at some unspecified date in the future. Because there was significant Republican and Democratic support for the concept, Congress took the lead on catastrophic healthcare coverage.

In 1987, Medicare helped 28 million elderly and 3 million disabled persons cope with their healthcare costs. Medicare part A—the Hospital Insurance program—helps pay for inpatient hospital or skilled nursing care. Anyone over 65 eligible for Social Security benefits is automatically eligible for Medicare part A benefits. Persons over age 65 not eligible may purchase coverage. The program is financed by an earmarked percentage of the Social Security payroll tax. Medicare part B—the Supplemental Medical Insurance program—is the optional portion of Medicare, in which 98 percent of those eligible choose to participate. Part B pays 80 percent of doctor bills and outpatient charges after an annual deductible is paid. The premium in 1987 was $17.90 per month, which covered only one-fourth of the government's cost. The rest of part B coverage is paid out of general revenues.

Jurisdiction over Medicare in the House of Representatives was shared between the Ways and Means and the Energy and Commerce Committees. In hearings and markup during the spring of 1987, both panels significantly expanded the coverage and benefits of the catastrophic illness legislation. H.R. 2470 provided acute-care coverage, contained a prescription drug benefit, created a "respite care" benefit for families caring for a seriously ill patient, and increased coverage for outpatient mental health, nursing home, home health, and hospice care.[39] The bill would cap out-of-pocket expenses by beneficiaries at less than $1,700 per year. Despite some concerns about the long-term costs, the House approved the bill on July 22, 1987, by a comfortable 302-to-127 margin.

The Senate had begun working on its own version of catastrophic healthcare legislation, S 1127, at about the same time as the House. The Senate Finance Committee version of the bill had one fundamental difference from the House version: It made catastrophic coverage entirely voluntary. By dropping Medicare part B coverage, enrollees could avoid paying any new premiums. In contrast, under the House bill, recipients in higher tax brackets would have to pay extra for part A hospital benefits, even if they dropped part B coverage. Despite some continued concerns about the cost of the bill, the Senate passed the legislation on October 27 by a vote of 86 to 11.[40]

House–Senate conferees appointed to work out differences in the two versions of the bills began meeting in February 1988. Throughout 1987, catastrophic healthcare coverage had been extremely popular (what some members call a "motherhood" bill), attracting strong bipartisan support with little White House opposition. As the conference committee began work, however, members became increasingly irritated by several intense lobbying efforts launched against the bill. Interest groups representing the elderly split over the issue. Although AARP supported catastrophic coverage, the National Committee to Preserve Social Security, headed by James Roosevelt, son of President Franklin D. Roosevelt, urged its members to oppose the bill. The National Committee already had a nasty reputation on Capitol Hill for using inflammatory tactics to frighten the elderly in order to fill its own coffers.[41] Opposition also came from the drug industry. Still, members of Congress remained broadly supportive of the concept despite vigorous lobbying efforts on the other side.

By June, conferees had reached an agreement, adopting House provisions instead of making the coverage voluntary. Because of deficit jitters, proponents all along had wanted a program that financed itself. This was accomplished by increasing the Medicare part B premiums over a five-year period and assessing the highest charges on those most able to afford it. The 60 percent of senior citizens who paid less than $150 in federal income taxes per year were required to pay only a small supplemental premium. The 40 percent with higher incomes were required to pay larger premiums. Those with the highest incomes (who paid more than $3,750 a year in income taxes) would pay an extra $800 per year in premiums, increasing to $1,050 per year by 1993. The most affluent group required to pay the maximum fees constituted fewer than 6 percent of all Americans over 65.[42]

Conferees agreed that this financing formula was both fair and fiscally responsible, and House and Senate members overwhelmingly agreed. On June 2, the House approved the catastrophic insurance bill by a vote of 328 to 72. Key Republican leaders, including Minority Leader Robert Michel, urged colleagues to support the legislation. Ways and Means Chairman Dan Rostenkowski noted that the bill "strikes a good balance between meeting the medical needs of the elderly and recognizing the limits on their ability to finance additional Medicare costs."[43] A week later, the Senate also ratified the conference report in a bipartisan vote of 86 to 11. In a July 1 ceremony in the Rose Garden, President Reagan signed the bill, stating that it will "help remove a terrible threat from the lives of elderly and disabled Americans."[44]

But the story of catastrophic healthcare coverage did not end with the signing ceremony. Many elderly citizens wanted the coverage but did not want to have to pay for it. Sponsors of the legislation, after years of effort to enact it, were confused. "I think most of the complaints are from people who don't understand it," one House Democratic sponsor noted.[45] But as the new premiums were assessed, the complaints in 1988 grew to an uproar from vocal senior citizens in 1989. Several bills were introduced in the 101st Congress to change the financing of catastrophic healthcare benefits, and others would have repealed the program altogether. Members went back to their districts only to be assailed about the program from every quarter. "It's the only issue out there," said one member after a series of town meetings in his district, which he called his "catastrophic tour."[46] Elderly demonstrators confronted Dan Rostenkowski after a meeting on the issue at a senior citizens' center. The elderly protestors, carrying placards, blocked his car and called him "Rottenkowski." Coverage of the scene on the national news and photos in the *New York Times* and *Newsweek* magnified public awareness of the controversy.

The tactics of Roosevelt's National Committee continued to infuriate Congress. In its mailings, the group urged its 5 million members to insist that Congress repeal the "seniors-only surtax."[47] By fall, supporters in both parties were in full retreat as repeal bills advanced in both the House and Senate. Members who continued to support the bill were incensed that those who could most afford the premiums were insensitive to the needs of the vast majority of low-income elderly who desperately needed the coverage. Ironically, because of the barrage of negative publicity, even those who paid the smallest premiums were calling for repeal. Many members simply had had enough. Representative Henry Waxman (D-Calif.) claimed that House members ultimately voted to repeal catastrophic coverage because they felt the elderly "were ungrateful, . . . so let them stew in their own juices."[48]

On October 4, 1989, the House voted to repeal the surtax and eliminate the expanded Medicare benefits. Two days later, the Senate voted 99 to 0 to eliminate the surtax but preserve some limited benefits. Six weeks later, the Senate finally gave up on the idea of preserving any of the additional benefits and accepted the House version. At 1:52 A.M. on November 22, 1989, the Senate joined with the House and voted to repeal Public Law 100–360. The Medicare Catastrophic Coverage Act, passed with such fanfare only 16 months earlier, was wiped off the books.

How did a pattern of congressional leadership occur? Congress appeared to have bipartisan support to solve a growing policy problem that also seemed to be a good political issue. The Reagan administration was internally divided and content to let Congress work its will. This was true even more so during the repeal; the Bush administration, which had taken office six months after the law had passed, stayed on the sidelines, out of the fray. Although HHS Secretary Louis Sullivan tried to preserve some of the benefits, the White House refused to take a position on the repeal, angering some on Capitol Hill. "I guess they don't have a dog in this fight," said one member. "They haven't even been involved enough to be ambivalent," quipped another.[49]

What were the results of the enactment and repeal of catastrophic healthcare? The case shows that Congress as a representative institution can lead policymaking but remains vulnerable to powerful, vocal interests. Congress lacks the "bully pulpit" of the president that can be used to inform, educate, and lead the public. In the end, Congress took the politically expedient way out. "By repealing the legislation, we have not repealed the problem," said Senate Majority Leader George Mitchell.

"The problem is bad and getting worse."[50] As of 2002, little progress had been made on this issue.

Cooperation/Consensus: Comprehensive Welfare Reform (1996)

President Bill Clinton's claim to be a "new Democrat" rested in part on his determination to reform welfare—a program developed by FDR and protected by Democrats. In the 1992 campaign, Clinton promised to "end welfare as we know it." Over the next two years, however, welfare reform took a backseat to deficit reduction and healthcare reform on his domestic agenda. Leadership on welfare reform would change dramatically with the election of a Republican Congress in 1994, which promised to overhaul welfare and turn it over to the states. Over the next year and a half, despite extreme partisanship, two presidential vetoes, and political posturing for the 1996 elections, Clinton and the Congress finally found a way to cooperate. On August 22, 1996, Clinton signed the Personal Responsibility and Work Opportunity Reconciliation Act of 1996, eliminating the federal entitlement to AFDC after 61 years.[51] It is a case that had all the markings of a political deadlock, but in the end, both sides found enough common ground to reach a compromise.

Clinton's credentials in welfare reform went back to his days as governor of Arkansas, where as a leader of the National Governors' Association, he lobbied Congress for the passage of the 1988 Family Support Act. Yet as president, he did not introduce a welfare reform plan until June 1994. The administration's bill required welfare recipients to work for their benefits and limited the amount of time that anyone could remain on welfare. The bill languished during the summer of 1994 as Republican delaying tactics ground legislative business to a halt. During the midterm election campaigns, Republicans claimed that Clinton had done little and had not kept his welfare reform promises.

After the 1994 elections, the Republican Congress put welfare reform at the top of its legislative priorities as part of the "Contract with America." The House moved quickly with a bill that was more radical and comprehensive than Clinton's.[52] The Republican plan denied benefits to unwed mothers, required states to cut off benefits after a certain time limit, capped spending for other antipoverty programs, and turned welfare over to the states. In his State of the Union address in January 1995, Clinton warned Congress that he would oppose any welfare reform proposal that was too punitive to the poor, especially children. During the first 100 days of the 104th Congress, House Republicans put welfare reform on the fast track. On March 24, the House passed H.R. 4 by a vote of 234 to 199, split largely along party lines. It converted AFDC into a block grant for states, allowing them to reduce their own source spending on welfare. The bill required recipients to find work within two years and be limited to five years of payments over their lifetime. Benefits for legal aliens were curtailed, and it became harder for children with behavioral disorders to qualify for Supplemental Security Income. President Clinton attacked the bill as "weak on work and tough on children."[53]

Progress in 1995 was slower in the Senate, where the approach was somewhat more moderate than in the House. In May, the Senate Finance Committee approved a bill that largely followed the framework of the House bill, but softened some of the provisions. The Labor and Human Resources Committee and the Agriculture Committee also took up parts of the welfare reform package. The Senate did not limit benefits to legal aliens, unwed mothers, and children born to welfare recipients. These differences with the House bill caused internal splits among the Senate Republicans, and Majority Leader Dole delayed bringing the bill to the floor for several months. Warning of a presidential veto of the Republican version, Senate Democrats readied their own welfare reform bill in hopes of having some influence on the legislation. Some of these provisions were included in the Senate bill, providing the basis for more bipartisanship than in the House. After two weeks of floor debate in September, the Senate passed its version of welfare reform 87 to 12.[54] The bill then headed for conference committee.

The conference began on October 24 with Republicans committed to getting a bill to the president's desk by the end of the year. The House and Senate versions shared the same basic premise of ending the federal entitlement and turning welfare over to the states, but differed on many significant details. Democrats were largely excluded from the negotiations. Parliamentary maneuvers abounded in the Senate, as the Republican leaders tried to attach welfare reform to the massive reconciliation bill that was working its way through Congress. Democrats, however, were able to use budget rules to strike certain provisions that they opposed.[55] They wanted welfare reform as a freestanding bill rather than under reconciliation, where rules would not permit them to filibuster the bill. Clinton continued to warn Republicans that he would veto a bill that was too punitive. Republicans continued to push welfare reform both through budget reconciliation and a freestanding bill.

On December 6, 1995, Clinton vetoed the massive reconciliation bill, leaving the freestanding bill as the remaining vehicle for welfare reform. Conferees finally reached agreement on that bill in the hectic days before the Christmas holidays. The House passed the bill 245 to 178 on December 21, while Senate approval by a vote of 52 to 47 came the next day. Believing that the Senate had accepted too many of the harsher House provisions, Senate Democrats turned against the conference report. On January 9, 1996, Clinton kept his promise and vetoed the bill, calling it "tough on children and at odds with my central goal of moving people from welfare to work."[56] The issue seemed deadlocked, with prospects for compromise looking dim.

When Clinton gave his State of the Union address in January of 1996, the political environment had changed drastically from the year before. He had survived the Republican onslaught in 1995 and saw his popularity rising after congressional Republicans were blamed for the unpopular government shutdowns. He challenged Congress to develop a bipartisan welfare reform bill, promising to sign it immediately. In February, the National Governors' Association endorsed the notion of reforming welfare together with Medicaid.[57] Congressional Republicans picked up on the idea, but the White House opposed it. As the presidential primary season gained steam, eventual Republican nominee Bob Dole was still Senate Majority Leader. He insisted that welfare and Medicaid reform be linked despite Clinton's repeated veto threats. Dole's view was that a third Clinton veto of welfare reform was more helpful to him in the presidential campaign than sending up a bill that Clinton could sign and take partial credit.

His campaign lagging, Dole resigned from the Senate in June to run for president full-time. New Majority Leader Trent Lott (R-Miss.) was under increasing pressure from Republican senators to get a bill passed that they could take credit for in the fall campaign. Republican leaders conceded, dropping their insistence that Medicaid reform be tied to welfare reform. Despite the partisan posturing that prevailed as the political conventions and fall elections neared, the prospects for cooperation and compromise began to improve. Members of both parties believed that actually achieving meaningful welfare reform would help them more than continued deadlock. A new House–Senate conference committee moved toward the more moderate Senate version of the bill, gathering some Democratic support. The House adopted the conference report on July 31 by a vote of 328 to 101. In a last-gasp effort to scuttle welfare reform, liberal Democrats continued to lobby hard for another veto. At a Cabinet meeting that day, however, Clinton announced that he would sign the bill despite opposing certain provisions. Knowing that it would become law, the Senate passed the bill on August 1 by a vote of 74 to 24. In both houses, Republicans were nearly unanimous in support, whereas about half of the Democrats voted for welfare reform.

Clinton signed the bill into law on August 22, 1996. It was the most sweeping overhaul of the welfare system since its creation in 1935. The final version of the bill turned welfare over to the states, with federal assistance in funding coming in the form of block grants. Recipients had to find work within two years or less, depending on state law, and were limited to a lifetime maximum of five years of benefits. Clinton signed despite his opposition to limits of benefits to legal aliens and cuts in food stamp eligibility. He promised to seek legislation to overturn those provisions. The bill would save the federal government $55 billion over five years, contributing to deficit reduction. At the end of his first term, Clinton was able to tell the voters that he had kept his promise about welfare.

How did the pattern of cooperation working through the regular legislative process finally emerge after a history of partisanship and deadlock? Much of it had to do with the perceptions of the political environment by the president and congressional members, as well as their own political interests. Welfare reform was an extremely popular issue. Both parties ultimately decided that it was better to divide credit for the bill rather than share blame for failure. Clinton had to resist significant pressure within his own party—he was denounced by a number of liberal Democrats. The change in Senate leadership also played a role, since Majority Leader Lott proved more willing to clear legislation, despite the campaigns, than Dole had.

Congressional Republicans played a greater role in shaping the overall legislation, but through the use of the veto and constant negotiation, the Clinton administration was able to eliminate some of the most onerous provisions. The budget rules also factored into facilitating passage. The final bill was enacted as a reconciliation bill, providing important procedural safeguards from delaying tactics, particularly in the Senate. In the end, the bill passed because enough of a bipartisan agreement had emerged on the broad outlines of welfare reform.

What are the consequences of comprehensive welfare reform? Initial results were impressive. Within the first year of enactment, welfare rolls around the states had dropped as much as 40 percent. Much of that decline occurred before the bill was actually passed, but came in anticipation of sharp new restrictions.[58] By 1997, 40 states had submitted new welfare plans to the federal government, 37 of which were approved under the new law. Some of these were even tougher than the federal requirements, requiring less time to find work and less than five years of lifetime benefits. By 2001, the number of welfare recipients had nearly fallen in half, thanks to a vibrant economy. But with a recession and many states reaching their five-year deadlines, further progress will be very difficult. The most employable welfare recipients got jobs first, leaving the more hard-core underclass yet to find work. Although the long-term impact of welfare reform is not yet certain, it is clear that its first five years was largely a success.

Deadlock/Extraordinary Resolution: The Social Security Bailout (1983)

In 1981, only four years after Congress and President Carter approved a Social Security rescue plan that promised to put the trust fund on a sound financial basis well into the twenty-first century, the program once again teetered on the brink of bankruptcy. The villains were not deceptive politicians but demographic trends and unforeseen economic developments. The elderly population was increasing, and more Americans were eligible for benefits. At the same time, double-digit inflation drove up Social Security COLAs (cost of living adjustments), while declines in expected wage growth resulted in diminished revenues from payroll taxes. America's favorite social welfare program returned to the center of a political firestorm.[59]

The political battle over the future of Social Security would center on two aging Irish-American politicians: President Ronald Reagan and House Speaker Tip O'Neill (D-Mass.). Although personally cordial with each other, they remained ardent political adversaries. President Reagan's "problem" with Social Security went back nearly 20 years. Campaigning for conservative Republican presidential nominee Barry Goldwater in 1964, Reagan urged that Social Security be made voluntary. The charge that he would destroy Social Security dogged Reagan in both his 1976 and 1980 presidential campaigns. Yet Carter's claim that Reagan would subvert Social Security did not prevent a strong Republican showing in the 1980 elections, and the political environment in 1981 seemed to favor the president as his budget and economic plan dominated the policy agenda. The high cost of entitlement spending was on the president's mind, but the administration decided against including large-scale cuts in Social Security in the initial plan masterminded by Budget Director David Stockman.[60] By May, after initial successes in its congressional blitz, and growing recognition of deep financial problems with Social Security, the administration decided to switch gears.

In an attempt to distract attention from the president himself, the administration's proposals were offered by Health and Human Services Secretary Richard Schweiker.[61] On May 12, 1981, Schweiker offered a plan to shrink the growing deficit in the Social Security trust fund by reducing benefits for those retiring before the age of 65, phasing out limitations on outside earnings, restricting eligibility for disability benefits, and delaying a scheduled COLA. The last proposal was the most controversial, because it affected all 35 million Social Security recipients. Public reaction and harsh criticism from the Democrats was swift. Representative Claude Pepper (D-Fla.), one of the most outspoken advocates for the elderly in Congress, called the plan "insidious" and "cruel." House Speaker Tip O'Neill called the administration plan "despicable" and promised that "I for one will be fighting this thing every inch of the way."[62] Groups representing the elderly screamed "foul." Save Our Social Security (SOS), a coalition of 83 senior citizen organizations, claimed that the administration plan was a "breach of contract."

Democrats, on the defensive because of the administration's tax and spending cuts, finally had an effective issue to use against Reagan. The House Democratic caucus unanimously adopted a resolution stating that the administration proposals were an "unconscionable breach of faith," pledging to oppose attempts to "destroy the program for a generation of retirees."[63] Congressional Republicans quickly found themselves in a precarious position and lashed out at the Democrats for politicizing the issue rather than dealing constructively with the growing crisis. President Reagan beat a hasty retreat, backing off from the proposals in a May 21 letter to Congress: "I am not wedded to any single solution" to the impending bankruptcy.[64] Congressional Republicans headed for political cover as well, voting for a nonbinding resolution disavowing cuts in minimum Social Security benefits.

Public opinion polls showed that the Democrats had a winning issue; a huge majority of the public opposed Social Security cuts. Some congressional Democrats, such as Senator Daniel Moynihan (D-N.Y.), downplayed the financial problems of the system, calling it an excuse for Republicans to cut benefits. By a large margin, the public perceived the Democrats as the party more likely to take care of the needs of the elderly. In late summer, Congress voted to protect minimum Social Security benefits by large bipartisan majorities in both houses. Yet the larger issue could not be wished or pontificated away. With each passing month, the impending insolvency of the Social Security trust fund became more apparent. By the fall of 1981, projections showed the program running a $1.5 trillion deficit over the next 75 years.[65] Recognizing the paralysis that enveloped the government over Social Security, Ronald Reagan announced in September the formation of a bipartisan National

Commission on Social Security Reform, to be headed by Alan Greenspan. The 15 member panel was composed of 5 members named by the president, 5 named by Tip O'Neill, and 5 by Senate Majority Leader Howard Baker (R-Tenn.). Although the commission made little progress over the next 15 months, it ultimately proved to be the vehicle for legitimizing an unpopular compromise.

The Social Security issue was dormant through the early part of 1982, although Democrats continued to bash Republicans with it in fund-raising for the upcoming elections. One successful letter to potential contributors stated: "The Republican party has raised millions of dollars to press for deep cuts in Social Security." The letter netted the Democratic National Committee over $1 million dollars in just a few weeks.[66] Meanwhile, the U.S. economy was sliding into recession while budget deficits mushroomed. As unemployment approached 10 percent, payroll tax collections sagged, and benefit payments continued to grow. Even Democrats who had minimized the Social Security crisis the year before were forced to admit the gravity of the problem. Equally clear was the political reality that nothing could be done before the 1982 elections, as congressional campaigns further politicized the issue. The "bipartisan" Social Security commission could do little but spin its wheels, because the commission itself was split down partisan lines. Democratic members opposed benefit cuts; Republicans opposed large payroll tax increases. Despite the lack of progress, Greenspan hoped to break the deadlock after the November 2 elections; he scheduled a three-day brainstorming session to begin on November 11.[67]

It became clear that the commission could not do it alone. For more than a year its members had done little, other than compare and criticize each other's alternatives for achieving solvency. After their three-day parley failed to achieve compromise, Greenspan announced that the direct participation of the two main protagonists—O'Neill and Reagan—was essential if any real progress was to be made. Congress could have returned in a lame-duck session to resolve the crisis, but this did not happen. The commission adjourned on December 10, reporting nothing but the fact that by mid-1983, the government would not be able to cover its Social Security checks.

The National Commission had initially failed, but it would ultimately serve as a cover in early 1983 for the real negotiations. With the president's blessing, secret meetings between Stockman, Moynihan, and O'Neill's personal representative opened the door to a smaller group who would negotiate in private.[68] In selecting the so-called "gang of nine," the most outspoken partisans on both sides, such as Claude Pepper, were excluded. Out of the spotlight, the tough give-and-take progressed for two weeks. The Democrats agreed to some COLA reductions, and the Republicans agreed to some tax increases. Finally, a deal was struck. The negotiators took their package back to the commission to give the compromise a bipartisan blessing before Reagan and O'Neill publicly gave final approval. Neither side liked it but, recognizing the gravity of the situation, held their noses, and approved the plan. Now it had to be sold to the rank and file of both parties in Congress.

What factors led to the extraordinary resolution of this policy deadlock? Ultimately, the impending bankruptcy forced an agreement. The compromise plan bailed out Social Security by raising revenues and lowering benefits. Revenues were enhanced by expanding coverage of the program to include new federal employees and preventing state and local employees from withdrawing from the system. Half of the benefits for taxpayers earning over $25,000 per year were made subject to federal income tax. Both payroll tax rates and the amount of earnings subject to the tax were increased annually through 1990. COLAs were delayed six months, saving billions of dollars. The package was not popular with either party, but most recognized that something had to be done. Final congressional approval was bipartisan, although the tenuous compromise nearly unraveled on several occasions. SOS and other groups opposed the bailout plan, but amendments that would have destroyed the fragile balance were defeated in both houses. On March 24, the House approved the plan by a vote of 243 to 102, while the Senate accepted it by a 58 to 14 vote in the early morning of March 25.[69] Representative Barber Conable (R-N.Y.), one of the key players among the gang of nine, commented, "It may not be a work of art, but it is artful work. It will do what it was supposed to do: It will save the nation's basic social insurance system from imminent disaster."[70]

What were the results of the bailout agreement? Despite the deadlock and divisiveness, the Social Security bailout clearly worked. By the 1990s, the trust fund was running huge surpluses such that some members were actually proposing a payroll tax cut. However, demographic trends continue to show that in the future, when the baby boomers begin to retire after 2010, Social Security would eventually face another crisis. Although the use of extraordinary means to resolve deadlocks may often look chaotic and desperate, the results can be satisfactory when a solution is finally hammered out.

Conclusion

Presidential-congressional policymaking in the arena of social welfare has shifted over time. Between the 1930s and the 1960s, when poverty and social programs were prominent on the agenda, most of the leadership came from the presidency. Since then, Congress has been a more equal player with the president and occasionally has been able to lead policymaking. After the Republican takeover of Congress in 1994, Congress was even more assertive in offering policy initiatives. Roosevelt and Johnson gained approval for their proposals from supportive Democratic majorities in Congress; Clinton had no success with Democratic majorities when it came to healthcare reform. In the case of catastrophic healthcare insurance, where Presidents Reagan and Bush stayed on the sidelines, Congress played a dominant role in shaping the policy. In reforming welfare in 1996, a policy priority for both branches, Congress took the lead in policymaking, but the president used his veto and veto threats to make major changes.

Interbranch conflict and deadlock frequently occur in social welfare policy. After the defeat of Nixon's Family Assistance Plan, welfare reform efforts were futile for over two decades. Underlying ideological differences about individual responsibility and the role of government made for heated disputes. Only the impending collapse of the Social Security trust fund forced the two sides to resort to extraordinary means—a bipartisan commission fronting for secret negotiations—to break the impasse.

Since the 1960s, the pattern of presidential leadership has been relatively rare in social welfare policy. Dominance by the legislature is also uncommon, although Congress regularly plays the larger role in formulating the details of policy. Most often, policies either get cooperatively resolved or simply die because of stalemate. Social welfare policy shares some common characteristics with economic and budget policy, in terms of partisanship and the frequency of interbranch conflict. It differs significantly, however, in the absence of a forcing mechanism such as the budget process. Congress has to meet through the night to reach a budget compromise to keep the government from shutting down, but deadlocked social welfare policies often have to wait for years to be resolved.

Notes

1. Quoted in *The Report of the Committee on Economic Security of 1935, 50th Anniversary Edition* (Washington D.C.: National Conference on Social Welfare, 1985): 145.
2. Gilbert Fite and Jim Reese, *An Economic History of the United States* (New York: Houghton Mifflin, 1965): 148.
3. Ibid., 149.
4. See Louis M. Hacker, *The Course of American Growth and Development* (New York: Wiley, 1970): 10–11.
5. Robert Hunter, *Poverty* (New York: Harper & Row, 1965): 62–65.
6. Congressional Budget Office, *Economic and Budget Outlook,* FY1991–95 (February 1990).
7. See David Stockman, *The Triumph of Politics* (New York: Harper Row, 1986).
8. Darrell M. West and Burdette A. Loomis, *The Sound of Money* (New York: Norton, 1999): Chapter 4.
9. Theda Skocpol, *Boomerang: Health Care Reform and the Turn against Government* (New York: Norton, 1997).
10. League of Women Voters, *Human Needs: Unfinished Business on the Nation's Agenda* (1981): 2.
11. U.S. Census Bureau, *Poverty in the United States: 2000* (September 2001).
12. Congressional Budget Office, *Economic and Budget Outlook,* FY1991–95 (February 1990).
13. Alison Mitchell, "Two Clinton Aides Resign to Protest New Welfare Law," *New York Times* (September 12, 1996): A1.
14. The figures in the following paragraph are taken from data published by the U.S. Bureau of the Census, 1997–2000.
15. "Cross-National Comparison of Attitudes on Government and Economic Equity," *The American Enterprise* (April/May 1990): 113.
16. Aage R. Clausen, *How Congressmen Decide: A Policy Focus* (New York: St. Martin's, 1973).
17. Charles Murray, *Losing Ground: American Policy 1950–1980* (New York: Basic Books, 1984).
18. Michael Harrington, "Crunched Numbers," *New Republic* (January 28, 1985): 7–10.
19. John E. Schwartz, *America's Hidden Success: A Reassessment of Twenty Years of Public Policy* (New York: Norton, 1984).
20. Congressional Budget Office, *Social Security: A Primer* (December 2001): 4.

21. Congressional Budget Office, *Long-Term Budgetary Pressures and Options* (March 1997): xix.
22. Social Security and Medicare Boards of Trustees, reported in *CQ Weekly* (March 24, 2001): 665.
23. Congressional Budget Office (December 2001): 3.
24. John C. Donovan, *The Politics of Poverty* (Indianapolis: Bobbs-Merrill, 1973):17.
25. Ibid., 26.
26. Ibid., 29.
27. Ibid.
28. See Anthony Downs, *Inside Bureaucracy* (Boston: Little, Brown, 1967).
29. *Congressional Quarterly Weekly Report* (May 27, 1964): 1037–1042.
30. Title II, Section 202, Economic Opportunity Act of 1964.
31. See Richard F. Fenno, *Congressmen in Committee* (Boston: Little, Brown, 1973).
32. Donovan (1973): 34.
33. *Congressional Quarterly Weekly Report* (July 24, 1964): 1533.
34. Donovan (1973): 37.
35. John F. Bibby and Roger B. Davidson, *On Capitol Hill* (New York: Holt, 1967): 238.
36. *Congressional Quarterly Weekly Report* (January 31, 1987): 207.
37. Ibid., 296.
38. *Congressional Quarterly Weekly Report* (February 8, 1987): 274.
39. *Congressional Quarterly Almanac* (1988): 282.
40. *Congressional Quarterly Weekly Report* (October 31, 1987): 2692.
41. *Congressional Quarterly Weekly Report* (March 26, 1988): 777.
42. *Congressional Quarterly Weekly Report* (December 3, 1988): 3450–3452.
43. *Congressional Quarterly Weekly Report* (June 4, 1988): 1494.
44. *Congressional Quarterly Almanac* (1988): 281.
45. *Congressional Quarterly Weekly Report* (December 3, 1988): 3451.
46. *Congressional Quarterly Weekly Report* (September 9, 1989): 2317.
47. *Congressional Quarterly Weekly Report* (October 14, 1989): 2713–2714.
48. Ibid.
49. *Congressional Quarterly Weekly Report* (November 25, 1989): 3239.
50. Ibid.
51. *Congressional Quarterly Weekly Report* (September 21, 1996): 2696.
52. *Congressional Quarterly Almanac* (1995): 7–36.
53. Ibid., 7–40.
54. Ibid., 7–48.
55. The "Byrd" rule, named after its author, Senator Robert Byrd (D-W.Va.), prohibits nongermane amendments and provisions that do not reduce the deficit.
56. *Congressional Quarterly Almanac* (1995): 7–52.
57. *Congressional Quarterly Weekly Report* (August 31, 1996): 2445.
58. Jason DeParle, "A Sharp Decrease in Welfare Cases Is Gathering Speed," *The New York Times* (February 2, 1997): A1.
59. Ibid.
60. Paul C. Light, *Artful Work: The Politics of Social Security Reform* (New York: Random House, 1985).
61. Stockman (1986).
62. *Congressional Quarterly Weekly Report* (May 16, 1981): 842–843.
63. Ibid., 842.
64. *Congressional Quarterly Weekly Report* (May 23, 1981): 896.
65. *Congressional Quarterly Weekly Report* (November 28, 1981): 2333.
66. Light (1985): 139.
67. *Congressional Quarterly Weekly Report* (October 9, 1982): 2615.
68. Light (1985): Chapter 15.
69. *Congressional Quarterly Weekly Report* (March 26, 1983): 596.
70. Ibid.

CHAPTER 9

Shared Governance

There is no structural or institutional or theoretical reason why the representation of a "single" broader constituency by the president is necessarily better or worse than the representation of many "separate" constituencies by several hundred legislators.

—JAMES MACGREGOR BURNS (1965)[1]

Congress and the president frequently work together in harmony.
Occasionally one branch defers to the other. At other times, Congress and the president engage in no-holds-barred political warfare. The House of Representatives' impeachment and Senate trial of President William Jefferson Clinton was an event of historic levels of political animosity between the White House and party majorities in Congress. Even at times when the best interests of the nation would seem to dictate cooperation, the two branches may be unable or unwilling to work together. For example, three months after the September 11, 2001, terrorist attacks, the U.S. economy appeared to be in trouble and there seemed to be both economic and political reasons for an economic stimulus package. Despite weeks of direct negotiations right up until the Christmas recess, President George W. Bush and the Democratic-controlled Senate could not reach a compromise. Yet at virtually the same time, Bush and liberal Senator Edward Kennedy (D-Mass.) appeared together in public to celebrate bipartisan cooperation that led to congressional passage of Bush's education program, the most important change in federal education policy in 35 years. These examples and the preceding cases support our assertion that *no single pattern characterizes policymaking today* and that *different patterns can occur across different policy areas at the same point in time.*

Our approach to analyzing Congress and the presidency is characterized by a shared governance perspective, a policy focus, and a belief that the best way to understand congressional-presidential relationships is by systematically observing how the two institutions make policy. Rather than the presidency-centered approach, we believe the evidence suggests that the two branches are nearly coequal partners, sharing responsibility for the governance of the nation. Initiatives spring from both ends of Pennsylvania Avenue, and in most cases, each branch helps shape the result.[2] Different patterns depend on the political environment, election results and policy preferences, institutions, leadership, and the policy agenda. In the following sections, we review each of the four patterns in terms of their characteristics, determinants, and consequences. In conclusion, we look at the prospects for presidential-congressional policymaking in the early twenty-first century.

Presidential Leadership

CHARACTERISTICS

The defining characteristic of the pattern of presidential leadership is that the presidency plays a greater role in shaping policy; Congress follows the president, regardless of whether congressional policy preferences are in conflict or congruent. Presidential leadership is different from the presidential "support" or "success" measures, since presidents may take a position on a roll-call vote that represents a policy largely shaped in Congress. Presidential leadership does not depend on which branch initiates the policy, although in most cases it reflects White House initiatives. Even in such cases, Congress has some degree of influence on the result.

Presidential leadership of the policymaking partnership with Congress occurs at varying levels of interbranch conflict. The degree of conflict often reflects differences in policy preferences between the president and congressional majorities, but also can be primarily political or based on constitutional issues. The Patriot Act of 2001 is a prime example of presidential leadership because the administration played the leading role in shaping the content of the legislation and Congress passed the bill several weeks after it was submitted. The Justice Department played a key role in developing the proposals but Congress was able to make several important changes in the law concerning detention of noncitizens and regulating money laundering.

In a case with high stakes for the nation, the Persian Gulf War of 1991 generated greater conflict between branches. President Bush Sr. initially received strong bipartisan support from Congress for his decision to commit U.S. troops to Saudi Arabia, but that support became weaker on the question of using force. An historic debate on that subject occurred soon after the 102nd Congress, under control of the Democrats, convened in January 1991. Despite the severe differences between the two sides, restraint and lack of recrimination characterized the debate. Although the margins of victory were close, enough Democrats in both houses crossed over to support the president that authorization was approved. While this cross-partisan vote allowed the president to conduct the war, Bush implicitly acknowledged Congress's war-making power by asking for legislative approval. The House and Senate votes enhanced the legitimacy of the war immeasurably. Bush might have pursued military force even without approval from Congress, but the level of interbranch conflict would have escalated and national unity would have diminished.

The level of interbranch conflict over President Johnson's Economic Opportunity Act in 1964 was moderate; majorities in Congress shared the president's general objectives. Johnson enjoyed strong support from his own party members, and many Republicans were reluctant to oppose a popular antipoverty program with elections just around the corner. The environment was ripe for enactment. However, criticism and controversy over the War on Poverty was greater in years after its passage than during its formulation and adoption. LBJ proved more attentive to passage than to implementation.

The case of George W. Bush's tax cut in 2001 reflected a newly elected president making economic and budget policy his most important priority. "Move it or lose it" fits this case well for a president that took office based on a disputed election. If Bush had waited for his tax cut, it probably would have never been approved or been much smaller. Because of the recession made worse by the terrorist attacks later that year, the budget surpluses disappeared. Even though Bush nominally enjoyed the first unified Republican control of government since 1955, some degree of "cross-partisanship"—attracting a handful of Democrats to join with them—was needed. Congressional voting patterns displayed the sharp party distinctions that have characterized budget and economic policy since the 1970s, but it was the opposition of several moderate Senate Republicans that forced the administration to reduce the size of its tax cut. In the end, faced with an unprecedented midterm change in the political environment—the loss of the Senate to the Democrats caused by a senator switching parties—President Bush decided to take the best deal he could get and declare victory.

Each of the last four presidents has had a major budget and economic package in their first year of office. Ronald Reagan's 1981 tax and spending package was most dramatic, also approved by cross-partisanship. George Bush Sr. had a less significant budget package in 1989, but it was notable in that it was a conscious effort to heal some of the wounds from budget battles in the Reagan years. Clinton's massive deficit reduction plan in 1993 was extremely partisan presidential leadership. His plan was adopted without a single Republican vote, and barely survived razor-close votes in both houses. Along with George W. Bush's tax cut, these cases suggest that economic and budget proposals by presidents in their first year in office are critical to establishing their leadership and priorities in national government. Congress will have much to say about the policies that result, but this seems to be the most advantageous time for a president.

WHAT LEADS TO PRESIDENTIAL LEADERSHIP?

In the cases of the Patriot Act, the Economic Opportunity Act, the 2001 tax cut plan, and the Gulf War, the political environment was highly conducive to decisive action and presidential leadership. Kennedy's death, LBJ's honeymoon, and growing popular concern with poverty and civil rights provided an opportunity for Johnson to move his domestic agenda quickly. President George W. Bush faced a far different environment in May 2001, when his tax cut passed, than he did in October 2001, after the terrorist attacks. The position of President Bush Sr. was shored up by the strong public support for military action in the Persian Gulf and heightened by Saddam Hussein's inflammatory rhetoric and intransigence. Johnson, Bush Sr., and Bush all used their personal prestige and popularity. Both Presidents Bush enjoyed record high popularity during the Gulf War and the war against terrorism. This certainly helps foster presidential leadership and in fact, no case better demonstrates the importance of the political environment and the nature of the times than the passage of antiterrorist legislation.

Personal leadership and institutions play a key role in cases of presidential leadership of the policy process. In all four cases, presidents had clearly defined goals and used the institutionalized presidency to achieve them. Johnson, who wanted a bold new antipoverty program, created a special task force to write the legislation and used his congressional liaison team to get it through Congress. Facing the same Congress that had thwarted Kennedy, Johnson fashioned a major domestic legislative victory. With the Patriot Act, Attorney General Ashcroft and the Justice Department represented the presidency, and pressured Congress for a speedy response. In early 2001, Bush and his administration pushed hard for the tax cuts, making it their top priority. A decade earlier, George Bush also acted quickly and decisively from the moment Iraq invaded Kuwait. He set definitive goals; explained them to Congress, the nation, and the international community; and gained the support of all.

Although it can occur in any policy area, presidential leadership is not equally prevalent in all areas. Despite the enhanced congressional role since Vietnam, and more recently the end of the cold war, presidential leadership is still more likely to occur in foreign affairs than in domestic policy. Even with strong congressional opposition to many free trade measures, President Clinton was successful with NAFTA and President George W. Bush was able to get the House of Representatives to approve "fast track" authority. When a national crisis occurs, the country still turns to the president. After September 11, partisanship did indeed stop at the water's edge, however. It was more business as usual in domestic politics. Absent such crisis atmosphere, Congress usually shares responsibility in policymaking. Trade, defense procurement, military construction, base closings, immigration, and foreign aid are all characterized by intense congressional involvement. In general, strong presidential leadership is contingent on a special combination of circumstances: effective presidential action matched with a favorable political environment.

CONSEQUENCES

Are there any common characteristics in the results of these four cases of presidential leadership? Policymaking led by the president appears to be more timely, non-routine, and responsive than the other three patterns. In all four cases we examined, presidents had clearly defined priorities and gained favorable congressional action in a period of months rather than years. In some cases, moving with dispatch may unavoidably lead to policy that is less representative, ignoring certain interests. The Patriot Act did not even provide a legislative history for courts to review in future years. The Economic Opportunity Act of 1964 overlooked many alternatives and potential problems with its approach.

In all these cases, presidency-led policymaking produced outcomes that were more substantive than symbolic.[3] The George W. Bush tax cuts totaled a massive $1.35 trillion over 10 years. The antipoverty program adopted in 1964 created a new agency and a host of new programs. The Gulf War achieved its main objective of driving Iraq out of Kuwait. The Patriot Act had concrete effects on civil rights and liberties, search and seizure, privacy, and the rights of the accused. At least in these cases, presidency-led policymaking also seemed to emphasize collective national benefits rather than more particularistic or regional benefits. Of course, each case also had important symbolic components as well, and presidents have pursued many policies that are more symbolic than substantive.

Despite a number of positive characteristics, the verdict on consistency, coherence, and long-term effectiveness of policies dominated by the presidency is mixed. One of the dangers of presidential leadership is the possibility that timely and decisive actions may prove to be hasty and ill-conceived. The Economic Opportunity Act was a disappointment, even to its most loyal adherents. Although there is insufficient evidence to support the claim that the War on Poverty actually worsened the plight of the poor, it is hard to find significant improvements that are attributable to the Economic Opportunity Act. The Bush tax cuts of 2001 remain controversial because of the sudden reversal of fortune in the federal budgets and the return to deficits. However, given the onset of recession, most economists agree that the timing of the tax cuts was actually favorable. The Patriot Act, passed quickly in times of national crisis, is also feared by its critics of being ill-conceived. That will be determined by how the law is implemented and whether it actually helps in the war on terrorism in the coming years.

National security decisions dominated by the White House are particularly susceptible to the demands for quick action, and the results can sometimes be disastrous. Irving Janis has documented a series of policy fiascoes that stemmed from the phenomenon of "groupthink" within the presidency—when presidents do not seek diversity of opinion but focus prematurely on a single policy alternative.[4] The ill-fated Bay of Pigs invasion of Cuba in 1961 and the decision to escalate the war in Vietnam are two prime examples. Even though the Gulf War succeeded in achieving its main short-term objectives, its long-term consequences were less clear. Ten years later, Saddam Hussein was still in power, hiding weapons of mass destruction. On the other hand, the war on terrorism in 2001 had positive initial results, toppling the Taliban regime in Afghanistan and damaging the Al Queda terrorist network.

Over the years, many presidential programs, such as Social Security in 1935, have been judged a success. In times of foreign or domestic crisis, the presidency is best equipped to respond quickly, but there are attendant risks. Although the pattern of presidential leadership usually leads to policies that are timely, responsive, and national in scope, they are not always coherent, consistent, or effective.

Congressional Leadership

CHARACTERISTICS

Congressional leadership is the pattern in which Congress plays a dominant role in shaping public policy—with or without presidential support. Leadership is also not dependent on which branch initiates policy; Congress may lead the policy process even if the original proposal was the president's. Under the domain of congressional leadership the degree of interbranch conflict can vary considerably. The amount of presidential involvement also varies but is generally less than in the other three patterns.

Although President Reagan first proposed catastrophic healthcare coverage, Congress led the process. Preoccupied with other matters, Reagan did nothing to resolve the deep divisions within his administration, essentially letting Congress carry the ball. Although he threatened to veto the bill if it was not to his liking, the level of interbranch conflict was moderate to low by the standards of most social welfare bills. Because he supported the concept, Reagan was happy to take some credit for the proposal when it was signed into law. President Bush's involvement in the process was even less so when catastrophic coverage was repealed in 1989. Sensing that the issue carried political risks, the administration took a hands-off approach and let Congress solve a problem it had created for itself.

The Cuba Sanctions (Helms-Burton) Act is unique among the cases in that a single external event—the shooting down of the airplane carrying Cuban Americans—allowed Congress to have its way by undercutting administration opposition. It is clear that the Clinton administration still thought the bill was a bad idea, would damage relations with allies, and might have been against international law. However, the incident simply made the political costs too high to oppose harsher sanctions on Cuba any longer. The president was limited to administrative actions to delay enforcement of the law.

The two cases of congressional leadership that have a common characteristic are the Civil Rights Restoration Act of 1988 and the Shareholder Lawsuits Act in 1995. In both cases, Congress mustered a two-thirds majority to override a presidential veto. In 1988, with a presidential election approaching, both parties felt civil rights was a critical issue: Democrats in Congress to show their continued support and the Republican administration to highlight its opposition to "quotas," reverse discrimination, and intrusive bureaucracy. The result was an acrimonious fight. The House and Senate ultimately overrode President Reagan's veto, making the Civil Rights Restoration Act law without the president's signature. In 1995, Clinton's first veto override was also based on political calculations as much as on policy considerations. The shareholder lawsuits bill was one of low visibility but intense special interest lobbying. In the end, President Clinton felt he had to shore up his political support among the trial lawyers more than high-tech businesses. Bipartisan majorities in Congress quickly and decisively overrode the veto, as the administration surely suspected it would. Nonetheless, the difficulty of getting a two-thirds majority in both houses over the active opposition of the president makes this type of congressional leadership relatively rare.

What Leads to Congressional Leadership?

Congressional leadership of the policy process is much more common than the presidency-centered literature would suggest. It often involves issues that have local or regional implications, generating more interest in Congress than in the White House. Congressional-led policymaking frequently involves routine or low-visibility policies, and inside-the-Beltway politics heavy on interest group participation, such as the shareholder lawsuits bill. Congressional leadership is not restricted to low-visibility or regional concerns, however. The Civil Rights Act of 1988 and catastrophic healthcare insurance were national in scope. Helms-Burton had important international and foreign policy implications. But all were policies that were much higher on the congressional agenda than on the presidential agenda.

Supermajority institutions, especially the veto, are one of the biggest obstacles to congressional leadership. Except in cases of veto overrides, congressional leadership is predicated on at least mild support or general disinterest on the part of the administration. In two of the cases, the president was content to let Congress work its will, within certain parameters. The cost of opposition was seen as greater than going along and taking some credit for the result. The political environment must also be right for congressional leadership of policymaking, and sometimes a weaker president improves the chances for congressional leadership. For example, it is unlikely that Congress could have enacted the Civil Rights Restoration Act over Reagan's veto before 1987, when the Democrats recaptured the Senate and the president was weakened by the Iran–Contra scandal. Congressional leadership can occur under unified control of government because of pressure from factions within the president's party in Congress, but is more prevalent under divided government. The 1994 election probably did more to promote congressional leadership of policymaking than any other in the century, propelling the Republicans to power with an articulated national agenda. Two of the cases of congressional leadership come from the 104th Congress. But a number of other cases of congressional attempts at leadership since the Republican takeover fall in the category of deadlock or cooperation. The Republicans learned that even under the most favorable of conditions, it is difficult to run the country from Capitol Hill.

Public support for the Congress can be related to legislative leadership of policymaking. Much more important is the size and policy preferences of congressional majorities. Conversely, presidential popularity can be an obstacle. The Republican Congress was not able to dominate President Clinton and force him to accept their balanced budget proposal in 1995. Congress's declining popularity and Clinton's surging approval strengthened his resolve. Enhanced institutional capability promotes congressional leadership of the policy process. Stronger party leaders, the use of omnibus legislation written by the leadership, and the use of restrictive rules in the House all facilitated congressional policy leadership from the 1980s to the 2000s.

Conditional party government tends to occur when the parties each have high internal cohesion and greater ideological distance between themselves. The data suggest that these conditions exist in the current era.[5] But Congress's ability to lead the policy process still depends, to some degree, on individual leaders and their skills. Newt Gingrich, for example, represented a dramatic departure from most of the previous speakers. His strategy of nationalizing the 1994 elections with the Contract with America gave him the opportunity to define a Roosevelt-like "100 days" to vote on the congressional agenda. His ability to handpick committee chairs, weaken committees vis-à-vis the leadership, and control the process was unprecedented in recent times, even if it did not last long. More than anything, Gingrich and the Republicans were a reminder of the potential of congressional leadership under the right political situation. Their failures also were a reminder of how quickly the political environment can change and the difficulties of dominating policymaking in a shared governance system.

Although party leaders are instrumental in facilitating the legislative process, policy leadership often comes from committees and policy entrepreneurs. Catastrophic health insurance was maneuvered through Congress by leaders such as Ways and Means Chairman Dan Rostenkowski and a handful of other representatives who had a special interest in the issue. Bipartisan cooperation within Congress makes enactment easier and reduces the likelihood of a presidential veto. Support from Minority Leader Robert Michel helped ensure passage of the catastrophic healthcare insurance bill. The Cuba Sanctions Act was largely the result of Senator Jesse Helms's (R-N.C.) hatred of Castro and determination to use the big stick against him. The Civil Rights Restoration Act was masterminded by a coalition of legislators led by Edward Kennedy in the Senate and the Black Caucus in the House.

Congressional leadership of policymaking is less dramatic than the highly visible legislative successes of a Roosevelt, Johnson, or Reagan. Speaker Newt Gingrich brought more visibility to Congress and the congressional agenda than any leader in memory. But both before and after Gingrich, the legislative branch sometimes sets the agenda, balances diverse interests, and crafts legislation.

CONSEQUENCES

Compared with policymaking led by the president, the legislative process is often careful, slow, deliberative, and less timely. Congress can approve the use of military force after a shocking attack or pass a continuing resolution in 24 hours when the pressure is on, but in most cases, major legislation takes many months or years to become law. Delay is tolerable in cases such as catastrophic healthcare or shareholder lawsuits, although the problems may worsen in the interim. In crucial decisions on the budget and foreign policy, however, deliberation and delay can cause serious problems and blunt the effectiveness of policy.

Congressional policymaking generally rates well on democratic criteria. It tends to represent a wide variety of organized interests, ideologies, and regional concerns—sometimes to a fault. The fragmented nature of the legislative process provides many access points with opportunities for amendment, logrolling, compromise, and modification. Narrow interests may dominate the issue networks of specialized groups, agencies, and subcommittees, but in major legislation, a broader array of organized interests usually are represented.[6] This tends to produce legislation that is more consensus-oriented, modest in nature, and incremental in approach. Congressional policymaking is undermined, however, when legislators prove timid in the face of powerful interests. The rapid repeal of catastrophic healthcare insurance is an example of Congress's abandonment of an important policy when challenged by a vocal minority.

The representativeness of congressional policymaking is reflected in the nature of benefits. As representatives of states and districts, members of Congress have a fondness for tangible district benefits and pork-barrel projects. There is a tendency to distribute benefits widely, rather than targeting them to regions or groups of individuals that have the greatest need. Although this may provide a measure of geographical equity, it often dilutes and diminishes the impact of policy. Revenue sharing is often cited as an example of a policy that gave states and cities benefits whether their need was great or nonexistent.[7]

Despite these well-known proclivities, the penchant of Congress for distributive politics is often overemphasized.[8] Pork-barrel spending on district projects constitutes only a tiny fraction of federal outlays, and its proportion has been dropping in recent years.[9] Congress also deals with issues that are national in scope—ranging from defense to tax policy to civil rights—and it can resolve regional disputes in areas such as immigration or energy policy.

Perhaps a more serious flaw in policy dominated by Congress is a tendency to promote symbolism over substance. When the political implications of legislation become as important as the policy implications, members act to protect themselves by adopting "motherhood" legislation, avoiding "dangerous" votes, and sidestepping tough issues. Such gestures may seem harmless or even politically useful, but they reinforce public cynicism about the Congress and congressional leadership.

Congressional influence in foreign policy is a two-edged sword. It can safeguard the country from dangerous entanglements or simply confuse and fragment U.S. policy. Helms-Burton caused problems with many allies and brought scorn and ridicule among the international community for trying to impose America's ideas about how to deal with Cuba on everyone else. It has brought threats of retaliation and action in the World Court for violating international law. This delights some of the law's most ardent supporters, but hardly gives Helms-Burton high scores for elements of good policy.

Representation of diverse interests, localized benefits, and emphasis on symbols rather than substance can have a negative impact on the consistency, coherence, and effectiveness of policies shaped by Congress. That explains in part why the federal government still subsidizes tobacco growers at the same time it spends hundreds of millions of dollars on cancer research and "stop smoking" campaigns. Because coalitions are unstable, policies may be contradictory. The political environment changes quickly, so congressional policymaking is often repetitive and redundant. Many issues return again and again without final resolution. This may be a necessary consequence of democracy, but it can have a damaging impact on the effectiveness of policy.

Despite these problems, policies shaped by Congress are not inherently less effective or less coherent than presidential policies. Because most policies are administered by the executive branch, Congress-led policies do not appear to differ significantly in effectiveness from policies dominated by the president. Presidents, too, engage in symbolic exercises, change directions, and produce results that are less than optimal at times. Congressional action tends to be slow, and the legislative process often appears chaotic and messy. However, when congressional leaders act responsibly, working carefully through difficult issues, the resulting policies can effectively balance diverse and competing interests in society.

Consensus/Cooperation

CHARACTERISTICS

Consensus/cooperation is a pattern characterized by moderate to low levels of interbranch conflict and a constructive mutual engagement in shaping the content of policy. Responsibility is not necessarily shared equally, but governance is more evenly shared than in the two previous patterns. In cases of consensus, there is no real opposition. In cases of cooperation, policy preferences diverge and conflict exists, but the two branches work in collaboration to achieve an acceptable outcome. Among our cases, the same-sex marriage bill comes closest to consensus. This was a case of both branches responding to a hot-button issue with the American people. In the face of overwhelming public opposition to homosexual marriages, both branches and both parties came together to enact a largely symbolic act.

Despite the media emphasis on conflict and deadlock, cooperation is probably the most prevalent pattern of presidential-congressional policymaking today. Initiatives may develop in either branch, from the thousands of bills submitted in Congress to the president's legislative agenda. Many congressional initiatives end up on the presidential agenda, such as tax reform and welfare reform. Others may be administration proposals, such as the Panama Canal treaties and the 1964 Civil Rights Act. Wherever the proposals originate, in cases of cooperation both branches perceive significant stakes and participate in the process.

The approval of the Panama Canal treaties is close to being a case of presidential leadership. The administration negotiated the treaties and then used all its resources to gain Senate ratification. However, this case involves significant differences from the Persian Gulf War and other instances of presidential leadership in foreign policy. First, the Senate's constitutional legitimacy in ratifying treaties is less ambiguous than the dispute between congressional war powers and the president's powers as commander in chief. Second, the Senate made important substantive revisions in the treaties, forcing the White House to accept a number of reservations. Finally, although ratification represented a significant victory for President Carter, capping one of his administration's more effective lobbying campaigns, final approval was made possible only by the bipartisan efforts of Majority Leader Robert Byrd and Minority Leader Howard Baker.

Despite President Clinton's promise during the 1992 campaign to "end welfare as we know it," Congress was the initiator and played the more significant role in shaping the Welfare Reform Act of 1996. Congress had been the leading force in enacting modest reforms in the Family Support Act of 1988, but that legislation had done little to change the underlying structure of welfare. The 1994 elections were critical for creating an environment leading to the enactment of the far-reaching welfare reform package agreed to in 1996. Yet this case had all the ingredients for deadlock. In general, the Republicans wanted to go much further in eliminating the federal entitlement for welfare than the Clinton administration, which had to deal with hostility from the liberal wing of the Democratic party. Clinton used his veto twice to force Republicans to make important concessions. The issue could have remained in deadlock, but both sides decided a deal was both good policy and good politics. Despite serious differences, both branches worked out a compromise that made historic and far-reaching changes in public policy.

The Tax Reform Act of 1986 is also a good example of the pattern of inter-branch cooperation in making a significant policy change. It was all the more remarkable given the hostility between Congress and the president over taxing and spending issues in the mid-1980s. The presidency and Congress shared responsibility nearly equally: The Treasury had drafted two detailed plans, and the House and Senate each adopted their own versions. All sides participated in shaping the final bill. Not only was bipartisanship essential, but the adoption of new policymaking ground rules were required. Despite concerted opposition from interest groups to virtually every part of the bill, cooperation between the two branches made it possible to do what most observers had thought impossible.

WHAT LEADS TO CONSENSUS/COOPERATION?

In the simplest terms, cooperation occurs when neither branch can dominate the other, and both partners place higher value on passing a bill than gaining a political advantage by blaming opponents for failure. Some degree of bipartisanship or cross-partisanship is essential to cooperation under divided government. Political experts considered tax reform impossible in 1986. The Republicans wanted lower rates and a tax system that did not distort investment decisions, and Democrats wanted a fairer system and an end to many of the loopholes enjoyed by the rich. In this and other cases of cooperation, collaboration took place in an environment conducive to accommodation and reciprocity. Cooperation in welfare reform occurred because the Democratic president moved significantly toward the Republican position in accepting the end of the federal entitlement, requiring work from all beneficiaries, and lifetime limits on benefits. Despite this movement, the bill easily could have resulted in a third veto, with welfare reform becoming a campaign issue. It did not because both sides believed they were better off claiming credit for the policy rather than pointing blame for its failure.

Consensus and cooperation can occur with or without supportive public opinion. In the case of the same-sex marriage bill, public opinion was paramount, eclipsing whatever policy differences may have existed between branches. In contrast, support for the Panama Canal treaties was soft, with a plurality opposed in most polls. In that case, cooperation occurred because a two-thirds majority of senators agreed with the president that it was the right thing to do, regardless of public opinion.

Tax reform exemplifies the importance of rules. In both houses, public sessions produced political posturing, special-interest amendments, and a steady erosion of the goals of each party. But new budget rules interpreted to require "offsets" allowed any amendment that reduced revenue to be ruled out of order unless offset with a provision that correspondingly increased revenue. Welfare reform succeeded in 1996 in a Congress with more centralized leadership than had occurred in decades. That made it possible for the Republicans to negotiate with the administration and to deliver the deal when it was struck.

In all four cases, individual leadership, particularly bipartisan leadership, was a crucial factor. President Jimmy Carter worked extremely hard and effectively with congressional leaders to get the Panama Canal treaties enacted. Senate Majority Leader Robert Byrd's personal leadership also played an important role in the ratification of the outcome.[10] Although Clinton was more reactive than proactive in shaping welfare reform, his previous vetoes established his credentials as a tough negotiator on this issue. Creative leadership by Senate Finance Committee Chairman Robert Packwood helped make tax reform a reality. His tactic of challenging committee members in a closed-door session to throw out their previous votes to get the top rate below 30 percent had a profound impact on the process.

Most of the instances of cooperation that we examined concerned policies that had percolated in the political system for many years. These issues had been carefully studied, explored, and debated inside and outside of government. Change was finally possible when both branches agreed that it was time to act. One of the most interesting questions concerns why some issues deadlock and others are resolved through negotiation and compromise. Why, for example, during 1995 to 1996, was welfare reform resolved but the balanced budget negotiations ended in standoff, when the political environment and key participants appeared to be the same? Why did Congress pass a bipartisan education bill in late 2001 but could not agree on an economic stimulus plan? It seems to come down to political calculations over policy concerns. We look more closely at this question when deadlock and extraordinary resolution are discussed in the next section.

CONSEQUENCES

Because both branches are involved in the process, policies emerging from a pattern of interbranch cooperation tend to represent diverse interests and perspectives. As the case of tax reform suggests, however, representativeness is not the same as catering to special interests or taking the lowest common denominator. Because of the long process of building coalitions to reach a policy consensus, this pattern is rarely quick or timely. Tax reform and welfare reform took years before they were finally enacted. Under some circumstances, however, consensus/cooperation can be timely. The Panama Canal treaties were debated and ratified under a deadline. The same-sex marriage bill was developed quickly in response to developments in Hawaii and intense media attention.

The cases of cooperation produced policies that were reasonably coherent and effective in comparison with other major legislation. Welfare reform has turned significant authority over to the states. In the first six years, the results have shown a dramatic reduction in welfare rolls in most states. However, the people who have left welfare are the most employable. As a number of clients reached their five-year limit on benefits in 2001, some states had to consider repealing the limits. In the case of the Panama Canal treaties, U.S. relations with Latin America would probably be much worse than they are today. The canal has remained open and fully operational.

The Tax Reform Act of 1986 achieved several important policy goals. The number of brackets was reduced. Hundreds of billions of dollars of tax loopholes were eliminated, enhancing the integrity of the tax system. However, Congress and the president have undone much of the Tax Reform Act in subsequent years, adding additional tax brackets in 1990 and 1993, and further complicating the tax system with a host of tax preferences in 1997. The Bush tax cut of 2001 lowered rates, but did little to reform or simplify the tax system.

The most symbolic, least substantive case in this category was the same-sex marriage law. Many legal experts argued the ban was unnecessary and duplicated existing state laws. The legislation did not solve any critical public problem. It simply expressed the sentiment of the American people in favor of traditional marriage and against same-sex unions. Symbolic legislation can play a useful social function in some cases, but is unlikely to really make a difference in slowing the pace of changing mores and social behavior.

We have seen that many of the policies that emerge from this pattern meet the test of good policy. On the other hand, the greatest danger of consensus/cooperation is that to reach an acceptable compromise, policies may become watered down and more symbolic than substantive, eroding their impact. Bipartisan cooperation is no guarantee of good policy if it simply papers over differences for the sake of appearing to do something about a problem. Consensus on an issue may ensure a democratic outcome but not necessarily effective public policy.

Deadlock/Extraordinary Resolution

CHARACTERISTICS

Deadlock occurs when sharp differences on visible issues lead to high levels of interbranch conflict, and neither branch is willing to compromise or able to lead the other. When a forcing mechanism exists (such as the annual budget), or the consequences of inaction are disastrous, deadlock may be resolved by extraordinary means outside the normal policymaking process. Deadlock can occur even during times when the environment would seem conducive to action.

Each of the four cases we examined generated unusual animosity between Congress and the presidency. Each took place under divided government (although deadlock can occur with unified control of government as well) and was characterized by high levels of partisanship. Social Security, aid to the Contras, and the budget conflict were prolonged struggles, evolving through a series of stalemates over many years until finally resolved. The two parties warred over Social Security for years before the 1983 bailout plan. The 1995–1996 budget standoff was preceded by a 15-year battle over how to reduce chronic deficits. Aid to the Contras was a dilemma that the political system seemed incapable of resolving throughout the 1980s.

The 1990 civil rights bill remained deadlocked at the end of the 101st Congress but finally was resolved in 1991 as a result of the Clarence Thomas hearings, the David Duke candidacy, and closed-door negotiations between Senate Republicans and the White House. As a case of presidential-congressional policymaking, it is very similar to the Civil Rights Restoration Act of 1988, except for one crucial difference. In 1990, Congress had been just short of the two-thirds majority to override Bush's veto, missing by one vote in the Senate. Perhaps the administration's fear that the one-vote margin would not hold prompted a negotiated settlement. Thus, in this case as in each of the other three, extraordinary means resolved the deadlock.

Use of a bipartisan commission resolved the Social Security crisis. The commission gave the administration and congressional leaders the political cover they needed to make the unpopular decision to raise taxes and cut benefits. Deadlock over the balanced budget plan throughout 1995 and 1996 remained unresolved until after the 1996 elections. Both sides went to the barricades, shutting down the government rather than compromising. Unlike in 1990, when the budget crisis was resolved by the use of a summit between branches, there was no extraordinary resolution for Clinton and the 104th Congress.

Aid to the Contras was characterized by a number of extraordinary actions by both sides, intended to outmaneuver the other branch. Congress passed the Boland amendments to handcuff the administration. In frustration, the White House devised the ill-fated plan to channel funds covertly to the Contras through private foreign contributions and diversion of the profits from secret arms sales to Iran. The result was the highly damaging Iran–Contra scandal that marred Ronald Reagan's second term. This issue was not resolved until 1989, when Bush and Congress reached an accord. Finally, when the Sandanistas were defeated in Nicaragua's elections in early 1990, the issue became moot.

WHAT LEADS TO DEADLOCK?

Deadlock in policymaking often reflects deep divisions in the nation, translated into sharp cleavages in the policy preferences of members of Congress and the president. We have seen that congressional parties have changed since the 1960s. Republicans are more conservative and Democrats are more liberal. Both parties are more cohesive with the disappearance of most Republican moderates and conservative Democrats. That means that when even centrist presidents like Clinton and George W. Bush confront one or both houses of Congress of the opposite party, deadlock may result.

Deadlock can occur when public opinion is divided, as it was over the question of aid to the Contras throughout the mid-1980s. Public opinion on budget questions was also inconsistent. The public strongly opposed big deficits, supported the Republicans' promise not to raise taxes, and at the same time supported Democrats who opposed further cuts in entitlements and domestic programs. Conversely, extremely strong public support for Social Security made it difficult for negotiators to raise payroll taxes and cut benefits, both of which had to be accomplished to solve the problem.

The pattern of deadlock emerges in a political environment in which policy preferences are divided and political stakes are high. The electoral consequences of these issues are extremely important at both the congressional and presidential levels, so compromise becomes even more difficult during an election year. The Social Security bailout became politically possible only after the 1982 midterm elections, and the final resolution of aid to the Contras occurred after the 1988 elections. The deadlock over the 1990–1991 civil rights bill reflected electoral calculations by both parties. The balanced budget plan remained in deadlock throughout the term of the 104th Congress. Only the 1996 presidential and congressional elections produced the needed conditions to break the deadlock.

Extraordinary resolution of policy deadlocks involves alternative institutional arrangements or innovative means to break the political impasse. Ad hoc devices such as summits and secret negotiations between branches have become more common in the last 20 years. Automatic mechanisms such as Gramm-Rudman mandatory deficit reduction were used in an attempt to force a political settlement on the budget conflict, but they restricted the options of both branches. Bipartisan commissions were used successfully in the Social Security dispute and have been employed in other controversial issues, such as military base closings, and have been proposed to deal with Medicare. George W. Bush used a bipartisan commission early in his term in an attempt to further his goal of partially privatizing Social Security. Restrictive rules limiting amendments in Congress made it possible to preserve unpopular solutions, including both the Social Security solutions and some of the earlier budget compromises.

While deadlock is not confined to any single policy area, it has been less common in foreign policy and civil rights. Historically, these issues have more often been characterized by compromise and cooperation, but interbranch conflict in both areas has escalated since the 1980s. Economic and budget policy and social welfare policy are more divisive, partisan, and prone to deadlock in the modern era. In terms of welfare reform, it took a generation to enact meaningful change, and the budget paralysis of the 1980s and 1990s looked like it would return in the 2000s when the surpluses disappeared.

CONSEQUENCES

Unresolved deadlock can result in drift and inaction in the face of pressing national problems. The specter of partisan intransigence—epitomized by government shut-downs—leads to public cynicism and disillusionment. Aid to the Contras and the 1995–1996 budget paralysis of are the best examples of the negative consequences of deadlock. U.S. policy in Nicaragua in the 1980s produced the worst of both worlds. It was a policy marked by contradictions—the approval of aid to the rebels one year, the denial of aid the next. It led Democrats in Congress to adopt means that may have been unconstitutional in their quest to handcuff the executive branch. Likewise, the Reagan administration reacted to the deadlock by breaking the law to achieve its objectives. The resulting policy failed to meet the objectives of either branch or to serve national interests.

Budget stalemate in the 1980s led to the largest deficits in history. The saga of budget negotiations between Congress and the president since this period is a combination of deadlock, negotiation, and extraordinary resolution. Significant progress was made in reducing the deficits in the 1990s and a balanced budget agreement was reached in 1997.[11] But after four years of surpluses, President Bush announced in 2002 that budget deficits had returned and would likely not be eliminated during his term.

The fact that the process is ugly does not always mean the results must be bad. Deadlock per se and extraordinary resolution of deadlocks are not always disastrous for the nation. Some deadlocks simply mean temporary delay, which can improve the policy in the long run. Other stalemates may be frustrating but not disastrous. The failure to pass the civil rights bill of 1990, despite its importance, had nowhere near the negative impact of inconsistent policy in Central America or chronic deficits. In addition, resolution by extraordinary means can sometimes produce very satisfactory results. The 1983 Social Security bailout ensured the solvency of the Social Security trust fund into the first third of the twenty-first century. Conversely, some economists argued that the deadlock over an economic stimulus package in late 2001 was actually a good thing. The watered-down compromise that finally passed in 2002 did little more than extend unemployment benefits.

Deadlock, by its very nature, fails many of the tests of good policy. It blunts the responsiveness of policymaking and fails to take action in a timely manner. Extraordinary resolution of deadlocks is often achieved only by limiting the participation and representation of competing interests. Summits and bipartisan commissions centralize policymaking in the hands of a few key decisionmakers in both branches.

The rank-and-file members of Congress and Cabinet officials may be cut out of the process, denied the right to amend or alter policy. Moreover, summits do not guarantee the resolution of issues. The 1989 budget summit agreement between Bush and Congress, for example, simply papered over differences, an exercise in "least-common-denominator" bipartisanship. Deadlock usually fails the tests of consistency, coherence, and effectiveness. Inconsistent policy in Nicaragua had costs, both in Nicaraguan lives and in the diminished international credibility of the United States. Deadlock over deficits significantly increased the portion of federal outlays that had to be devoted to paying interest on the debt, diverting resources from other pressing needs. Extraordinary resolution of deadlocks can ultimately solve problems, but the political system pays a price in terms of public confidence, international credibility, civility in government, and national unity.

COLLABORATION AND COMBAT: AN ASSESSMENT

Table 9.1 summarizes the 16 cases that have been examined. Based on the conclusions to each of the substantive chapters, we suggest, in summary form, which patterns are most prevalent by policy area. Based on the discussion in this chapter, Table 9.1 also suggests some of the policy consequences associated with each pattern of presidential-congressional policymaking. Of course, the prevalence, causes, and consequences of these policymaking patterns defy simple conclusions.

What are the policymaking strengths and weaknesses of Congress and the presidency? Perhaps most important, no single pattern guarantees good policy, although some patterns seem more promising than others. The presidency does have certain advantages of dispatch and clarity, but presidential-led policymaking does not always result in well-managed, effective policies (or, conversely, in less democratic policies). The Congress has the advantages of representativeness and openness, but Congress-led policy can also be well managed and effective. Of course, it can also be ineffective, symbolic, or worse. Cooperation and extraordinary resolution reflect a mix of the strengths and weaknesses of both branches as they cooperate or mutually resolve differences.

The election of 2000 revealed an electorate very closely split between the two parties. It was virtually a tie for both Congress and the presidency. There is some evidence that the American people want divided government, taking to heart Madison's view that ambition should counteract ambition.[12] Yet recently, more than 75 percent of voters cast their ballots for congressional and presidential candidates of the same party.[13] It is clear that divided government does not preclude effective policymaking.[14] But it is also clear that divided government matters. Major legislation is more controversial and more likely to fail under divided government.[15] It increases the probability for deadlock to occur and often lengthens the time that it takes to address problems. Issues that lack the urgency of a government shutdown or trust fund bankruptcy may go unresolved indefinitely.

Clinton and the Republican Congresses after 1996 had about as antagonistic a relationship as any in American history. The Republicans were determined to drive Clinton from office for lying about his relationship with White House intern Monica

Table 9.1 Cases of Presidential-Congressional Policymaking, by Pattern and Policy Area

POLICY AREA	PATTERN OF INTERACTION				
	PRESIDENTIAL LEADERSHIP	CONGRESSIONAL LEADERSHIP	CONSENSUS/ COOPERATION	DEADLOCK/ EXTRAORDINARY RESOLUTION	MOST PREVALENT PATTERNS
Foreign policy	Gulf War (1991)	Cuba Sanctions Act (1996)	Panama Canal treaties (1978)	Aid to Contras (1983–1989)	Presidential leadership more frequent, especially in crisis, but growing congressional role, particularly when domestic implications are substantial
Civil rights policy	Anti-Terrorism Act (2001)	Civil Rights Restoration Act (1988)	Same-Sex Marriage Act (1996)	Civil Rights Act (1991)	Congress more important in recent years under Republican presidents; cooperation diminishing as partisanship increases
Economic and budget policy	Tax cut (2001)	Shareholder Lawsuits Act (1995)	Tax Reform Act (1986)	Balanced budget plan (1995–1996)	Dominance by either branch rare; deadlock common; extraordinary resolution frequently needed
Social welfare policy	Economic Opportunity Act (1964)	Catastrophic healthcare insurance (1988–1989)	Welfare Reform Act (1996)	Social Security bailout (1983)	Greater congressional leadership; neither branch dominant; periodic deadlocks punctuated by compromise
POLICY CONSEQUENCES	Timely and decisive but can be hasty or ill-conceived; responsive if not always representative; nonroutine, major change	Often slow but representative; favors local and dispersed benefits; often more symbolic than substantive; modest and major changes	Not timely but can be decisive; representative and consensus-oriented; generally substantive and effective, but compromise may dilute impact	Inaction in the face of demands; less representative; politics over policy; extraordinary resolution can sometimes be effective but strains system	

Lewinsky. The House pursued impeachment but could not find any bipartisan support for its efforts. Although the House was successful at impeaching Clinton, the public perceived it as a partisan witch hunt by the Republicans and Clinton's approval ratings actually climbed. The Senate held a brief trial and Clinton was acquitted on all charges. But despite vetoes, attacks, impeachment, and government shutdowns, Clinton and the Republican Congresses also produced welfare reform, approval of the line-item veto, major trade legislation, and a balanced budget agreement. Even at a high level of institutional combat, some policymaking can take place.

Our analysis to this point suggests that the key to more effective policymaking is not strengthening either the president's or Congress's role; rather, it is to enhance the ability of both branches to enter into a constructive engagement with each other. This could be accomplished in various ways.

Can Shared Governance Be Improved?

Constitutional Reform

The most outspoken critics of presidential-congressional deadlock propose a radical solution: changing the basic structure of the Constitution. Constitutional reformers make the case that, however brilliant a solution the separation of powers may have been two centuries ago, it is simply inadequate for the governing needs of today. However, over the years, there has been remarkably little sentiment for tinkering with the Constitution. In an attempt to break down resistance to change, a group of scholars and public officials, including Douglas Dillon, Lloyd Cutler, Charles Hardin, and James Sundquist, formed the Committee on the Constitutional System.[16] Although interest in constitutional reform has peaked for the moment, their proposals are still useful for thinking about improving presidential-congressional policymaking. The checks and balances designed to prevent despotism, in the words of the committee, have led to "government stalemate and deadlock, to indecision and inaction in the face of urgent problems."[17]

Accordingly, the Committee on the Constitutional System drafted a series of proposed constitutional amendments that would fundamentally restructure the way the American political system works. To prevent divided government, they proposed electing candidates for the House, the Senate, and the presidency on a single ticket.[18] To provide greater consultation and collective responsibility in policymaking, they suggested amending the Constitution to allow members of Congress to sit on the president's Cabinet. This idea was first introduced in Congress in the 1880s. To achieve a similar result, another proposal called for Cabinet secretaries and administration officials to participate in the deliberations in Congress, including floor debate. Other alternatives to avoid divided government included awarding bonus seats in Congress to the party winning the presidency and repealing the Twenty-Second Amendment, which limits the president to two terms.[19]

If deadlock occurs, the constitutional system of the United States provides no method for breaking it, short of waiting for the next election. The committee suggested several daring constitutional changes to break deadlocks between Congress and the president. One proposal provided for a congressional vote of no confidence, making it possible to remove the president and call new elections. Conversely, the committee also proposed giving the president the power to dissolve Congress once during his presidential term and call for new legislative elections. Less radical amendments to reduce political deadlock included a one-house veto override, a presidential line-item veto, reduced majorities required for treaty ratification, and the establishment of a national referendum to break a stalemate.[20]

These and other dramatic proposals to make the United States more like a parliamentary democracy are interesting and provocative, but constitutional reform is not the answer. There are serious flaws in both the diagnosis and the cure. Scholars have analyzed and criticized the major reforms proposed by the committee and found that each is based on an incorrect diagnosis of the problems or does not match political needs.[21] As we have seen throughout, deadlock is not the only pattern of policymaking that occurs under divided government, nor is unified party control of Congress and the presidency any guarantee that deadlock will be prevented. The patterns of presidential leadership, congressional leadership, and cooperation also occur under divided government and often result in effective policymaking. Even when deadlock occurs, leaders of both branches have increasingly relied on extraordinary means to resolve deadlocks.

PARTY REFORM

Assuming that improvements must be made within the current constitutional system, the reforms most frequently proposed to bridge the separation of powers are to restructure and strengthen political parties. The notion of disciplined, responsible parties has long held appeal to political scientists.[22] Critics believe that the American people have for too long been lulled by bland appeals to compromise, centrism, bipartisanship, and national unity. Nicholas von Hoffman urges the two parties to "politicize, polarize, ignite the rancors of politics, disunite, crack open the one-party state."[23] To accomplish these changes, party reformers advocate a return to old values: party caucuses rather than primaries, uncommitted party convention delegates, laws to strengthen the national parties, and the single-minded pursuit of a partisan agenda. Others advocate increased party services to members, expanded party fundraising, better education of the public, and party sponsorship of presidential primaries. Government-assisted reforms would include state deregulation of parties; legislation to make the parties the main conduit of campaign funds; free media time for parties; and requirements for party registration, party labels on ballots, and the option of voting a straight party ticket in all states. Taking a different approach, some propose the creation of a multiparty system.[24]

Party reform is not likely to be the answer to improving shared governance between the president and Congress. Ironically, the United States already has much of what responsible party advocates wanted a generation ago: more cohesive parties that represent significant policy differences, better financed national parties, and stronger party leaders in Congress. We have seen trends leading to conditional party government including party cohesion, party voting in the House and Senate, and differences in policy positions (see Figure 4.1) in Chapter 4. Party leaders in Congress have more tools at their disposal to foster party discipline, even in the Senate. In the early 2000s, the number of strong party identifiers is stable and split-ticket voting is declining. Nonetheless, party government still cannot sustain consistent governing coalitions today, especially under divided government.

COLLABORATIVE POLICYMAKING

Over the past 30 years, Congress has greatly enhanced its capacity to shape the policy agenda, formulate and enact legislation, and hence, negotiate as an equal partner with the president. With the addition of more cohesive parties, it means that unless parties achieve absolute majorities and control of the presidency and Congress, some kind of bipartisan or cross-partisan coalition must be built. As one Democratic senator observed, "We have coalition government now. It only works when both sides are on board."[25]

This situation enhances the influence of members who are near the median in terms of ideology in Congress. Moderate centrists in both parties are more important as parties use cross-partisanship to win on important issues. That pattern was apparent with the Bush tax cut of 2001 and seems to be more prevalent now. Although bipartisan coalitions can blur party differences, the cases suggest that cooperation tends to produce more satisfactory policy outcomes. If deadlocks occur, extraordinary means of resolution can be sought. They may prove useful in dealing with tough issues, such as getting a handle on the growth of Medicare and Social Security before baby boomers begin to retire. In the final analysis, arriving at effective foreign and domestic policies, which respond to the rapidly changing environment, is more important than clarifying party differences.

Cross-partisanship can preserve party differences. Both parties can establish a record on which to run, based on their negotiating positions, and use the media to clarify their differences. Collaboration does not mean that all issues will take the pattern of consensus/cooperation. If political conditions are right, certain policies can still be led by either Congress or the president, particularly if the other branch believes that the costs of opposition are high. Governing by cross-partisan collaboration in a separated system is comparable to a multiparty governing coalition in a parliamentary system.

The presidency-centered era of national policymaking is over. Even the national unity following the tragic terrorist attacks of September 11, 2001, did not displace shared governance for long, and perhaps not at all in areas unrelated to the war on terrorism. The postmodern presidency in the aftermath of the cold war shares governance with an assertive and capable Congress. Until one party or the other can dominate both branches, collaborative policymaking in some form seems necessary for national policymaking.

Notes

1. James MacGregor Burns, *Presidential Government* (Boston: Houghton Mifflin, 1965): 284.
2. Steven A. Shull, *Domestic Policy Formation: Presidential-Congressional Partnership?* (Westport, CT: Greenwood Press, 1983).
3. The major investigation of political symbolism is by Murray Edelman, *Symbolic Uses of Politics* (Urbana, IL: University of Illinois Press, 1964).
4. Irving L. Janis, *Victims of Groupthink* (Boston: Houghton Mifflin, 1972).
5. Steven A. Smith and Gerald Gamm, "The Dynamics of Party Government in Congress," in Lawrence C. Dodd and Bruce L. Oppenheimer, *Congress Reconsidered,* seventh edition (Washington, D.C.: CQ Press, 2001): 245–268.
6. See Randall B. Ripley and Grace R. Franklin, *Congress, the Bureaucracy, and Public Policy* (Homewood, IL: Dorsey, 1988).
7. Richard P. Nathan et al., *Monitoring Revenue Sharing* (Washington, D.C.: Brookings Institution, 1976).
8. Theodore Lowi differentiated among distributive, regulatory, and redistributive policies in "American Business, Public Policy, Case Studies, and Political Theory," *World Politics* 16 (July 1964): 677–715. For an empirical treatment using his typology, see Shull (1983).
9. John Ellwood, "Comments on Shepsle and Weingast," in Gregory B. Mills and John L. Palmer (eds.), *Federal Budget Policy in the 1980s* (Washington, D.C.: Urban Institute Press, 1984).
10. See discussion of Senator Byrd as "trustee" in David Vogler, *The Politics of Congress,* third edition (Boston: Allyn and Bacon, 1980): 82.
11. CBO and Senate Budget Committee estimates, reported in *Congressional Quarterly Weekly Report* (May 17, 1997): 1118.
12. Morris Fiorina, *Divided Government* (Boston: Allyn and Bacon, 1996): 64–65.
13. Ronald D. Elving, "Partisanship Belies Rhetoric of Peace," *Congressional Quarterly Weekly Report* (January 18, 1997): 198.
14. David Mayhew, *Divided We Govern* (New Haven, CT: Yale University Press, 1991). Other critiques of divided government include Fiorina (1996); Gary W. Cox and Samuel Kernell (eds.), *Politics of Divided Government* (Boulder, CO: Westview Press, 1991); and Steven A. Shull, *Presidential-Congressional Relations* (Ann Arbor: University of Michigan Press, 1997).
15. George C. Edwards III, Andrew Barrett, and Jeffrey Peake, "The Legislative Impact of Divided Government," *American Journal of Political Science* 41 (1997): 545–563.
16. Donald Robinson (ed.), *Reforming American Government: The Bicentennial Papers of the Committee on the Constitutional System* (Boulder, CO: Westview Press, 1985).
17. Ibid., 69.
18. Ibid., 175–188.
19. Authors writing on the Twenty-Second Amendment include Bruce Buchanan, "The Six-Year One-Term Presidency," *Presidential Studies Quarterly* 17 (Winter 1988): 129–142; Thomas E. Cronin, "Two Cheers for the 22nd Amendment," *Presidency Research* 9 (Spring 1987): 6; David C. Nice, "In Retreat from Excellence: The Single Six-Year Presidential Term," *Congress and the Presidency* 13 (Autumn 1986): 209–220.
20. Robinson (1985): 254–264; see also John Orman, *Presidential Accountability* (Westport, CT: Greenwood Press, 1990).
21. Mark Petraca et al., "Proposals for Constitutional Reform," *Presidential Studies Quarterly* 20 (Summer 1990): 503–532.
22. The American Political Science Association issued a report entitled, "Towards a More Responsible Two-Party System," in 1950.
23. Nicholas van Hoffman, *Make-Believe Presidents* (New York: Pantheon, 1978): 213.
24. Theodore J. Lowi, *The Personal Presidency* (Ithaca, NY: Cornell University Press, 1985): 203–209.
25. *Congressional Quarterly Weekly Report* (December 30, 1989): 3354

Index